Published in April 2009

A catalogue record for this book is available from the British Library

ISBN 978 1 84425 485 9

Library of Congress control no. 2009924795

Published by Haynes Publishing,
Sparkford, Yeovil, Somerset BA22 7JJ, UK

Tel: 01963 442030 Fax: 01963 440001
Int. tel: +44 1963 442030
Int. fax: +44 1963 440001
E-mail: sales@haynes.co.uk
Website: www.haynes.co.uk

Haynes North America, Inc.,
861 Lawrence Drive, Newbury Park, California 91320, USA

Design and layout by Richard Parsons

Printed and bound in the UK

Photo credits (t = top, m = middle, b = bottom)
Penny Adie 66b
Alamy 22, 48t, 67t
Besbrode Pianos 68
John Colley Piano action shots
Forsyth Brothers Ltd 65
istockphoto.com 6, 8b, 9t, 10, 18b, 42, 44, 46, 47, 54, 56b, 58t, 61, 62, 64, 67b, 69b, 70, 73, 80, 82, 86, 88, 152, 170, 182
Kemble 9b, 24, 60
Korg 176
Lebrecht 12, 14, 15 (both), 16, 20, 53, 74, 108
Wikimedia commons 5, 8t, 17, 18t, 18m, 19, 23, 59b, 65b, 69t, 184
Yamaha 7, 50t, 56t, 58b
John Bishop All other images

The publishers would like to give particular thanks to Eleanor and Elbie at Lebrecht, along with Kemble and Yamaha for help with images.

Acknowledgements

The authors offer their thanks first and foremost to those customers who allowed us to photograph their pianos, and especially to those who were aware that our comments were unlikely to be kind. Not one refused.

Specific thanks are due to Steve Cook at Fletcher and Newman for supplying, at very short notice, all manner of components for us to photograph; to Central Wheel Components, Coleshill, for the penny farthing bicycle wheel spokes that we hope look convincing as piano wire in our photos of the piano action models; and to Nic Kilminster at Academy Pianos, who was generous in letting us photograph his stock and pester him for obscure information. He played Bach while we worked, and provided lashings of tea into the bargain.

We're also grateful to Louise McIntyre at Haynes Publishing for commissioning this book in the first place and for being hugely supportive thereafter. This may sound like crawling and indeed it probably is, but having a good relationship with your publisher really does produce better books.

Piano
Manual

John Bishop
Graham Barker

Buying, problem-solving, care, repair and tuning

Contents

Introduction

This book is about...

All pianos, but particularly ordinary, working pianos: certainly the ones owned by serious players, but equally the ones bought more in hope than expectation for beginners, the ones in equatorial living rooms and freezing church halls, the ones that take every manner of punishment in schools, pubs, hotels and clubs. It's mainly about uprights with many miles already on the clock, because they're the overwhelming majority; but newer pianos and grands are covered too.

This book is for...

Anyone who has ever come within ten paces of a piano – and yes, I do mean to include those who are only reluctantly interested because a child or partner plays under the same roof as them. I have strained every sinew to make this book essential, money-saving, even enjoyable reading for the entire piano owning and playing community, from first-time bargain hunters to virtuoso professionals.

My starting point was the fact that most piano owners know little about an instrument that has done its best to help them out by remaining remarkably unchanged for two centuries. This is a shame, because the piano as a piece of technology is definitely worth knowing. It looks and undeniably is complex, but not *that* complex: it's essentially a union of stellar design and down-to-earth materials.

True, there is an intimidation factor. The first thing you'll see inside most pianos is the massed, forbidding ranks of the *action* – the main playing mechanism and the seat of the piano's design genius. But once you grasp that what you're actually seeing is the same handful of basic components duplicated seven dozen times, the inside of a piano starts to become a fascinating place. Without a doubt, understanding how your piano makes and manages sound will increase your pleasure in owning it, and enrich your appreciation of its music. It may even make you a better player.

This book covers...

■ Looking after your piano at any level, from cleaning and light maintenance to advanced repair. If you yearn to take your piano to bits and put it confidently back together, the information you need is here. If you're content to leave the hands-on stuff to a tuner or piano technician and simply want to widen your knowledge of this wonderful instrument, this is the book for you. And if you've been playing the piano professionally for decades, I bet I can teach you more than a thing or two.

■ Tuning your own piano. Not everyone can do this, and professional piano tuners exist to make it unnecessary. But you'll get more pleasure from a piano that is constantly rather than periodically in tune, so it's worth trying my procedure for tuning one or two strings to see how you get on. If going the whole hog isn't for you, at least you'll acquire a greater appreciation of the skills of your piano tuner, and that alone is a decent reward.

■ How to buy a piano wisely. This matters because as a piano technician I still condemn on average a piano a fortnight as unfit for use, and that in just one small area of the UK. The piano has usually been recently bought, often at a price many times its worth. In my experience the number of bad pianos in circulation is growing, as it becomes easier for those outside the reputable trade to sell rubbish to the unwary on the internet. And far too often, a barely playable piano is bought as a first instrument for a child. This is desperately sad, for there is no surer way to undermine a child's

enjoyment of music than to start him or her off on what is literally an instrument of torture. This book is therefore invaluable for anyone planning to buy a piano for a child. If you want that child to cherish you in your old age, think of Chapter 5 as part of your insurance.

■ Equal temperament. The tuning concept without which there would be no piano. It surprises most people, including many competent musicians, to learn that a perfectly tuned piano is for the most part slightly out of tune. The reason for this is notoriously difficult to explain simply, but it's my duty to take on such challenges and I hope I've succeeded in Chapters 1 and 10.

Why the piano?

The piano is an extraordinary instrument. It is technically formidable, yet wears its complexity lightly enough to be played by children and given pride of place in millions of homes. It is one of very few instruments capable of making complete music, and has a far bigger repertoire than any other. It is the pre-eminent instrument of innovation and experimentation, particularly in 19th-century classical music and 20th-century jazz. Envy and admiration is the social reward of anyone who goes through the pain barrier of learning to play it.

It's also living history. The piano is the most sophisticated *wholly mechanical* device to survive and thrive in the 21st century. At heart a masterpiece of 18th- and 19th-century engineering, most of its 10,000 or so parts are made of hopelessly old-fashioned materials – wood, cast iron, felt, leather – yet all work in concert to a degree of precision that would seriously challenge modern manufacturers in any industry.

The piano is supremely man-made, yet no other instrument feels quite so responsive, soulful and *alive*. Keyboards producing digitally synthesised sounds may challenge its utility, but I doubt whether they can ever be as expressive or emotionally compelling. One might perform the complete works of Chopin on a digital keyboard as a curiosity, but probably not as a serious artistic endeavour. No matter how convincing an electronic piano might sound, at least one listener will know it's not the real thing: the person playing it.

Why the pianist?

Nothing, however, is forever. One ambition of this book is to give pianists the knowledge and skills they need to help the piano survive for another few centuries. At present, too many pianists are non-swimmers in the sense that if a piano is in trouble, they can't rescue it.

The piano is unusual in that by tradition, its players don't have to learn any basic maintenance or understand the technology of the instrument *at all* – and for some strange reason the rest of the musical world lets them get away with it! Most other instruments need regular tuning by the player, often even as a performance progresses. That breeds useful self-confidence. But if the piano is out of tune or out of sorts, someone else is responsible for putting it right: the function manager, the orchestra leader, the piano tuner… definitely *not* the pianist.

Pianists, of course, regularly perform on unfamiliar instruments, but this excuse is worth at best half a fig leaf. Every tuner has a story of getting a panic call from a top-drawer venue where the piano won't play properly. The audience simmers with impatience; the pianist frets.

Within seconds the tuner has pulled off the keyboard lid, reached into the piano and extracted a calcified cheese roll, a beer mat, or a pencil lost by the last performer. The piano is cured! The tuner may get a round of applause but no one thinks to yell at the pianist for displaying such a total lack of gumption.

Will this book produce a new breed of more confident, capable and well rounded pianists? I hope so. Music is going from strength to strength. Pianos are still going from strength to strength. Long may it all continue; and long may you enjoy reading and using this book.

PART 1

Selecting your piano

Owning a piano is a big musical milestone for millions of people worldwide. But many budding musicians fall by the wayside because they're playing, or trying to play, the wrong piano. Part 1 aims to ensure that *you* find the *right* piano.

It also explains what makes the piano such a magnificent and enduring instrument. There's some necessary history, some necessary technology and some necessary musical theory – but no unnecessary stodge.

CHAPTER 1

Where did it all come from?

Starting from a dinosaur period almost a thousand years ago, the modern piano finally emerged in around 1850. It has remained largely unchanged since then, and its last major technological improvement happened around 1914. Yet the piano probably sells more strongly now than ever. So how did it all happen?

Distant beginnings

A history of the piano could easily fill a substantial book on its own, so by covering the essentials so briefly I'm bound to upset someone. I can only offer my sincere apologies to any historian who knows better and can still keep it short. More constructively, the *References* section lists further reading for anyone who wants to learn more.

A piano is in essence two music-making concepts in one: a *stringed* instrument that is played indirectly by means of a *keyboard* borrowed from the organ, which predates it by several centuries.

Keyboards evolved from the technologies used to play 11th-century (or thereabouts) church pipe organs. The earliest versions bore no resemblance whatsoever to a modern keyboard; they were levers or sliders acting directly on the pipes, and it took considerable strength and stamina to operate them.

Medieval plainsong was a spare, undemanding form of music – all melody and no harmony – so at first only a very limited scale was needed. It took until the 15th century for organs with a head-swimming three octaves to appear. Over a similar period remote mechanisation emerged, which freed players (or 'organ beaters') from having to rush manically from pipe to pipe. The two developments together produced the first keyboards that actually started to look like keyboards, albeit primitive ones.

Stringed instruments go back much further. The idea of stretching a string secured at both ends and plucking it to make sound probably emerged the week after the wheel was invented. The ancient Greek polymath Pythagoras is thought to have been one of the first to study the behaviour of a stretched string and the relationship between mathematics and sound (*see Problem 2: Equal temperament tuning, page 17*).

Remote playing

The whole family of lutes, viols and guitars seems to have been present in Europe by medieval times. Their common denominator is strings stretched across two bridges, one of which is attached to a resonator box – usually the body of the instrument – to amplify the sound. With the addition of more strings, the zither was born. This evolved into the dulcimer, the first known instrument where the strings were intended to be struck with hand-held hammers rather than plucked or bowed.

By the early 15th century someone had had the bright idea of attaching an organ-type keyboard to a dulcimer so that the strings could be played remotely.

This was a bold move. Manual dulcimer hammers allow soft and hard strokes, and are double-ended so that they can be turned to change the tone completely. There is no doubt that in moving to remote mechanical operation, players sacrificed a large measure of expressiveness. On the other hand, they gained something revolutionary and exciting: the ability

Polygonal virginal made from Cypress, Italy. Made by Joseph Salodiensis, Italian, 1559–1574. (Frank B. Bemis Fund)

to play many more notes at once, and to play them much more rapidly. The die was cast. The dulcimer still exists, but no longer as an instrument of significance.

Thus was born the class of instruments that includes harpsichords, virginals, spinets and clavichords. It subdivides into those where the string is plucked – harpsichords, virginals and spinets – and the clavichord (sometimes simply clavier) whose strings are struck dulcimer-style. Their collective evolution was slow, and instruments based on this pre-Renaissance technology were still being made in the early 19th century.

Clavichord made from Fir, Italy.
(Leslie Lindsey Mason Collection)

Not quite the sound of the future

All these instruments produced a pale, insubstantial sound judged by modern standards. Only the harpsichord had the potential to evolve into something loud and strong enough to fill a large room or hold its own alongside other instruments. Its build quality improved, and it became so successful that despite the piano's appearance from around 1720, the harpsichord remained the more popular instrument until well into the 19th century.

The piano was far from an instant success because three great obstacles stood between it and the instrument we know today: it lacked true expressiveness; what could be played on it was limited because J.S. Bach's equal temperament tuning system was still a few years off; and contemporary materials science couldn't yet meet the challenges inherent in the piano's design, especially its need for high-quality strings.

Let's see how these problems were overcome.

Harpsichord made from Walnut, France. (Edwin M. Ripin Collection, Friends of the Collection Fund)

Problem 1: Expressiveness

In the clavichord, the hammer is metal and it remains in contact with the string – reducing its freedom to vibrate – until the note fades or is ended by releasing the key. This produces a pleasing enough sound, but not a loud one.

Bartolomeo Cristofori (1655–1731), who is generally credited with inventing the piano some time around 1700 in Italy, realised that much greater volume could be produced if a hammer with a softer surface could strike the string and bounce straight back off it, allowing the string to carry on vibrating. This, and the mechanism that enables it to happen, is the very essence of the piano.

Cristofori chose felt as his hammer material – doubtless mindful of the dulcimer's felt-covered hammers – and so astute was his judgement that felt has remained the conventional piano hammer material ever since.

The best way to appreciate the magnitude of Cristofori's innovation is to open up the top lid of an upright piano and peer inside. Then:

- Depress any key and see which hammer moves forward.
- Press a finger lightly on the hammer to resist, but not prevent, its forward motion.
- Depress the key slowly.
- When the hammer is precisely an eighth of an inch (3.17mm) away from its string there will be, if the piano is correctly set up, a quiet but definite dull thud from inside the works.
- As you hear it, you will feel the hammer being released from the key.

In normal playing, this is the point where the hammer leaps off the mechanism and flies through the air. For a microsecond, it acts as though shot from a catapult. This is called *set-off* or *let-off* and the mechanism that makes it happen is the *escapement*.

Cristofori's escapement is such an elegant mechanism that even pianos made today incorporate a remarkably unchanged version of it, which I explain in more technical detail in Chapter 2. All I want to say here is that it's one of those things that looks obvious and simple when you see it, but making the first one really was a feat of genius.

At the time, Cristofori's mechanism was considered fiendishly complex – then as now, to function correctly it had to be engineered to fractions of a millimetre, but working in felt and wood – and the piano's early reputation suffered when other builders produced cruder, simplified versions to keep costs down. In attempting to overcome the resulting deficiencies, later piano makers did little more than reverse

engineer back to Cristofori's original design! (It must be remembered that there would have been no equivalent of modern technical drawings to follow. Knowledge of Cristofori's work spread largely through written descriptions. It would have been impossible to convey it accurately this way, so in a sense Cristofori's work was 'lost' almost as soon as it appeared.)

For a long time, musicians compared the piano unfavourably with the clavichord, which was easier to play and was itself the focus of a great deal of improvement effort. I have to return to my theme of *expressiveness* to explain why the piano eventually rendered the clavichord all but extinct as a working instrument.

In the clavichord and harpsichord the string is struck with the same rather meagre force no matter how hard the key is depressed. Neither would be the instrument of choice of a Vladimir Horowitz or a Little Richard. By contrast, and as the name suggested, notes on Cristofori's *pianoforte* could be played loudly, softly, or anywhere in between, giving it a similar range of expressiveness to the human voice. The keener musicians and composers of the day grasped how much of an advantage this could give them, and as the piano's technical efficiency started to match its expressive potential, more and more of them became converts. Soon the piano was streets ahead of any other keyboard instrument.

Cristofori named his invention *arcicembal che fa il piano e il forte* – 'harpsichord that plays both softly and loudly' – which over time was contracted to pianoforte and then piano.

Problem 2: Equal temperament tuning

To own or play a piano you don't need to know a thing about equal temperament. This is fortunate, because it's difficult to explain in non-technical terms. But without equal temperament the modern piano wouldn't exist and all Cristofori's work might have been for nothing, so it's worth at least a few paragraphs.

Equal temperament was developed as a solution to a problem. It wasn't a perfect solution but it was the only workable solution – because, as we'll see, a mathematically perfect solution is impossible.

The problem lay in tuning any keyboard instrument so that it could do what we now take for granted – play harmonies that sound 'right' whichever keys they're played in. At the start of the 18th century the clavichord was good for one-note-at-a-time melodies but not much else. The more harmonically ambitious a player or composer got, the more out of tune it would sound. This deficiency was inherited by Cristofori's piano.

For a long time these tuning limitations were tolerable because harpsichords and clavichords produced a fairly feeble sound. What you couldn't hear without straining, you didn't worry about too much. Most composers were also fairly feeble, content to write within the instrument's constraints. But as technology advanced and organs, harpsichords and clavichords became louder and more powerful, the problem could no longer be ignored. And then along came Johann Sebastian Bach – a musical genius who wasn't just a prolific composer and performer, but also a master craftsman and organ builder who had no trouble transferring his skills to the clavichord. Impatient to use much more challenging harmonies than had ever been attempted, he decided that enough was enough and Something Had To Be Done.

What he did transformed keyboard playing forever – though ironically, he wasn't at all enthusiastic about early pianos. And unavoidably, we now have to get to grips with what the problem was. In fact, what it still is.

The Pythagoras solution

The problem is how to find the best intervals between notes, based on the vibration each note makes. Two notes an octave apart – for example C – produce a pleasing, harmonious sound when played together. The vibration rate of the higher C is twice that of the lower C. A note a fifth higher than C – G – also sounds like some sort of relative, if not so close. Thus any note sounded together with its fifth, like C+G, is a basic building block of musical harmony. It provides an accompaniment of sorts, if a rather tedious one. (It's the drone sound heard from bagpipes.)

The problem of intervals has been around a long time. Legend has it that Pythagoras (he of the square on the hypotenuse) was the first to analyse it and propose a solution in around 500 BC, but Babylonian texts from 3500 BC apparently contain something similar.

Finding all the fifths was Pythagoras's first task. (Or maybe someone else's, as almost nothing is known for certain about Pythagoras. But he was clearly brilliant anyway, so he might as well have the credit.) In the absence of electronic measuring instruments, he used blacksmiths' hammers. He discovered that two hammers, one half the weight of the other, produced notes an octave apart when the anvil was struck. He then found that if he made two more hammers, two-thirds of the weight of his first pair, each produced a note a fifth above its full-weight companion. This was his *eureka!* moment. By becoming a small-scale hammer manufacturer, he produced a series of fifths for the full 12-note scale, based on his two-thirds ratio.

In theory, by step 12 he would be back at the note he started with, only an octave higher. In practice, he wasn't. He was 'off', in a way familiar to any DIY enthusiast who tries to draw a precisely horizontal line right round a room and get the two ends to meet up. His end note was very sharp of, or higher in pitch than, the one he started with.

This happens because the vibration frequency of the strings doubles every octave – an exponential series, if you're mathematically inclined – whereas the harmony building blocks of music are expressed in whole fractions. There was, and still is, no mathematically perfect way of reconciling these two different 'natural' methods of creating intervals between notes.

Whether or not Pythagoras realised what was going on, at this point he more or less shrugged and walked away. The musical outcome was that hundreds of generations of keyboard players had to live with a tuning system that frustrated any attempt to play in more than one key without making listeners wince.

impossible to improve the sound of any key without making one or more other keys sound worse. So if we want to play any piece of music in any key, or want to play music that modulates into other keys, and if we want to use the same instrument without having to retune it, there is no other option.

That, then, is equal temperament in a nutshell. It depends not on how a piano is designed or made, but purely on how it is *tuned*. We're all playing pianos on which, when correctly tuned to equal temperament, every interval except the octave is slightly out of 'natural' tune. The reason our ears can accept this is simple: we've been hearing music played this way for so long that it sounds right. It's an enormous conspiracy, which we all become party to from birth.

Bach publicised his new system with *The Well-Tempered Clavier (Das Wohltemperirte Clavier)*, a series of 48 preludes and fugues – two in each key, major and minor – which would have been impossible to play without his tuning. Nonetheless, it took a substantial time for equal temperament to become universally accepted, and some of the great composers stuck doggedly to other systems, perhaps for particular effect. For example, one has to assume that Chopin wrote his *Funeral March* in B♭ minor, with the familiar lament of the third movement in D♭ minor, for some good reason other than deliberately making it difficult to play.

For what it's worth, there is academic evidence that Bach's tuning system wasn't quite our modern system, and a distinction is now made between *well tempered* and *equally tempered* tuning. A well tempered system permits music to be played in any key, but it won't sound exactly the same in every key. In equal temperament, it will sound the same in every key. Had Bach been better at mathematics, he might have gone straight to equal temperament. But it hardly matters. Bach got the piano out of a hole, and for that we should be eternally grateful to him.

The Bach solution

In Chapter 10 I'll explain in much more technical detail what today's professional piano tuner does to achieve equal temperament tuning. All I need do here is state that J.S. Bach painstakingly, and entirely by ear, devised a system of smoothing out the 'bumps' at the boundary of each octave. What he produced was a system in which some intervals on a correctly tuned piano are out of tune but are *equally out of tune in every key*. This is a difficult concept to sell to some people, and even now a piano tuner rash enough to try to explain it to a customer risks being regarded as an unsafe pair of hands. (One can imagine Bach's friends eager to let him play their clavichords, but ready with an excuse should he offer to tune them.)

For example, in the inversion G C E of a C major chord, the G is left slightly flat relative to the C, while the E is very sharp – arguably too sharp, were in not for our collective cultural familiarity with it. If the E was flattened and the G slightly sharpened, this chord would sound better. But that would just create a problem somewhere else: if we now played the minor chord G# C# E – that is, C# minor – the E would be too flat for comfort.

In other words, Bach's system is a glorious compromise. Mathematically, it solves the problem only optimally, in the sense that although there are 'faults' in every key, each key sounds equally 'bad'. The crucial practical point is that it is

Problem 3: Strings

Of all the problems that held back the development of the piano, the most stubborn was the lack of decent strings. Contemporary industry supplied nothing that was really suitable for the job. This was intensely frustrating for the growing number of musicians who could see the potential in this new instrument. Desperate measures even included making strings by sawing thin strips of metal and filing them round – a terribly laborious procedure for such disappointing results.

It was nearly a century after Cristofori's and Bach's contributions before German foundries started drawing cast steel bars through progressively smaller holes to produce strong, thin wire. Rapid technology improvements after 1820 resulted in wire of consistent quality, great tensile strength and uniform thickness. Manufacturers also discovered that the drawing process itself made the wire stronger, so that the thinner the wire, the stronger it was relative to its cross-section. Later the wire was improved even further, by drawing it through holes in gemstones.

Piano string manufacture still isn't perfect. One of the problems that plagues modern piano making and tuning is that any manufacturing imperfection in piano wire causes 'falseness' or false beats. Sometimes a tuner will find a single string that produces a beat, a slight dissonance, which usually occurs when two strings interact and are slightly out of tune with each other. This is a real difficulty. The most common cause is wire that is slightly oval. As the plane through which the string vibrates changes, the string isn't quite sure how

thick it is. A thicker string vibrates more slowly and therefore sounds flatter than a thinner string. When the delinquent oval string vibrates through its thinner plane, it is sharper than when it vibrates through its thicker plane. It behaves like two slightly out of tune strings all on its own!

Further developments

Once the problem of wire manufacture was solved, piano development accelerated through the 19th century. Strings were made longer, and their greater strength meant that they could be put under a higher tension. All this greatly improved sound quality.

The next focus of attention was the frame, the main load-bearing component of the piano. The more tension the strings were under, the greater the string load on the frame. The original wooden frames, looking very much like a harp, were unable to cope with the increasing load. All-wood frames were replaced by iron-braced wood frames, and then by cast iron frames.

In 1859 the German piano manufacturer Steinway patented the cast iron overstrung frame and the 'roller' action, or more correctly the *double escapement* action. (This will be explained in Chapter 2.) Other makers quickly took licences for these features

from Steinway or adopted them later, when the patents expired. In effect, Steinway completed the development of the modern piano, as all changes since 1859 have been incremental or cosmetic rather than genuinely innovative. Overstrung frames were developed for uprights, and the tape check underdamper action (of which also more later) was added. And that was about it.

Manufacturing processes have improved enormously since the later 19th century, and so a piano made in 2000 is likely to be significantly *better* than an equivalent factory-fresh piano made in 1900. But it won't be much *different*, and that is a large part of the piano's universal appeal. Five years after it comes out of its box, a digital keyboard will be obsolete. Fifty years after it trundles off the production line, a well-maintained piano could still be going strong.

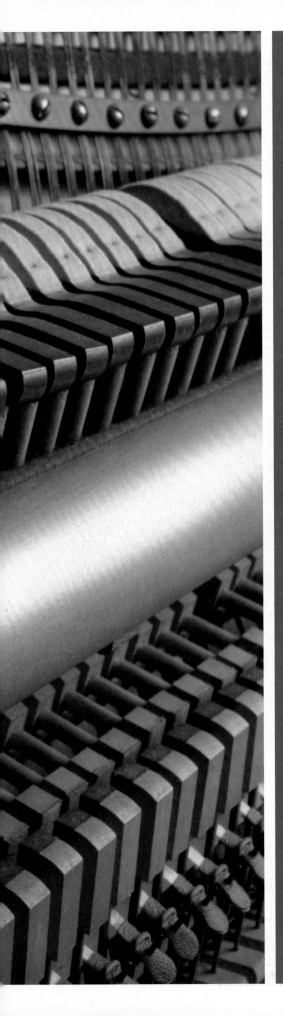

CHAPTER 2

How a piano works

The basic technology of the piano and how to identify the fundamental differences between good and bad, modern and obsolete.

What's where?

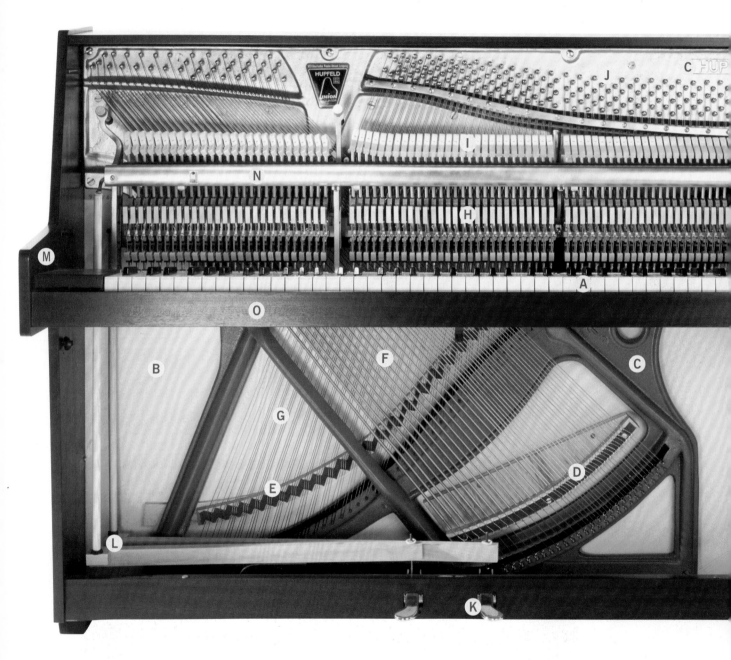

A keyboard

B soundboard

C cast iron overstrung frame
(Plate in US usage)

D bass bridge

E treble bridge

F bass strings (copper wound)

G treble strings

H action

I hammers

J tuning or wrest pins

K pedals

L pedal operating mechanism

M case

N hammer rest rail

O keyslip

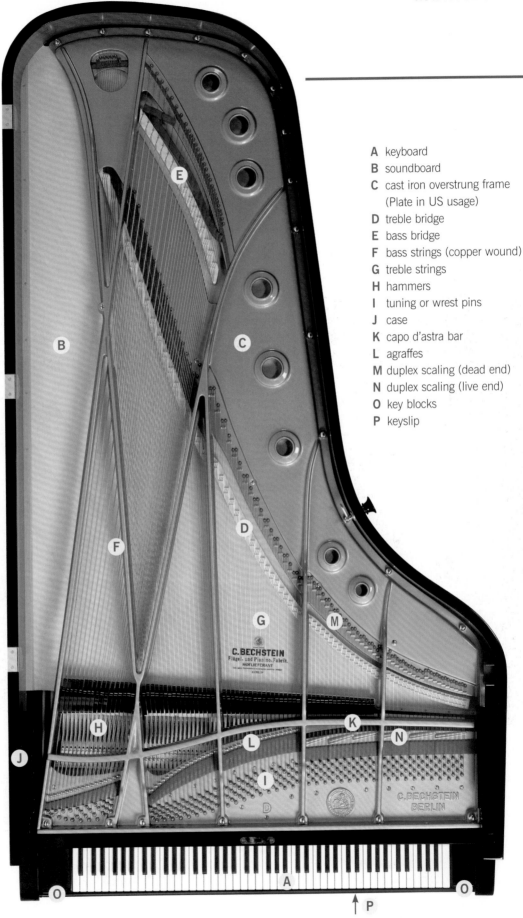

A keyboard
B soundboard
C cast iron overstrung frame
   (Plate in US usage)
D treble bridge
E bass bridge
F bass strings (copper wound)
G treble strings
H hammers
I tuning or wrest pins
J case
K capo d'astra bar
L agraffes
M duplex scaling (dead end)
N duplex scaling (live end)
O key blocks
P keyslip

How modern is modern?

In this chapter I'll outline how modern pianos are made and how they work. Because Chapter 5 advises you on how to buy a used piano, I'll also tell you here about some of the pianos that are still around but technically obsolete.

An immediate problem is defining 'modern'. In most manufacturing industries it's easy to be confident about dates, as for many decades any significant technological improvement has usually been adopted rapidly by everyone, while anything deemed obsolete has usually vanished equally quickly.

By comparison, the piano market is a bastion of extremely slow and asymmetric change. Often, a design or technology innovation from one of the top-quality grand piano makers has taken up to 50 years to filter down to the budget end of the upright piano market. Thus, calendar dates are in themselves no guide to modernity, as it's perfectly possible for a piano made in 1900 by one company to be more technologically modern than a piano made in 1950 by another.

Some manufacturers clung on to obsolescence because they couldn't afford to adopt new technologies; others because obsolete designs became cheaper to produce and easy to sell as better pianos became more expensive. Whatever the reason, in a piano context any use of the term 'modern' has to be accompanied by all sorts of qualifications.

My own main get-out clause is this: while it's easy to describe what to expect from a piano made in the last 20 years or so, pianos made not much earlier than that may be an unhappy marriage of ancient and modern. I'll return to this theme in Chapters 4 and 5. For the time being, wherever I state that something started or ended by a particular date, I mean only roughly. Sometimes very roughly.

Modern pianos – design and construction

Frames (or 'plates' in the USA)

The frame is the major component, usually harp-shaped and usually made of cast iron, across which all the strings are stretched. (As noted in Chapter 1, frames were first made wholly of wood, then of wood with metal brackets, then of wood braced with metal. No pianos with such frames will now exist except in museums, so that's all I'll say about them in this book.)

All upright pianos made today, and all good-quality uprights made since around 1920, will have a full-height, overstrung frame. Therefore the first two important things to learn about the frames of pianos still around today, and so likely to be offered for sale, are:

- The difference between a three-quarter frame and a full frame.
- The difference between a straight-strung frame and an overstrung frame.

Three-quarter frame versus full frame

The three-quarter frame is the earliest form of cast iron frame. The name indicates that the frame doesn't go to the full height of the piano, but stops about three-quarters of the way up. Three-quarter frames are now totally obsolete technology. They're bad mainly because they leave the exposed wooden wrest plank (see *Wrest planks and tuning pins* on page 30) to do all the work of coping with the many tons of string tension.

Around 1900, good piano manufacturers introduced a far superior full-height frame known as the bushed frame, which I explain in more detail later (see page 31).

Unfortunately, less good manufacturers kept on producing three-quarter frame pianos for many years, which is why there are still some around. I can only assume that they must have been cheaper to make, possibly because anyone wanting to manufacture a full-frame piano would have had to pay a licence fee to the owner of the intellectual property. However, knowing full well that their pianos were inferior, many later makers of three-quarter frame uprights used visual trickery to fool the gullible into thinking they were buying an instrument with a full frame. Common practices included painting wood gold to make it look like metal, or adding impressive but structurally useless pieces of extra metal. (See *The three deadly sins* on page 32).

The two top photos show a three-quarter frame ending below the tuning pins. The pins appear to be driven into sturdy metal. In fact, it's just a thin sheath of brass or tin that does nothing structural but covers up the bare wooden wrest plank (of which more later). What look like large bolt

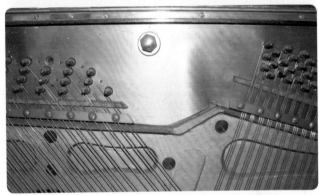

heads are actually wood screws holding the wrest plank to the wooden framework of the piano. There are no excuses – this is a deliberate attempt to deceive. Older pianos and larger modern pianos have a stout wooden frame behind the cast iron one. A typical one is shown below.

Straight-strung frame versus overstrung frame

An overstrung piano is not necessarily good simply because it's overstrung, but straight-strung pianos are *never* good. They haven't been made for several decades so their numbers are declining fast, but there are still plenty around to tempt the unwary. Many old straight-strungs were well made and can still look beautiful, but if they sound even moderately good the chances are high that they've just been tuned and will very quickly sound much worse.

Straight-strung frames

Note that straight-strung frames are often called 'vertically strung' frames. However, in the USA the term 'vertical' means an upright piano of any kind. Therefore to avoid any possibility of confusion I'll use only the term 'straight-strung' from now on.

A straight-strung frame is conceptually simple. You make a sturdy, harp-shaped frame – see above – usually of cast iron, and stretch all the strings across it vertically from top to bottom. Harpsichords and clavichords were strung this way, so it was logical to do the same for pianos.

Straight-strung pianos had a good run, but overstringing was seen to have so many advantages that it quickly rendered the straight-strung piano obsolete. By about 1918 no quality piano manufacturer was still making straight-strungs.

However, fringe manufacturers kept on turning them out for the bottom end of the market, certainly until around 1960 and possibly into the 1970s. These were all poor-quality models

of obscure branding and usually untraceable provenance. They only sold because (a) they were easier and cheaper to make than overstrung pianos and (b) there were still enough retailers and customers around who didn't know or care how bad they were. Plenty of these pianos still exist, so make sure you don't end up owning one.

From the very beginning there were two fundamental problems with straight-strung pianos, especially in their upright form:

- No string can be longer than the height of the piano. This means that the more bass sound quality you want, the taller the piano has to be.
- The taller the piano, the more of a monster it looks – and the more easily it falls over.

Now that all surviving straight-strung pianos are old, a third problem eclipses the other two:

- Straight-strungs almost inevitably need a lot of work to keep them playable, but replacement parts are no longer available. Many repairs will therefore be either impossible or their cost will exceed the value of the instrument. I hardly ever find a straight-strung piano worth repairing, and that situation will only get worse with time.

And that is almost all you need to know about straight-strung pianos. Never, ever buy one. At best they're museum pieces.

Overstrung frames

Overstringing is a more complex design, but both the technology and the resulting sound quality are far superior to straight-stringing in almost all respects (though see *In defence of straight-strung pianos*, page 29).

The strings are still stretched across a single frame but the big differences are:

- The strings are divided into two sets – bass strings in one set, treble strings in the other.
- In an upright piano the bass set is strung across the frame *diagonally* at an angle of between 40 and 60°. Stand facing an upright and the bass strings run from top left to bottom right; treble strings from top right to bottom left (though to be strictly accurate, they're vertical at the right-hand end and progressively fan out into a diagonal. See below).
- One set of strings has to cross over the other at some point – hence the 'over' of overstrung. This is easy to see on a grand with the lid up, but on an upright it's approximately behind the keyboard. So that the two sets of strings don't interfere with each other, the frame is skewed to provide a clearance of about 5in (130mm) between the treble and bass strings in the crossover zone. See below, at the line that slants down to the action post left of centre.

Overstringing has two distinct advantages over straight-stringing. The first is that across the same size of frame, diagonal strings can be longer than vertical strings. The extra length amounts to only a few inches, but it's enough to make a significant difference to the sound quality.

The second and more complex advantage is that in a straight-strung the bass bridge has to be sited deep down in the left-hand corner of the piano, near two edges of the soundboard. Usually, the closer the bridges are to the middle of the soundboard the better the sound quality. The straight-strung is therefore condemned to have an unsatisfactory bass tone, and the lower you go the worse it gets. As early as 1820 piano maker John Broadwood followed scientific advice and created a separate bass bridge, moving it in from the very edge of the soundboard. This paved the way for overstringing.

The main benefits of overstringing are:

- A much superior bass sound compared with a straight-strung piano of the same size – or, alternatively, the same quality of bass from a less tall piano.
- A longer string means a smaller diameter and thus fewer harsh harmonics in the sound.

In an overstrung grand piano, the bass and treble strings cross at only 20–30°. The smaller angle means that little extra length is gained compared to an overstrung upright, but this doesn't matter because a full-size grand is longer than a full-size upright is tall, so its strings are longer anyway. The claimed benefit of overstringing grands is that it enables a superior load-resisting structure to be achieved, and moves the bass bridge away from the edge of the piano. It also uses less cast iron than a straight-strung would, so there is a manufacturing benefit as well as a musical one.

Is it straight-strung or overstrung?

An at-a-glance indicator is the wooden blocks at the ends of the keyboard – see below. In an overstrung piano the block at the bass (left) end is normally wider than the block at the treble (right) end. Unfortunately this isn't a foolproof test, so if you're seriously interested in the instrument you'll need to look inside.

If the strings are arranged in two sets, and both sets slope towards and then across each other – thicker ones from left to right, over the thinner ones which slope from right to left – it's an overstrung piano. The treble strings (right-hand end) start out vertical and fan out gradually, which is why I suggest

To do this, lift up the top lid (*not* the keyboard lid, which is correctly called the *fallboard*). If you're in someone's home, ask the owner to remove any ornaments, plants, family photographs etc. *Don't do it yourself* – this is how priceless items get damaged, piano cases scratched, and relationships impaired.

Once the lid is up, you'll immediately see the top end of the strings. A torch isn't necessary but you'll see much more if you have one. Look at the bass strings (left-hand end) in particular. If they and all the other strings go straight down at 90° to the floor, the piano is straight-strung. Don't even consider buying it. The photo below shows this view with the front removed.

looking mainly at the bass strings to quickly spot a straight-strung – see above.

Finally, an uncommon variant of the straight-strung is the *oblique*. Here, all the strings run parallel to one another but at a slant of around 15–20° to gain a little extra length. Don't consider buying one of these either. (The 1890s Schiedmayer below is a three-quarter frame with oblique stringing. This example was recently rebuilt and already its tuning pins are loose: not money well spent. It was in any case obsolete within a few years of being made.)

In defence of straight-strung pianos

In technology terms, the progression from straight-stringing to overstringing has been somewhat over-hyped. It wasn't a giant leap, but more like three steps forward and one back.

In theory, straight-stringing has something going for it that overstringing has lost. This is why a few good makers – for example Bechstein in Germany and Collard & Collard in Britain – continued to make some straight-strung pianos for a short while even when other quality manufacturers had shifted entirely to overstrung production.

Overstringing had, and still has, a small but significant design weakness. Where the two sets of strings cross, there isn't enough room for full-size dampers (see below). This crossover area is called the *overstringing break*. It can be up to 6in (150mm) wide where the tuning pins are separated, and when you play across it you don't need acute hearing to detect that the dampers there are not as effective as on the rest of the piano. Worse, there can be a distinct difference in tone across the break, especially if it coincides with the point where the stringing goes from plain strings to wound strings, and from trichords (three strings per note) to bichords (two strings per note).

The better made the piano, the less obvious the overstringing break. A good test of the quality of any piano is whether a skilled player can find the overstringing break just by playing it, rather than looking inside.

In the light of this, a strong argument ought to exist for a slightly larger straight-strung frame, which would be better than an overstrung because it wouldn't have these problems. Everyone would have to learn to live with taller pianos, but that would arguably be a small price to pay for technical superiority.

In practice, overstringing quickly became synonymous in the market-place with quality, and that's what really killed off straight-stringing. An analogy is the market triumph in the 1980s of the VHS video format over the superior technology of Betamax. Whatever reservations they might have had, all serious piano makers *had* to change to overstringing if they wanted to stay in business.

And that's the end of the theoretical defence of straight-strung pianos. The reality is that no good ones have been made for nearly a hundred years, and even the very best of their day will now be well beyond practical use. Nonetheless, it's quite possible that a seller somewhere will try to persuade you that his straight-strung or oblique upright is a good buy because its bass strings are as long as, if not longer than, the bass strings on a small modern overstrung. Get a tape measure out and he'll probably be right, but that doesn't change anything. Unless it's the last piano on earth, it still won't be worth having.

Wrest planks and tuning pins

Frames need to be strong and rigid so that they can withstand the enormous stresses – over 10 tons in a small upright and up to 20 tons in a concert grand – of having up to 200 strings stretched tight across them. And by and large they are strong. With reasonable care, a cast iron frame will last indefinitely.

Not so the wrest plank – or 'pin block' in the USA – a piece of laminated wood about 2in (50mm) thick, the shrinkage and deterioration of which is inevitable and is the cause of death of most older pianos.

It's impossible to predict how long a wrest plank will last. A reasonable estimate used to be 60–70 years, but central heating now greatly reduces life expectancy. I increasingly find pianos having to be written off after about 30 years, and in extreme cases after as few as 20. It follows that if you want your wrest plank, and thus your piano, to have a long life, keep it in an environment where the central heating is switched off or turned down as low as possible. (See Chapter 6.)

The function of the wrest plank

Each string is wound at the top of the frame round a cast steel tuning pin which, as the name suggests, is the means of tuning it. But the tuning pins are not held by the metal frame; they're secured in holes in the wooden wrest plank, whose sole job is to hold them firmly. There is little finesse in installing the pins; it's simply a matter of walloping them into tiny holes with a large hammer. Thus, all that keeps the tuning pins in their holes is friction – the tightness of a metal peg in a wooden hole barely big enough for it.

Each string is then tuned by tightening or slackening its tuning pin. 'Wrest' and 'wrist' are related in origin, hinting at tuning as essentially an application of brute force; and brute force is rarely good for wood.

In pianos still in existence, you're likely to see one of three wrest plank configurations:

■ Exposed wrest plank

The oldest, most failure-prone and least tuner-friendly wrest plank design. As the name implies, the wrest plank is in full view (see page 25, top two photos). It gets no support from the cast iron frame, which means that throughout its life the plank has to cope with many tons of string pressure trying to drag the pins downwards and rip them out of the plank. The pins in turn are trying to pull the whole plank off and fold the piano up. It's a testament to the skill of the piano builders that the pins stay in at all.

An exposed wrest plank does tuners no favours, as they have to make extremely fine adjustments to the tiny tuning pins without 'stirring' them around or putting any downward pressure on them. Even when great care is taken, the wood around the pins will gradually be crushed and the holes enlarged.

After some years it becomes a losing battle as the combined effects of natural shrinkage and the crushing of the wood round the pin holes after each tuning take their toll. It's a vicious circle of loosening pins needing more regular tuning, which only loosens them more. Sometimes just one or two pins are affected, sometimes all of them. The better the build-quality of the piano, the more likely it is that the looseness will be even across all the pins, but that isn't much consolation.

Sooner or later even the most carefully built piano will not stand in tune for more than a few hours – especially if the wrest plank has started to split as well as shrink, and even more especially if the splits run from one pin hole to another. The photo below shows splits running right across the three tuning pins for one note, despite someone's clumsy past attempt to fill and paint them. These splits may be tiny, but they're sufficient to bring this piano to the end of its life.

Even without splits, loose pins usually spell doom for a piano. The only remedy is to replace all the original tuning pins with oversized new ones – available in size increments of five thousandths of an inch (0.127mm) – to fit the enlarged holes, and it's usual to fit new strings too. But this is the equivalent of major orthopaedic surgery in humans, and it's usually uneconomic in uprights as the cost of the parts alone is likely to exceed the value of the instrument when rebuilt.

■ Bushed frame (Mark 1)

Somewhere between 1900 (the top makers) and 1950 (the stragglers), piano manufacturers started making what are usually termed bushed frames. In engineering terms they weren't properly bushed for some time, so I've used my own designations Mark 1 and Mark 2 to distinguish the earlier and later types.

The Mark 1 is a full-height cast iron frame that covers and is attached by large screws to the wrest plank, which as a result is no longer visible or 'exposed'. Only improvements in casting technology made this possible, as it requires the casting of a large area of very thin metal.

A bushed frame has holes drilled through the metal – one for each tuning pin. The hole, however, merely allows the pin to pass through on its way into the wooden wrest plank, so it may seem that not much has changed. The process of shrinkage and gradual demise described above applies equally to bushed frames, but crucially at a much slower rate compared with an exposed wrest plank kept in a similar environment.

The advantages of a bushed frame are that (a) the attachment of the wooden wrest plank to the metal frame slows the rate of shrinkage; and (b) surrounding the pin with metal makes it harder for incompetent tuners to crush the wood round the pins.

In the best-made pianos there is a (c): the holes in the frame and the wrest plank are so aligned that the heads of the tuning pins rest on the bottom rim of the holes in the casting. This arrangement relieves the pins of some of the enormous string pressure without generating any extra friction, as cast steel runs smoothly over cast iron.

Therefore, an early bushed frame can substantially extend the life of the wrest plank, and thus of the piano. But much better is possible.

■ Bushed frame (Mark 2)

In this design, which is now standard, the cast iron frame carries most of the string load. The Mark 2 bushed frame first appeared around 1920. It's basically the Mark 1 with the addition of a hardwood plug (usually rock maple) inserted into each tuning pin hole in the metal frame, prior to the insertion of the wrest plank into the frame. The plugs are mushroom-shaped and the head is on the inside of the hole. The pins still pass through the holes in the frame into the wrest plank, but each one is now also gripped firmly in a tight-fitting collar or 'doughnut' of wood. (The technical term is *wrestpin bushing* or *tuning pin bushing*.) In the photo above the wood surrounding each tuning pin is clearly visible.

Compared to a Mark 1 frame, the wooden bushing transfers much more of the downward string pressure from the tuning pin to the frame, and effectively shifts the load from the wrest plank to the frame.

The advantages of this simple and arguably obvious and long overdue design improvement are considerable. Reduced loading on the wrest plank means it will stand in tune longer, and the rigidity of the pin in the bushing makes the tuner's job so much easier that wear and tear on the wrest plank holes is almost eliminated. The wrest plank will still shrink, but so slowly that it should last the lifetime of a well maintained, well-kept piano.

The three deadly sins

These photos show the inside of a straight-strung upright. They illustrate three classic design and manufacturing flaws, any one of which will make a straight-strung an even worse proposition than it is already:

■ An overdamper action
■ A three-quarter frame
■ An exposed wrest plank

Photos C and D give a closer view of the treble and bass ends respectively. It's now more evident that the real cast iron frame is the black lower portion, which is clearly well short of being a full frame. This is a three-quarter frame, or 'half plate' in the USA. The shiny gold upper part is a fraud. It's called a cap or capping piece and adds nothing to the piano except weight.

Most straight-strungs have only one or two of these 'deadly sins', so it's something of a privilege to be able to show you all of them in one instrument – a cornucopia of obsolescence.

In Photo B the overdamper action (known from its appearance as a 'squirrel cage' by US piano technicians) is still in the piano. The wires down the front of the action operate the dampers. Overdampers never functioned well, even when new, and deteriorate rapidly as the felt wears out. Astonishingly, some overdamped pianos were still being made in the 1950s. They were hopeless then and are worse now.

Note also what appears to be an impressively shiny cast iron frame, reaching right up to the top of the interior. Look at its five huge retaining screws – solidity incarnate. Or perhaps not...

As explained earlier, three-quarter frames are a bad idea because they leave the wrest plank to do all the work of holding the tuning pins without any help from a cast iron surround. This piano has a double dose of bad luck because photos C and D also show that it has an exposed wrest plank, which means that the pins and their many tons of pressure are held solely by wood. (The gold paint seen here is original and would have been applied deliberately to make the wrest plank look like metal, so this piano has now chalked up two attempts at deception. Both were common practice at the budget end of the piano industry.)

This piano is over 80 years old, and the visible splits running from pin to pin mean that the wrest plank is irreparably damaged and will now never stand in tune.

The casework

The case or casework of a piano – all the wood you can see when you stand looking at it – simply holds the instrument together. It adds much to its aesthetics but nothing to its tonal quality. This may surprise some people, so it needs explaining.

Sound is vibration, and when a piano is played every bit of it vibrates to some extent: a tuner can feel the vibration even through the tuning pins. The case certainly vibrates too, but this doesn't add significantly to the volume or tone of the instrument. The soundboard (see page 34) is specifically designed to amplify the piano and generally does an excellent job, so any additional vibration is unlikely to make a noticeable difference. Indeed, piano designers strive to stop energy 'escaping' from the soundboard into the case precisely because the shape of the casework makes it an inefficient amplifier of sound.

It's admittedly difficult to look at the big, sturdy, beautiful mahogany case of an old upright and not believe in its sound-enhancing qualities. But this is, I regret to say, no more than a romantic notion. The piano would probably sound just as good in casework knocked together from old floorboards.

'Stripped' casework

In fact the piano will almost certainly sound louder and more dramatic with parts of its casework removed. Perverse though it may seem, the very design of both uprights and grands compresses the sound into a small, enclosed space where reflected sound will self-cancel and some of the initial sound will be stifled. Stifled sound is not what most players want, which is probably why the classic image of a grand piano is always with the lid propped elegantly open.

In the case of the upright, the best part to remove is the front board. This is not at all elegant – it makes the piano look as though it's in for repair – and you lose the music desk. However, the player of an upright benefits much more from the increase in decibels compared to the player of a grand. Raising the lid of a grand reflects the sound mainly outwards at the audience. The unleashed sound of an upright has to pass the pianist first, so it's always better to play a 'stripped' upright if you want to *really* hear it, as long as family and neighbours don't object too much.

As a compromise, the top lid can be raised to get useful extra volume. It's a little-known fact that most uprights have a small wooden latch somewhere inside, enabling the lid to be propped open. People

are often amazed when I show them this feature in a piano they have owned for decades. The photo below shows a modern brass version. When the lid is closed on the prop, it will be left open by around 3in (75mm).

Modern casework – mover beware!

In older pianos, the cases are substantial and provide rock-solid support for the rest of the components. Old-fashioned uprights and large modern uprights have a large wooden frame in the back with four or five large, upright timbers and an outer rim of similarly stout construction (see page 25). In engineering terms this is overkill and most modern uprights omit the wooden frame, exposing the cast iron frame to the whole string load. The photo above shows that almost the entire back of a modern piano of this design is soundboard. This is good news for trees, but it reduces the margin for error when moving pianos.

When there is a wooden frame in the back the cast iron frame is sandwiched in the middle of the piano, close to its centre of gravity. You can tilt the piano backwards up to 20° from vertical and it won't fall over. But move the heavy cast iron frame right to the back, just inside the soundboard, and the piano falls over much more readily – at as little as 5° from vertical. (Please don't put my figures to the test. See Chapter 6.)

This is an argument for using professionals to move pianos any distance, and especially up or down stairs. That said, the most common accident is toppling the piano while manhandling it in situ, for example to clean behind it. The best safety precaution is more care all round, really – and always keep an upright piano against a wall.

In a grand piano, the case is actually load-bearing. Therefore, while some makers have followed the reduced timber trend and dispensed with a wooden frame, most grands still have one, easily visible from below. Some modern grand piano makers also fit a steel 'spider' tensioner into the wooden rim of the outside case to improve stability.

Soundboards and bridges

The soundboard is the large, apparently flat expanse of pale-coloured wood (usually spruce) that lies behind the frame and the strings in an upright, or below the frame and the strings in a grand. It is traditionally constructed from diagonal strips of wood first glued and clamped, then held together by ribs running in the opposite diagonal along the back. The photo on page 33 shows the soundboard of an upright. The photos below show the bottom of a grand piano soundboard: the ribs run at 90° to the component strips, the screws, with large 'button' or load-spreading washers, go through into the bridges.

Better pianos have the strips cut 'on the quarter' – that is, the planks are cut along the grain out of a quarter of the log. This yields fewer planks than the more economical 'through and through' cut right across the log, but they're less likely to shrink and warp.

The soundboard is more complex than it looks. It is actually a huge diaphragm, similar in function to the vibrating cone in an audio speaker. For a start it isn't flat, despite its appearance, and is 'feathered', or thinner at its edges. It is installed in the piano slightly crowned – that is, raised or 'bellied' in the middle. When the piano is first assembled in the factory this crowning is obvious to see; but as the string load of up to 20 tons of tension is applied, the soundboard is progressively squeezed down until almost, but not quite, flat.

The strings run up and over bridges fixed to the soundboard (see page 28, top right). These too appear flat but are not, though the angle formed over the bridge is usually less than 2°. To explain the job the bridges do, it's useful to detour into guitar technology, as guitar bridges perform the same basic function as piano bridges but are much more visible. (The guitar isn't the only example I could have used – the violin would do almost as well.)

The higher the bridge on an acoustic guitar, the louder the instrument will be – but it will also be more difficult to play. For example, photos of Django Reinhardt show him using guitars with exceptionally high strings – punishing to play, but a necessary trade-off to get maximum volume in pre-amplification days. Another characteristic of a high bridge is that louder notes decay faster. This happens because the higher the bridge, the greater the string-load on the soundboard, and so the less readily it will vibrate; therefore, a greater proportion of the energy released by plucking a string goes into trying to make the soundboard vibrate. The louder the note, the more energy is needed to move wood. Result: a much shorter resonation.

The same applies to the piano. The angle the strings form over the bridge is called *downbearing*, and the greater the degree of downbearing, the louder the piano will be. Because the strings are relatively long this angle is so small that it can only be measured with a special gauge that straddles the bridge.

Since the materials used in soundboard manufacture are natural products, the degree of downbearing varies slightly from piano to piano, despite the best efforts of quality control. And once assembly of a piano is complete, it can be very difficult to iron out any variations. This is the main reason why even pianos of exactly the same age, make and type often sound different from one other.

Glue or screw?

As a postscript, it's worth noting two different approaches to the assembly of soundboards and bridges. Some piano makers rely almost entirely on glue to hold the soundboard together, and even glue the bridges on to the soundboard, all in the conviction that this produces a superior sound. The photo below shows screws holding the bridges on, but the modern upright on page 33 evidently relies on glue. As a hardly surprising result, the bass bridge sometimes comes off. (See Chapter 8, section D.)

Other makers both screw and glue the ribs and bridges, insisting that this is structurally better and doesn't affect the sound. My experience tends to bear them out. Whenever I reattach a bass bridge I always put three screws in as well as glue, even if it was originally just glued. I have never been able to hear any difference in sound.

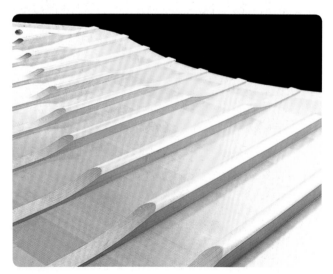

The keyboard

A key consists of two parts – a visible, familiar white or black front part that you play, and an invisible 'behind the scenes' part that activates the action. The whole key is made of wood and a set of keys is made from large, flat pieces of wood fed through the equivalent of a bread slicer.

When the front of the key is depressed 7/16in (12mm), the action moves the hammer forward 2in (26mm). This makes the key a *reversed lever* – small travel, large load movement – rather than the more normal lever, which requires a large travel for a small load movement. In mechanical terms the keyboard is therefore a collection of levers, which occupies the *keybed* and sits on three rails collectively known as the *keyframe* (see photos below):

- The middle or balance rail has upon it the fulcrum for each key – a polished steel pin with a small felt washer on it. The keys rock backwards and forwards on these pins, some of which are slightly offset to compensate for the shorter length of the black keys and the need to equalise the leverage on both white and black.

- The front rail comprises two rows of pins, one row near the front for the white keys, the other a little further back for the shorter black keys. These pins fit into a hole in the bottom of the key and guide it in its up-and-down movement. They have a thick felt buffer washer on them so that the key doesn't make a noise when it reaches the bottom of its stroke.

- The keys are weighted so that at rest they are ready to play. The back 'rail' – it isn't really a rail – is the *backtouch*, a thick piece of felt running the length of the keyframe. Its job is to ensure that the keys land at rest quietly.

In both uprights and grands, pressing the front of the key makes the back of the key rise up. The difference is that in an upright the action produces forward motion of a hammer, while in a grand the action produces upward motion of a hammer.

So what is the action? From this point on, nothing is simple.

Key coverings

Traditionally, the white key coverings were made of ivory and the black key coverings of ebony. It's now illegal to trade in ivory and ebony is scarce, so neither material is used any longer. Plastic is the usual substitute for both, though celluloid was and can still be used.

Surviving ivory key coverings are often discoloured and yellow, like bad teeth, especially in the middle of the keyboard where sweat has reacted with the material. Only the most expensive pianos had one-piece ivory coverings: most were made in two parts – the *heel* (front half) and the *stem* – joined at what appears to be a thin pencil line along the white keys, level with the end of the black keys (see below).

Only a small portion of an elephant tusk is grain free; the rest has marks in it like those on human fingernails. Thus only expensive pianos had keys of ungrained ivory. The next grade down had ungrained heel but grained stem. Finally came grained in both portions. When celluloid was developed as an ivory substitute for cheap pianos, an immediate problem was that it looked *too good*. So guess what? They invented grained-look celluloid so that it was no longer the stark white of expensive ivory! This must have been a huge relief to the marketing people.

Today, white keys are plastic, and in my view plastic is absolutely fine. It clearly disturbs some makers though, who claim that their keys have a covering of something with a fancy name suggesting ivory, and make a fuss about what a good ivory substitute it is. Call me obtuse, but ivory is over so I can't see what's so wrong about calling plastic plastic. Celluloid is still available but has to be fitted with specialist equipment, whereas plastic can be fitted in any workshop. I explain how to do it in Chapter 8, section A.

The action

The most important component by far in a piano is its *action* – the bit that converts the effort of your fingers into musical notes.

More correctly, the action isn't a component but a sub-assembly: several components grouped as a self-contained unit that can be installed or removed as a single item. The photo below shows an action in all its glory, removed from the piano. As you can see, it is actually a large collection of individual actions, one for each note.

Actions are such highly complex and precision mechanisms that most piano manufacturers don't make their own. Instead they specify what they want and a specialist supplier produces it for them. Over the years many variants of the action have been produced – some better than others – so it's quite possible to see actions of several different types. The biggest visual difference is between grands and uprights. But however much an action may vary in detail or materials, every action in every piano works in a similar way.

Sheer genius

It's easy to be almost reverential about the action of a piano. In an instrument packed with cleverly designed and crafted components, the action stands out as a work of engineering and musical genius. Its design was so perfectly conceived that it has remained essentially unchanged since 1720, and was last significantly improved in 1849.

This mechanism is incredible in performance, capable of lasting for decades and millions of working cycles without maintenance. I explain how to repair the upright action in Chapter 8, section B, and the grand action in Chapter 9. Both will, I hope, provide an insight into just what an exceptional piece of engineering the action is.

Explaining the almost impossible

Explaining the piano action in simple terms is perhaps the toughest challenge of this book. The main factors that make it so difficult to understand are:

- It's unlike any other mechanism most people are familiar with.
- Everything it does, it does at the same time.
- It has dozens of parts, each with a separate and often archaic name.
- For complication, it probably beats anything inside your PC or car engine.

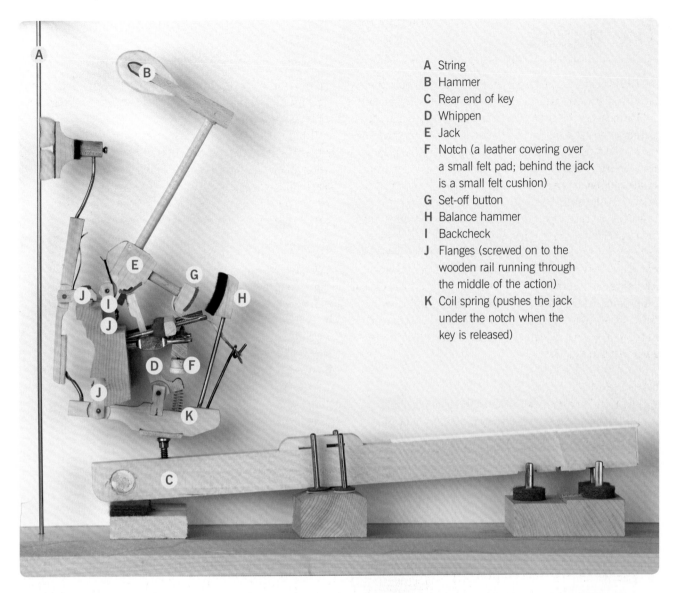

A String
B Hammer
C Rear end of key
D Whippen
E Jack
F Notch (a leather covering over a small felt pad; behind the jack is a small felt cushion)
G Set-off button
H Balance hammer
I Backcheck
J Flanges (screwed on to the wooden rail running through the middle of the action)
K Coil spring (pushes the jack under the notch when the key is released)

These are the jobs the action does:

- It converts the small downward motion of the key into a much greater forward motion of the hammer (upward motion in a grand, whose strings are hit from underneath).
- It reduces almost to zero the delay between pressing the key and hearing the note.
- It 'kills' the note the instant the key is released.
- It enables notes to be played in very rapid succession.
- It enables the player to control the length, expressiveness and volume of any note.
- It stops unplayed strings producing any unwanted sympathetic vibrations.

We'll now look at these functions in more detail, first for the upright and later for the grand.

Making the sound

The action assembly on pages 38–39 has been stripped out of a 30-year-old Kemble upright. For ease of understanding I've left out all the parts that are not strictly necessary, so this is essentially a 'lite' version of a typical upright action. Also, only those components mentioned in the text are identified. (It would be possible to name around 80 separate parts, but I doubt you'd thank me for it.)

When a key is depressed, the hammer starts to move forward (in an upright) or upward (in a grand). But if it just *kept* moving under key power, it would collide with the string and produce nothing better than a dull thud. Something has to release the hammer from the key *before it reaches the string*. The part that makes this happen is the escapement or jack (part E in both keyed diagrams). There is, of course, a large supporting cast of other components, but if you want a true action hero, its name is jack. Now let's see what happens, step by step:

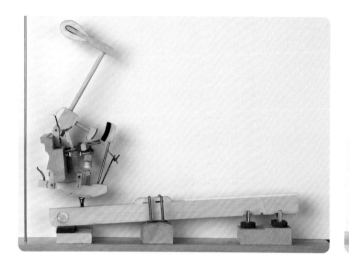

1 The action is *at rest* – that is, waiting for something to happen – 2in (26mm) from the string.

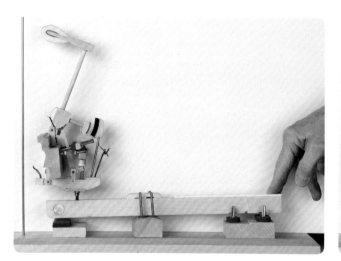

2 The player has pressed a key, causing its rear portion to rise.
- It lifts the whippen and jack.
- The jack pushes into the hammer notch, the little piece of leather *under* the hammer butt.
- This propels the hammer forward.

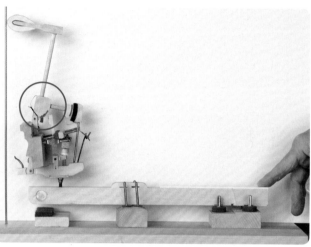

3 The hammer is still hurtling forward and is now nearing the string.
- By now, the heel of the jack is caught under the set-off button.
- This makes the jack come out from under the hammer butt…
- …which means that the hammer is no longer being pushed forward. The hammer is in fact flying through the air towards the string.

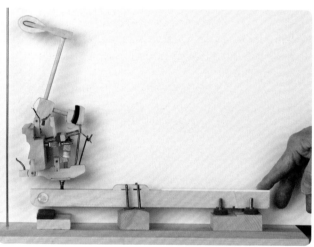

4 The hammer is 'in check'. It has collided with the string, bounced back and stopped.
- It stops in this position because the buckskin-covered balance hammer has collided with the backcheck (identifiable by its dark felt covering).
- If the key is pressed again *without being fully released*, the hammer will strike the string again. And again and again, as often and as rapidly as desired. It won't be as powerful as a full stroke, but it will do the job!
  NB: With a grand piano action (see below) 'in check' enables rapid repetition *at full force* without completely releasing the key.

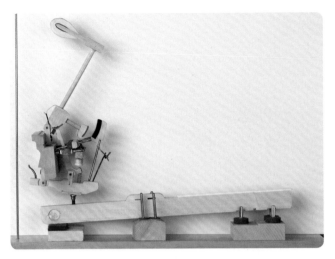

5 The player has released the key fully and the action is back at rest. The cycle is complete, ready to start all over again. This will happen millions of times over the lifetime of the piano.

Killing the sound

We've just explained how the action makes the string vibrate. But it also has to kill the sound when the key is released. This is achieved by a *damping* mechanism.

The top 20 or so treble notes on the piano are left free to vibrate until the sound dies of natural causes. These are short, light strings whose vibration fades rapidly, so no intervention is required.

However, from somewhere between note 60 and 70, depending on the make and quality of the piano, pianos need a damper mechanism to stop the vibration more quickly.

In essence, the damper consists of a spring that presses a felt pad against the string when the player releases the key. Each string has its own spring and pad, so a damper mechanism consists of a large number of individual dampers.

The damper pads are different shapes and sizes. They start small at the treble end, becoming larger as they head towards the thicker, longer and more powerful strings of the bass end. In the monochord section they are shaped to wrap around the string; in the bichord section they are wedge-shaped to fit between the two strings; and the pads for the lower trichords are a double-wedge shape. These are visible on the bottom photo on page 36.

The damper springs become progressively stronger, and the hammers heavier, into the bass. Because of this, the bass keys are noticeably harder to depress. This is especially marked in a grand piano, where the hammer is lying flat on its back rather than almost vertical as in an upright.

Where does damping fit into the action cycle?

In steps 1–5 there is a small steel 'spoon' on the front of the whippen. As the whippen moves up, this releases the damper off the string.

■ Below left shows the damper lifting from the string as the key is depressed.

■ Below right shows a damper in the rest position with the pad against the string, stopping the sound.

And that, basically, is how the piano action creates sound and then stops it.

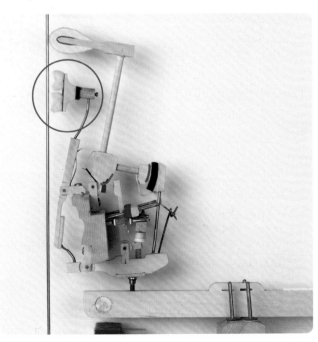

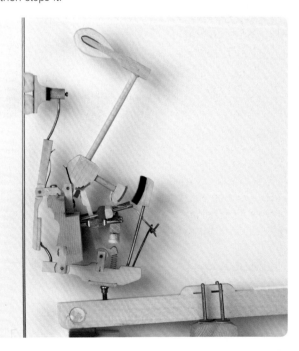

The grand piano action

From the player's point of view, the grand piano action differs most significantly from the upright action in two ways:

- More rapid repetition of notes is possible, and without loss of volume. This is an advantage for both loud and soft playing, and it makes the grand the more flexible instrument for many kinds of music.
- However, this advantage comes at a cost. Grands take more physical effort to play than uprights, because the damper mechanism is heavier and the hammers have to be raised from a flat rather than a near-vertical position.

Many players are dismayed by their first encounter with a grand; they find it heavy and ponderous, and have trouble playing fast. There's no doubt that to play a grand well you need to be something of an athlete. But the harder you work, the harder the piano will work for you.

To explain how the grand action works, I have constructed the model below of a single key and single action part. Photos 1–5 show the action working in stages as a key is played.

A grand piano action looks very different from an upright action for three main reasons:

- The damping mechanism isn't visible – it stays inside the piano (but is shown in the model below).
- The action is attached to the keyboard and keybed. They're shown on separated on page 161.
- The hammers lie on their backs. In the upright they stand almost vertical.

A String
B Hammer
C Rear end of key
D Whippen
E Jack
F Roller or knuckle
G Set-off button
H Backcheck
I Flanges
J Repetition spring
K Repetition lever
L Drop screw
M Damper

1 The action is at rest.

4 The hammer has now bounced off the string and landed on the backcheck and so is in check.
- The roller is pushing down on the repetition lever. This raises the tension in the repetition spring, which is straining to force the protruding upper end of the jack back under the roller.

2 The player – out of shot to the right – starts pressing the key down, which raises the rear or left-hand end. (Note the clearance above the square, green felt pad of the backtouch.)
- The damper starts to rise from the string, leaving the string free to vibrate.
- The right-hand end of the whippen rises…
- The jack pushes the hammer up, via the leather-covered roller…
- The heel of the jack moves towards the set-off button…
- The repetition lever jams up against the drop screw.

5 The player has now *partially* released pressure on the key, intending to repeat the note.
- As soon as the backcheck and hammer part very slightly, the repetition spring pushes both repetition lever and hammer up equally slightly. This allows the protruding end of the jack to slip gratefully back under the roller.
- The note can now be played again at full volume *without full release of the key*.

3 A microsecond later, the jack protrudes through an aperture in the repetition lever (not easy to see – look closely to the right of the roller). The repetition lever is still hard up against the drop screw.
- The jack disengages from the roller as its heel catches on the set-off button.
- The hammer hits the string, having flown through the air for the last 1/16in (1.59mm).

The action thus allows the player a wide range of expressiveness. In both upright and grand, the harder the key is struck, the louder the note sounds. The grand especially may be played very quietly *and* very rapidly. And if all that isn't enough, the pedals offer players even more opportunity for expressiveness.

The pedals

All pianos have at least two and often three foot pedals, each of which alters the sound of the instrument in a different way.

The sustain or damper pedal (right-hand)

This is often incorrectly called the *loud* pedal. I have already explained that when a key is depressed, its damper lifts until the key is released. When the sustain pedal is depressed, *all* the dampers lift. This means that each note played continues to ring out until the pedal is released or the string vibration fades away naturally.

It also means that all the strings are free to vibrate sympathetically. This will be most marked in close relatives like octaves and fifths; but whichever notes are played, all the sounds will run into each other. (This has a cacophony potential that children love experimenting with. It's particularly excruciating if discords are allowed to sustain. If the pedal is used correctly, this should not happen.)

The sustain pedal gives players much more scope for expressiveness, and makes possible a more complete accompaniment to the melody. Many formal compositions have the pedal strokes notated on the music, but most pianists like to devise their own pedalling.

The soft pedal (left-hand)

The soft pedal has a longer history than the sustain, as Cristofori's 1720 piano had a lever-operated equivalent of a soft pedal. Called *una corda* (one string), it shifted the whole keybed slightly to one side so that the hammers struck only one string of each bichord (two-string) note. (On Cristofori's piano, every note had two strings.) This produced a quieter note, but there were also other subtle effects, partly from the sympathetic vibration of the other string and partly from exposing a different part of the hammer to the string.

This is worth explaining as the mechanism is very similar on a modern grand: the whole keybed shifts. Where there are three strings, two are struck; where there are two, one is struck; and where there is one, one is struck. Presumably because there is no snappy Italian for all this, *una corda* it remains.

If you've never pressed the soft pedal on a grand, it can be disconcerting to find the whole keyboard shifting before your eyes. Many children and adults first encounter it during an examination on a grand when they've never played one before. A bad time to be disconcerted!

The soft pedal on a modern upright is quite different. Here, the pedal shifts the hammers to about halfway towards the string. Over their shorter travel they don't develop as much momentum, so the notes are quieter. This is called *half-blow*. Though effective in softening the sound, this mechanism is

crude and progressively damages the leather in the notch of the hammer butts.

On older uprights, the soft pedal mechanism is different again: it makes a felt pad rise up in front of the hammers. The hammer blow is transmitted through this felt, which reduces the sound to about a third or less of its unfettered volume. The technical name for this is *celeste*, which makes it sound a lot less crude than it is.

The middle pedal

Many modern grands and uprights have three pedals. The function of the middle pedal is quite different in each.

On the grand, it is usually *sostenuto*. This sustains, like the sustain pedal, but *only* those notes held down when the pedal is depressed. This is quite tricky to learn to operate, but it adds yet more potential for expressive playing. Many cheaper grands fake *sostenuto* by having a middle pedal that sustains just the bass section. This is a reasonably acceptable substitute.

On a modern upright, the third pedal is generally a *practice pedal* which brings a felt pad down in front of the hammers. It is usually softer than the celeste pad described above, and so is slightly less effective than the celeste. However, unlike the celeste the practice pedal can be locked over to one side and so does not have to be held down continuously. As the name implies, the advantage here is that it can be locked on for a full practice session at times when full volume might not be welcomed by others within earshot.

All this, though, is generalisation. Over three decades of working on pianos, and especially on older instruments, I have seen grands with half-blow soft pedals, uprights with *sostenuto* and even *una corda* on an upright. These are some of the chance finds that make it impossible to be too categorical about pianos!

Underdampers and overdampers

All modern upright pianos now use a damping system called underdamping, introduced around 1914. As the name suggests, the dampers go under the hammer. You won't be able to see them without dismantling your piano, but the photo below shows a part of a typical underdamped upright action with the dampers under the hammers as if looking from the strings.

Underdampers are near to the middle of the string, so they kill the vibration close to the point where it is created. This is about as effective as the laws of physics allow. Each damper is also mounted on a spring, which allows the felt to wear down considerably before the damping effect starts to fail.

string to be effective, and have to be very small to fit between the hammer and the end of the string. The last 13 dampers seen in the bottom photo will be completely useless.

As the devisers of the underdamper system recognised, the fastest way to stop a string vibrating is to arrest it at its centre, where the greatest amount of vibration occurs. Overdampers, then, are doomed by their design to be bad at killing a note rapidly. The piano may sound discordant or 'honky-tonk' as notes last too long and run into each other. Worse, overdampers tend to wear out rapidly, becoming even less effective.

There is hardly any chance of buying a piano with an

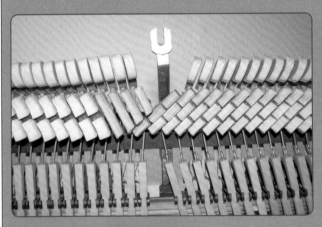

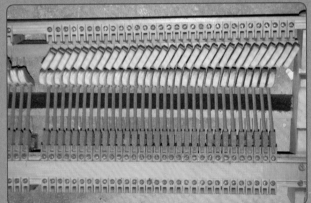

Overdamper action

What you *don't* want to see in your own piano is an *overdamper* mechanism, so called because the felt damper pads operate over the top of the hammers. The photo below shows a typical overdamper mechanism.

If in doubt, how do you spot an overdamper action? Simple. Underdampers can't be seen, so if you can see the dampers at all they're overdampers. The photos on the right show the overdamper action as if looking from the strings (compare them with the photo above, showing underdampers from the same viewpoint). The dampers are too close to the top end of the

overdamper action that works. It's not too much of an exaggeration to state that their purpose in life was to go wrong. That does not, however, stop people trying to sell them, especially at auctions or on the internet. I've heard sellers claim that while most overdamped pianos are indeed to be avoided, theirs is acceptable because it's German, and before 1914 the Germans built some big, fine pianos of exceptional quality. Yes they did, but they're still overdamped. That makes them useless a hundred years later.

CHAPTER 3

Choosing a piano

Before buying either a new or a used piano, you first need to form a clear idea of what you want and don't want. Even if you find yourself surrounded by excellent pianos, not all of them – and perhaps very few of them – will be suitable for you.

Selection criteria

Pianos don't lend themselves to impulse buying. It's one thing to exchange an item of clothing that you loved in the shop but hated as soon as you got home; it's another thing entirely to take back a piano that weighs several hundredweight and should only be moved by professionals. If you think about the following points before and during your quest for a piano, you're much more likely to get it right first time.

When choosing a piano, the criteria that matter are:

Technical

- In the case of a used piano, it must be tuneable. It doesn't matter how good it looks, or how good it sounds on the day you try it. If it isn't tuneable, it's useless. Anything older than about ten years and you may need professional advice on this.
- It must be playable by the person who will spend the most time playing it. Children have smaller fingers and a shorter reach than grown-ups, so a piano that feels comfortable to an adult may be awkward for a child.
- If it's to be played in a school, club, theatre, church etc it must effortlessly produce enough volume to fill the venue. This means larger rather than smaller pianos, but beware the assumption that a grand is always louder than an upright. Small grands are often hopeless in even a moderately sized auditorium.

Aesthetic

- It must produce a pleasing sound. In a home environment, the judge of this shouldn't be just the main player, but everyone who will share the noise. Different pianos deliver varying degrees of pleasure to different ears.
- It must look good in its intended environment, especially if it will occupy a prominent position in your home. Music isn't everything, so think hard before buying a large, ugly or incongruous piano for its superlative sound quality.
- If the piano you want doesn't suit the room, consider altering the room layout or decor to suit the piano. If the alternative is a more expensive piano, a partial room makeover may work out cheaper.

Can you live with it?

- Volume matters. In a small house with thin walls, you may not want a piano with enough natural volume to fill a town hall. (Many used pianos do in fact come from concert halls, schools and other places where a seriously large sound is necessary.) On the other hand, too quiet a piano may be frustrating for a naturally vigorous player. See also *Quiet practice*.
- How much space can you spare? Grand pianos, even baby ones, are a tight fit in most homes, unless, like legendary jazz pianist Thelonious Monk, you're willing to live in whatever space is left over. Upright pianos were designed

▥ Quiet practice

A solution to the common problem of practising after children have gone to bed, or at other unsocial times, is a practice pedal (see Chapter 2). This enables the piano to be played at about a quarter of its normal volume, which isn't great but is better than no practice at all. A practice pedal is present on most modern uprights as a third or middle pedal which, when depressed, locks over to one side and muffles the sound by bringing down a felt pad in front of the hammers.

If need be, a mechanism that has the effect of a practice pedal can be retro-fitted to most upright pianos. It is operated not by a pedal but by a lever hidden under the top lid. It's hard to find commercially, so you may only be able to source one through a piano dealer. Or you may find a piano with one already. I occasionally come across pianos whose owners are unaware that they have this mechanism installed, so look for it if an instrument you're interested in doesn't have a practice pedal. It's a long shot, but you never know.

to be home-friendly, but this was in the days when rooms tended to be bigger. These days many people want small upright pianos, and are willing to lose some sound quality to save space. But the keyboard is more or less the same size on any piano, so all a small piano really does is take up less *wall* space. There may therefore be an argument for buying a taller piano with almost the same footprint but a much better sound.

■ Will the chosen location suit everyone? I don't want to sound too *feng shui* here, but the positioning and orientation of a piano within a room can significantly affect both sound quality and player satisfaction. For example, many pianists don't like playing with their back to the room. A good supply of natural light is also important. Satisfying the player may, however, dissatisfy others, and I've known this become a source of friction within families. And don't think that the piano can be moved around like a tea trolley. At a stretch it can, but in practice it nearly always stays put.

Piano fashion

Piano casings are subject to fashion just like everything else, so if you want a particular 'look' your choice may be limited. Your search may take longer and you may have to recruit professional help to track down what you want, or an acceptable substitute.

Here, extremely briefly, is the design history of the modern piano.

Nineteenth-century pianos were often highly decorated with marquetry, usually floral in pattern. Extravagantly swirly wood grains were popular too, particularly walnut. Towards 1900 a plainer looking instrument was favoured, often with a rosewood finish.

After 1918 mahogany became the fashion and has remained so ever since. There might be an occasional walnut or even teak casing, but anything other than mahogany could be difficult to sell. Oak pianos were around, but found mainly in schools, churches or other institutions.

There have always been plenty of black pianos around, because it was the colour preferred by many German makers.

Indeed, for most of them it was the *only* colour, well before the days of Henry Ford. Perhaps for that reason, English pianos were rarely black – I've only ever seen one.

The German fondness for black bordered on the irrational. I once stripped the French polish off a battered old black Ritmüller upright, only to uncover the most exquisite rosewood casing. When repolished *sans* black it was barely recognisable as the same piano. (As an added touch of German eccentricity, the frame was decorated with beautiful, hand-painted enamel flowers – just for the occasional benefit of the tuner! It felt like a privilege to tune it.)

For the last few decades a shiny black finish has been increasingly popular, probably because black goes with anything. It might also conceal inferior wood, of course. And it conveniently lends itself to being sprayed on rather than hand polished.

In recent years several piano makers have sold new versions of old or classic models. For example, Bechstein produced an upright in the 1980s that copied one of their models from around 1900. Whether this is a passing marketing fad is difficult to say, but if you hanker after a piano from a long-gone era, it's not beyond the bounds of possibility that there are new or recent versions of it to be had.

Design disasters

During the 1940s and '50s, there was a trend towards smaller pianos and cases that were then considered modern. Some seemed to have been inspired by the art nouveau of Odeon cinemas. In the 1960s and '70s smaller pianos started to take on a slab-sided look similar to the Hammond organ. In my view the Hammonds of this era still wear it well, but the pianos look terribly dated.

From the 1940s to the 1970s there was an unfortunate and never successful fashion for 'modernising' existing pianos, in line with a popular home decoration mania for smoothing and squaring off everything in sight. (Anyone brought up in the 1950s and '60s will remember hardboard and plywood triumphing over good taste – fielded doors rendered flat, turned banisters boxed in, etc.) To their shame, some piano parts suppliers still list the bits and pieces necessary for this extreme cosmetic vandalism.

The earliest and most common minor modernisation was the removal of the sconces (candle holders) from old pianos. There was obvious sense in this as gas or electric lighting made them redundant. The casing became easier to polish, if at the expense of sometimes unsightly screw holes and differently-coloured surface patches.

But most post-1950 modernisation was so severe that anyone experienced in the trade can recognise it at once. Typically:

- Front panels were removed and replaced with slabs of plywood. (Sometimes I've found and restored original, elegantly inlaid panels left inside the instrument – possibly someone's conscience at work.)
- Corners were smoothed off and decorative fluting removed.
- Grand pianos had their turned legs squared off or entirely replaced with square legs.
- And – ultimate horror – many grands had their fretwork music desks replaced with plywood.

Pianos fitting any of these descriptions are still around in large numbers and prices tend to be low, so you may find yourself having to decide how you feel about the desecration of a once fine (or at least better-looking) instrument. My own view is that such a piano can be excellent value if it's up to pitch and playing well with plenty of life left in it. But it'll be purely a functional instrument, never an object to cherish.

Grand or upright?

Uprights vastly outsell grands for the simple reason that grands are too big for most homes. Broadly speaking, uprights are designed for the home and small performance venues, while grands are designed for larger venues where there is also likely to be a higher requirement for technical and musical quality.

The line between them, though, is decidedly blurred, because so many piano makers have produced smaller grands supposedly suitable for homes. This has always involved some degree of compromise, and the results have rarely been completely successful.

Therefore, if you're tempted to consider a grand, my first observation has to be that a grand isn't necessarily better than an upright. Many uprights are much better than many grands.

What, then, are the facts about grand pianos?

Small is not grand

It constantly amazes me that so many people who want a grand piano want a small one. I suspect that what they really want is the status value of a grand at the least possible cost. If it's social standing you want, fine. But if you want the best sound quality for your money, think again.

As I explain elsewhere about uprights, the bigger the instrument, the better the sound quality. This relationship is even more marked with grands.

Relative to the size of the instrument, the soundboard of a grand is *smaller* than that in a full-size upright piano. In an upright, the soundboard can be almost the whole height of the piano. In a grand, the space available for the soundboard is much reduced by the space needed for the keyboard and action.

The strings of a grand are also relatively shorter than those of a full-size upright. In an upright they can be almost the whole height of the piano, plus the extra allowed by the diagonal overstringing. In a grand, the strings end well before the keyboard and the extra length achieved by overstringing is less than in the upright.

Therefore, unless you're prepared to buy a grand piano over 5ft 6in (1.68m) long, sound quality won't be noticeably better than that of an upright of similar quality.

By 6ft 4in (1.93m), it's a different matter: you're now getting into powerful technology. In my view, this is the minimum size at which a grand piano comes into its own and is significantly better than an upright. (The size of a grand, by the way, is measured from its keyboard edge to its furthest point, along a line at 90° to the keyboard.)

Apart from size, there are three other reasons for preferring a grand piano:

- Principally, the superior performance of the double escapement action (see Chapter 2). It's simply more responsive and even on a baby grand feels better than an upright. Notes can be repeated more rapidly and at full volume.

- The superior damper arrangement. The dampers of a grand are larger, because there is more room for them. They're also longer and heavier, and helped by gravity. They're therefore bound to be more effective, though to some extent this advantage is reduced because there's a greater length of string to stop vibrating, especially in a concert grand. Furthermore, the hammers and dampers in an upright work on the same side of the string, but of necessity at different points along it. In a grand, the hammers and dampers work on opposite sides of the string, making it possible for both to operate at the same point on the string. The difference is small but significant. When the key is released, the sound really does stop dead. Play a good upright and then a concert grand, and you'll notice the difference.

- A less evident overstringing break. This is admittedly a marginal advantage that will be inaudible to most players, but it's there nonetheless. The photo below shows typical grand dampers. Only one damper is slightly shortened to accommodate the overstringing break. By contrast, the photo on page 29 shows a typical upright underdamper arrangement, in which three of the dampers are progressively shortened, down to about an inch (26mm).

Baby grands

Baby grands are popular, but are they any good? Here's a clue: they're often called *vanity pianos* in the trade. This implies that quality has been sacrificed to appearance.

To many people, first impressions may suggest the opposite. Because of the double escapement action in all modern grands, a new baby grand will undoubtedly feel better to play than an upright, and this probably sways many buying decisions. The blunt fact, though, is that grands less than 5ft long (1.52m) simply don't have enough string length to produce quality sound, and a full-size upright will be a far better choice.

Added value features

Because grands represent the top end of both the price and quality scales, some manufacturers are keen to add special 'de luxe' features that are unlikely to appear on uprights. Some of these have debatable technical value but presumably help the sales people deliver a more impressive performance. For example:

Top bridge arrangements

Different makers use different techniques for bridging the strings. Any improvement in sound quality is likely to be slight and subjective, but for serious players it could be a factor to consider. Some grands have *agraffes*, or individual bridges for each string, while some have a cast iron bridge and pressure bar.

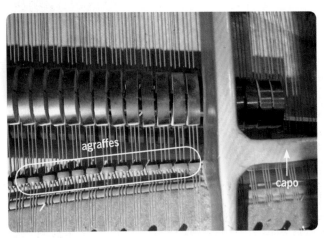

Others have a *capo d'astra*, a bar in the treble section *under* which the strings pass on their way to the tuning pins. It may be either cast into the frame, or bolted on. The photo below shows, to the left, agraffes with the strings passing *through* them; and to the right, a capo bar with the strings passing *under* it. (This instrument sounded very weak in the capo area. I suspected the capo as the cause, but wasn't able to confirm it.)

Duplex scaling

Duplex refers to the non-speaking part of the string – the 'spare' bit at each end, after the string has passed over the top and bottom bridges. In most grands and uprights, a strip of usually bright-coloured fabric is wedged under or woven through one or both of these non-speaking lengths to prevent any sympathetic vibration: it's visible on the top photo on page 51. In most smaller modern pianos, this is done only at the 'dead' or bottom bridge end of the string. The 'live' or tuning pin end has such a short non-speaking length that sympathetic vibration is unlikely.

In bigger and more expensive grands, the length of the non-speaking ends is calculated or *scaled* and sympathetic vibration is allowed. This is normally at an octave above the speaking length, though some pianos use different intervals. The small photo shows the bass strings deadened by a felt strip in a modern Kawai. The larger photo, however, shows the treble section where the string passes from the bridge to another small bridge and is free to vibrate sympathetically.

On some makes (for example, concert grands from US maker Mason & Hamlin), the duplex length is tuned by tapping a little wedge – one for each note – back and forth under the non-speaking segment of the string. It won't vibrate unless properly tuned.

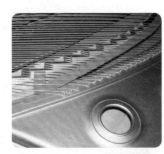

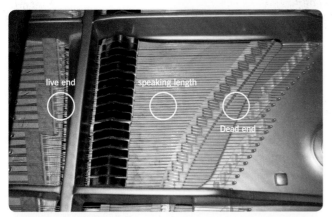

On many pianos with duplex scaling, only the 'dead' or bottom bridge end is calculated, but when the 'live' end is also calculated it is called *double duplex scaling*. This is visible in the boxout photo, in the length marked 'live end'. This is the section between the capo bar and the tuning pin end of the strings of the same Kawai, calculated in length and free to vibrate.

Aliquot stringing

The pinnacle of esotericism was perhaps reached in the 1870s, when Blüthner produced a grand with *aliquot stringing*. (Aliquot is a mathematical term meaning something contained an exact number of times in something else. For example, 4 is an aliquot part of 16.) Each trichord from about the middle of the piano upwards had another string stretched above it, tuned an octave above the fundamental. The hammer did not strike it, but if a note was struck and held down, the aliquot string would absorb some energy so that the tone would change and the note would die more rapidly.

Aliquot stringing may have been more of an attempt at product differentiation than a serious contribution to piano design. Perhaps unsurprisingly, Blüthner stand by it but in my view pianos are not noticeably better for it and in most of the examples I see the aliquot strings have been either deadened or removed. I'd like to interpret this as an act of justified rebellion by tuners or technicians, exasperated beyond endurance by an embellishment that burdened them with extra and possibly unpaid work for no improvement in sound quality that they were aware of.

🎹 Are the 'extras' worth it?

Is all this going just a little too far in the pursuit of perfection? Possibly. I doubt that even experts could detect the presence of any of these features in a piano by listening to it from a front-row seat in an auditorium. Nevertheless, they're all symbols of peerless quality and craftsmanship, of an honourable striving to create exquisite and 'perfect' musical instruments. Perhaps the most reasonable verdict is that they were all worth a try.

But they do, of course, come at a price (though some of the cheaper pianos now emerging from China and Korea have duplex scaling). If you want and can afford pianos with features such as these, compare their merits by playing as many of them as you can.

Otherwise, the main tests that I detail in Chapters 4 and 5 for the quality of a new or used upright apply equally to grands. Watch especially for buzzing bass strings and a weak treble. Even the most expensive pianos can have these problems.

Don't forget the stool!

To get maximum enjoyment out of your piano playing – or even to play well at all – you need to be comfortable. And for health and safety reasons it's absolutely vital to sit in the correct position for playing the piano. This is especially important for children, whose developing physique can be damaged by prolonged sitting in the wrong posture. It's therefore much more important than you might imagine to have a proper piano stool. Yes, they can be expensive and yes, they do take up room. But the most common alternative – a dining-room or kitchen chair – just isn't good enough.

The main arguments in favour of piano stools and against chairs are:

■ All serious musicians are at risk of repetitive strain injury (RSI), and poor posture caused by inappropriate seating is just going to make it happen that much sooner.
■ If you take the piano seriously, you may well spend more hours sitting on whatever you use as a piano stool than on any other single piece of furniture. (For hours clocked up in one place, only bed may beat it. And there you're horizontal.)
■ Most chairs are designed for bodies at rest, but a body playing the piano is often highly active. An adult of average build playing pieces that demand a lot of energy can destroy a chair in fairly short order, so never use the Chippendale. Piano stools are designed to cope with the dynamics of vigorous playing. That's why they don't look like chairs.
■ Height is critical, and it's unlikely that the nearest convenient chair will be the right height for your body. (It can be so difficult to find something exactly right that in my pub pianist days I've preferred to sit on stacked beer crates than on chairs.)

There can be no hard and fast rule on height as pianos vary and so do humans, but for most adults and most pianos a minimum seat height is 22in (560mm). For children it may have to be considerably more than this.

The ideal posture for an adult is to be seated with:

■ Feet flat on the ground.
■ Back straight.
■ Forearms flat or slightly downward sloping – never upward sloping.
■ Wrists horizontal or slightly downward – never angled upward.

The same checklist applies to children, but if there is a shortage in the leg department it's more important that the child's back is straight than that he or she can reach the pedals. It's possible to buy a pedal extending mechanism, but this is an investment perhaps only worth making if the child is keen and shows real promise. In most cases it won't harm to delay learning

pedal technique for a few years until the child grows. There really isn't that much to it.

Never, ever use a height-adjustable typist's or office chair, unless you want to injure yourself or someone else. They're tempting because they're cheap, comfortable and easy to adjust to the right height, but they have wheels. This makes them frisky and unstable. For comic effect they can't be beaten, but for serious playing they're dangerous.

The best seating solution by far is a *rise-and-fall* or adjustable height stool. These have large 'door knobs' on the ends which, when turned, operate a scissors mechanism to raise or lower the seat. Though not cheap, such a stool should be regarded as essential in schools and other environments where there will be more than one player.

Cheaper versions have bolt-on legs and are sold flat-packed, and in my experience deteriorate fairly rapidly. Those with permanently fixed legs are dearer because they're more substantially made and can't be flat-packed.

The supreme version of the rise-and-fall is the concert stool. It has a large, comfortable flat top in leather (usually buttoned) and is ideal for prolonged playing. It's expensive but probably essential if you have a grand piano.

If you're thinking of letting your child take lessons from a piano teacher, one clue to their suitability is whether or not they provide an adjustable piano stool. But even if they do, in my experience many piano teachers don't pay much attention to how their pupils sit, so make a point of asking the teacher to demonstrate good posture. If they're clearly not familiar with the checklist above, your child may be better off elsewhere.

Care of piano stools

Though designed to be robust, an adjustable stool will last longer if it's spared unnecessary stresses. Adults shouldn't try to adjust the stool while sitting on it, and also for safety's sake don't let children play with it or adjust it on their own.

A conventional, non-adjustable piano stool with a lift-up lid and room for music storage should only be used to store the few pieces of music in current use. It's a mistake to do what many people do, and cram every piece of music they own into the stool. The base of these stools is usually flimsy plywood and if you fill it up until the lid is resting on the music, your bottom will exert force via the stack of music against the stool's base. As wood shrinks and joints loosen with age, the pressure may split the base or even cause the whole stool to disintegrate.

If you're offered an attractive old stool, beware piano stool amnesia. This is the surprisingly common condition that allows otherwise fiercely house-proud owners to overlook the fact that the seat of their piano stool hasn't been cleaned in living memory.

Inspect its condition carefully. In many cases a quick sniff will be enough, but don't get too close – it may be flea heaven, especially if the family cat likes curling up on it. Once the stool is yours, take the lid off and give the cover fabric and its padding the deepest clean it will stand, or go the whole hog and get it reupholstered.

Buying piano stools

If you're buying a piano that has a matching stool, do insist on the stool as well – even if you don't intend to use it. Matching items shouldn't be separated as a matter of principle, and a matching stool may help you get a better price for your piano when you come to sell it.

Bear in mind that most new pianos have always come complete with a matching stool. So if that stool is missing when you come to buy a piano, even after several changes of ownership, you should ostentatiously mourn its absence for two reasons. First, because you'll have to buy a replacement, and even a good used one may not be cheap; and second, because whatever you buy is unlikely to match the piano. You may get lucky and find a dealer who has an orphaned stool for your model of piano, but the chances of one turning up exactly when you need it are remote.

Therefore, when buying a new or good quality used piano from a dealer, it's reasonable to use the piano stool as a bargaining counter. Top of your wish-list should be a *matching* rise-and-fall stool with a leather seat. Ask for one. If it can't be done, negotiate for a significant discount – preferably pausing just as you're about to go through the motions of paying. Nothing improves one's bargaining position quite like a disappearing cheque-book.

Most piano dealers will either have a choice of stools in stock or be able to order one for you, perhaps on approval. Stool prices can vary widely, but this is an area where you tend to get what you pay for, so there's a big advantage in being able to try a few before buying. If that isn't possible, there are always plenty of new and used stools for sale on the internet. However, the usual notes of caution apply to anything bought unseen. In general, don't expect the 'bargains' to be much good.

Finally, always check that any stool you're offered hasn't been shortened. This is quite a common problem. Victorian and Edwardian piano stools are collectable in their own right, but will usually have been made for big pianos kept in big rooms in big houses. When both pianos and homes became smaller, many owners kept the attractive old stools but couldn't resist the temptation to cut them down to a more 'convenient' size – typically to around 18in (450mm). This enabled them both to fit under the keyboard and double as an extra dining seat. Unless you're seven feet tall this will be no good as a working piano stool, so always take a tape measure with you and settle for nothing less than a 22in (560mm) minimum from floor to seat top. If it's a rise-and-fall stool, cutting it down may mean that even when fully extended you don't get the minimum height you need. In my opinion any piano stool that has been vandalised in this way is unlikely to be a good buy, even as an antique.

CHAPTER 4

How to buy a new piano

If you can afford it, buy new. But not all pianos in the same price range will be the same. There can be many differences, even between two supposedly identical instruments. I explain how to 'test drive' a new piano to maximise your chances of buying one that will be right for you.

If you can, buy new

■ New piano prices have been falling for some time. Against a background of rising incomes in many countries, a new piano is now more affordable for most people than ever before.

■ There are no really awful pianos being made any more, so it's difficult to buy a lemon. In the quite recent past there were horror pianos like the Lindner, made in Ireland until 1975, which gets a brief mention in Chapter 5; but if you buy a new piano today you're almost guaranteed to get one that will meet all modern standards and give many years of excellent service.

This doesn't mean that there is nothing left to consider, and that all new pianos are as good as each other. Like many types of consumer product, you tend to get what you pay for. At entry level there is a fairly high but somewhat uniform standard of quality. Beyond that, the choice is yours and the more you're prepared to spend, the more you can specify what you get for your money. Nevertheless, even within a typical owner's price range there will be plenty of options – so how do you go about making a choice?

Play the pianos

It's going to be impossible to make an informed choice if you don't personally play or listen to several instruments. So if you can play, take some music to the showroom and play a selection of pianos until you feel you know which suit you and which don't.

If you can't play, take someone who can. You could even consider paying a professional, or an impecunious music student, to come. (There are few gigs around during piano showroom hours, so daytime fees tend to be modest.) A good piano dealer won't pressure you for a decision, so don't feel any embarrassment about taking your time – even if that means coming back for a second or third visit.

You could also consider paying a piano technician to come with you, perhaps on the visit where you make your final choice. The advantage is that you get the opinion of someone who can hear and interpret *all* the sounds generated by a piano. The point here is that a piano is a mechanical apparatus,

many of whose working parts make some kind of non-musical noise. Most of those noises will go unnoticed and that's the way it ought to be, but they will be there nonetheless. A piano technician knows what to listen out for, and can differentiate 'right' from 'wrong' sounds.

Is this level of scrutiny really necessary for a factory-fresh piano? I'll be the first to admit that most buyers get by perfectly well without it, but read on and you may appreciate that I'm not suggesting it just as a luxury. Even though pianos are made on production lines with very high standards of quality control, they're made of natural materials assembled largely by hand. Some variability is therefore inevitable. This doesn't mean that some new pianos are good and others bad, but it does mean that (a) some pianos have minor imperfections that need fixing, and (b) every piano has its own 'voice' resulting from an accumulation of tiny and perfectly natural variations. A piano technician can guide you to a better understanding of the pianos you're trying out, and can help you make choices that will be right for you.

However you test your pianos, observe these general guidelines:

- While playing or listening, concentrate on the *tone and feel* of the piano. Is it what you want? Even identical pianos can have quite different tonal and tactile characteristics.
- Assuming you want an upright, ask the dealer to remove the front top board from the piano you're most interested in, and the bottom board too if you feel bold enough. *Don't risk removing anything yourself* – that's a good way to fall out with the dealer. Now play some more. Just like opening up the lid on a grand, the piano will burst into life. (As a general point, it's always better to play an upright this way if you want to unleash its true potential, but family and neighbours may need to be very understanding.)
- The more expensive the piano, the better it's likely to sound. This means that if you don't want to spend what it takes to get that better sound, you'll have to accept some kind of compromise.

Now I'll get down to a few specifics, which you can use to refine your choice. These tests will help you identify the perfect piano or – perhaps more realistically – help you find the piano that offers best value within your budget, and that you'll be happy to live with.

Find the break

Play scales across the overstringing break. As I explain in Chapter 2, this is a design weakness on overstrung pianos, and all new pianos are overstrung. Can you hear any change in tone as you play across this break? Play single notes, then play with both hands. If you can find the break simply by listening

for it (that is, without looking inside), the piano designer or builder has not done a good enough job.

Around this point too, the dampers are shorter than the rest (see page 29), so play your scales staccato. Are any of the notes in this area decaying less rapidly than over the rest of the piano? If this is noticeable now, it may become a source of mounting dissatisfaction later.

Find the string changes

The next test is to see if you can detect, again just by listening, the points where the strings change (though it's no secret that it all happens around the overstringing break).

If you can hear the changes in tone without having to 'cheat' by looking inside, there is a question mark over the quality of the piano. There are two critical string changes (see photo below).

- From trichord (three strings per note) to bichord (two strings per note).
- From plain strings to copper-wound strings.

There is a third change further into the bass, when the stringing changes from bichord to monochord (single) strings. However, in most pianos it's normal to hear this quite plainly. Indeed, there tends to be such an improvement in tone that many pianos would probably benefit from more monochords. And at some further point, the bass monochords will have a double copper winding on them. For example, this Challen baby grand (right) has its bottom six bass strings double wound. Can you hear this point?

Find the unusable notes

The point at which notes become unusable is another measure of piano quality, so keep playing your scales right down into the bass. Even on top concert grands, the bottom few notes tend to 'growl' so much that many players consider them unusable. Any kind of improvisation often means going up or down an octave.

Even if you don't currently need the piano's full *compass* (all its notes), that may change in the future. You really do need a piano that works flawlessly down to bottom C. If bottom C growls horribly, this is not the piano for you. (On some Bösendorfers, the bass end key block is actually a small lid which flips off to expose more keys, down to F. Jazz pianist Oscar Peterson famously demonstrated them on TV from Ronnie Scott's Club in the 1960s. They were only usable when played with the octave above, and rapidly.)

Listen for bass buzz

While at the bass end, listen *very carefully* to every bass note. In my experience, about one in four pianos – including new ones – has at least one bass string with a loose copper winding on it, audible as a metallic buzz.

Even though this is a common problem, most people are unaware of it and don't hear it – at least not in the showroom. If you do hear a buzz you should certainly mention it, and note carefully what happens next. Because it's so rarely mentioned, some sales people dismiss it as a trivial problem that can be cured by tuning. *No it can't*. No amount of tuning will fix it. This false claim is a recurring source of embarrassment to tuners, especially if they're being paid to provide the 'free' after-sales tuning typically included in the price of a new piano.

I explain how to tackle a buzzing string in Chapter 7, but it's obviously best avoided in the first place. If the person selling you a new piano tries to mislead you in this way, either make it clear that you know better in at least this one aspect of pianos, or take your custom elsewhere. (In the interests of stamping out this deception, do both. Scrupulous dealers, and most piano tuners, will thank you for it.)

Find the fade

The next trial is at the treble end. Treble notes on many pianos fade away quickly and the top octave, or even two, may have little volume. The string speaking length is so short, and the volume from it so small, that the mechanical noise of playing the note can exceed the volume of sound it produces. The symptom of this is a 'thunk' from the top handful of notes. (You'll know it when you hear it.)

This problem results from tiny differences in downbearing – the angle of the strings as they pass over the bridge, as explained in Chapter 2. Too much departure from the ideal downbearing will be especially noticeable in the treble.

Downbearing can also vary between two otherwise identical pianos, so if the treble sounds acceptable on the piano you're trying out, make sure *either* that this is the one you actually buy (assuming it passes all other tests) *or* that you have a chance to test and approve a substitute before agreeing to buy it.

Nothing can be done to correct a downbearing problem short of dismantling the piano, so if the top end is feeble, reject that instrument. Don't let anyone persuade you that this is the natural sound of the treble end! While it's true that in some pianos it's almost impossible to tune these top few notes, there are plenty of others where they play perfectly well.

Agraffes

Most pianos have a cast iron top bridge and a pressure bar to hold the strings against it. In the bass section, the strings will pull tightly around a pin on the bridge.

Some pianos have instead a series of agraffes. The top photo shows an older piano and the bottom, a more modern piano. Agraffes are, in effect, separate bridges for each string. This is generally regarded as a much superior system, but also an expensive one, as fitting agraffes takes more time and skill than fitting a pressure bar and bass pins. Nonetheless, agraffes are found on some East European pianos – for example, those from Petrof. If you come across an affordable piano with agraffes, try it and see if you can hear the 'rounder' sound quality claimed by some players. If you can, this might be a factor to take into account.

Tone too harsh?

You might find a piano that you like in all respects except for a slightly harsh or strident tone. If this is the only barrier to buying it, ask the dealer to *needle the hammers* (Chapter 8, section B). Be warned, though, that although this is a routine operation it requires a lot of skill and so may be better entrusted to a piano technician than a tuner. If badly done, the tone will be uneven from note to note.

🎹 The world of piano manufacture

The centre of gravity of world piano manufacturing has shifted a considerable distance since 1900. Then, the main producing countries were Germany, Britain and the USA, each of which had many manufacturers. But numbers dwindled throughout the 20th century as companies merged, were taken over or quietly closed down. Smaller makers in particular couldn't produce enough pianos to enjoy the economies of scale, and so couldn't compete on price. Even great names finally succumbed: Bentley in the 1980s, Broadwood in the 1990s. (Pianos branded 'Broadwood' continued to be made in the UK, as the name was owned by Birmingham company Ladbrookes, but they too went out of business in 2007.)

Rather in the way that Japanese cars have conquered the world, so have Japanese pianos. Two names, Kawai and Yamaha, now stand head and shoulders above everyone else. I don't want to promote their products above those of other companies, but I'd be ignoring the elephant in the piano showroom if I didn't mention them specifically. Their market dominance may, however, be short-lived.

On 2 April 2005 came news that Steinway's affiliate US company Boston was to have its Essex line of pianos made in China, at the Pearl River factory. (Evidently the adjectival status of 'Essex' remains high in the USA.) The earth shook beneath the feet of the traditionalists, but a glance at a current list of US piano manufacturers shows the extent of globalisation: nearly all are merely US divisions of non-US companies. Very few original indigenous firms remain.

The likelihood is that within a few years, China will be the main source of volume production of the most popular types of piano, with only marginal contributions from much smaller makers in other countries. For example, good quality and moderately priced instruments are currently available from makers in Poland and the Czech Republic, but whether or for how long they can compete against even cheaper Far Eastern imports can only be guessed at.

Buying unseen and unheard

I would always advise that you buy a piano that you have tried out and are happy with. I hope I've made the point that no two pianos are truly identical, so I would further urge you to buy *only* that piano and not one still in its crate in a warehouse, no matter how many reassurances you're given that it will be 'exactly the same'.

This makes it difficult to recommend buying a new piano on the internet, even though many reputable dealers now provide this option. If an offer tempts you and the seller has a showroom, go there and put the piano through its paces as suggested above. It may well be that the showroom price is higher than the internet price. If you're happy with the instrument, you might try to close the deal there and then at the lower price. You may or may not be successful, but the more important principle is *only buy the one you have tried*.

Increasingly, there are new pianos for sale online where there is no possibility of trying them out. While I would never buy this way, the low advertised cost is tempting a growing number of buyers who presumably enjoy taking risks. For example, one of my customers bought a new piano off a major auction site. It eventually arrived from China via Poland. The delivery driver and his mate spoke no English and would unload only on to the road outside the buyer's house – in the rain. The buyer was fortunately able to round up enough friends to get it indoors. There was no stool and of course no free first tuning, which was by now definitely needed. The piano itself was a good make and in many ways an excellent instrument, but the buyer later admitted that if he'd had the chance to try it out, it wouldn't have been his first choice. Caveat emptor.

Closing the deal

Assuming you've found the piano you want, it's time to talk price. It's difficult to give detailed advice on negotiation, as what works well in one situation may backfire in another. A few general pointers may, however, be harmless enough:

■ Almost all new pianos are offered with a free first tuning, qualified free delivery (for example ground floor only, within a 20-mile radius), and free stool. If not, you should insist on these things as you're definitely paying for them even though it's all described as 'free'. For more detail on stools and what to ask for, see Chapter 3.

■ Don't commit yourself to an immediate buying decision. The adage about acting in haste and repenting at leisure can apply with full force here. Like pets, a piano is not just for Christmas. Unlike most pets, a piano is bigger than you and noisy. If it turns out to have the wrong room presence or make the wrong noise, you will quickly understand the meaning of 'buyer's remorse', so always go away and have a good think about it before parting with your money.

■ It may even be worth waiting until the dealer makes the inevitable follow-up phone-call, because you may find the price suddenly dropping significantly if you sound undecided. If, on the other hand, you're told something like, 'It's the last one at the low price you were quoted,' this is the dealer trying the opposite tack.

■ However it plays out, don't be persuaded into a sale if you have any doubts about that piano. It's better to wait and get it right than buy a piano you can't 'bond' with. And the more pianos you try, the more likely it is that you'll know instinctively when you've found the right one. A good piano dealer will understand this and be patient, recognising that satisfied customers are much more valuable than disgruntled ones.

■ Don't pester the dealer for one concession after another, to the point where any profit disappears. Most piano dealers have their heart in the right place and try to do their best for customers anyway, so the risk is that you'll lose any goodwill you might have built up.

CHAPTER 5

How to buy a used piano

While you can get a perfectly satisfactory used piano for much less than the cost of a new one, buying used is always a risk. Here's what you need to know about used pianos and the way they're sold, so that you can avoid the many pitfalls.

Because of its all-encompassing nature I'm going to focus on the most common piano-buying scenario in the world: parents who know little or nothing about pianos want to buy a first instrument for a child.

In this scenario, there are nearly always two powerful and often unspoken factors at work:

■ Even when the child seems keen to play (a rarity in my experience), a wise parent won't bet on this enthusiasm lasting.

■ Therefore most parents don't want to buy an expensive instrument that after a few weeks may just sit there collecting dust and scratches. Their compromise position will be: *we want a bargain*.

More often than not, this means that they can be persuaded to go for cheap rather than quality. The rationalisation is: 'We'll get an entry-level piano to see how it goes. We can always upgrade later.' This tends to assume entry through the basement. For some silver-tongued dealer with few scruples, it's then easy to pass off the piano equivalent of a car with a blown engine as 'just the thing for a beginner'.

I've been getting called out to just-bought, untuneable cheap pianos about once a fortnight for 30 years, so it's perhaps fair to conclude that the risk of being landed with a dud piano isn't much different from the risk you run when buying a 'bargain' used car.

I'd argue that the real loss when caught this way isn't the money, as most bad pianos change hands for relatively modest sums (even if they're invariably well above the trade value of the instrument). The loss is the likelihood that it will be difficult and perhaps impossible for anyone, especially a child, to get any enjoyment from playing a bad piano. Buy a rubbish car and it shouldn't affect your driving ability. Buy a rubbish piano and you could snuff out a lifelong source of pleasure and possibly a great musical career before it's even begun.

If that isn't bad enough, a child may not realise what the problem is, so when playing is rapidly abandoned the parents may congratulate themselves for not having wasted too much money on the piano. It's the kid's decision that swung it, not anything they or the dealer did. And of course they can't blame the child, so it's basically nobody's fault. Ho hum.

🎹 Bargain pianos

'Bargain' can mean different things to different people, but to most of them it means cheap. Using my formula on page 65, I'll define a bargain piano as one priced at up to 25–30 per cent of the cost of an equivalent new one.

If you take your time and heed my advice, it should be possible to find a playable bargain piano that might take a learner up to Grade 5 or 6. (If a student is good enough to reach Grade 6, it's time to consider a *serious* investment in a quality piano.)

This, though, is definitely the main 'buyer beware' zone, where bad pianos outnumber good by a wide margin. I buy the occasional quite good instrument in this price range, but over the same timescale I'll condemn many more that to the non-expert look or sound no worse than the good one. Many of them will have been bought for children to learn on. And all of them, almost by definition, will have been overpriced.

Therefore, the less you want to spend on a piano, the more you really need the guidance of a professional!

Does buying used make sense?

Many people who buy a used piano have no idea about the cost of new pianos. They simply assume that buying new will be unjustifiably expensive, especially for a child to learn on. They then go out and buy a used piano that may be so overpriced that it ends up costing them – once removal, tuning and repair costs have been added on – about the same as a new piano. In many cases where the piano needs a lot of work to make it playable, a new piano might be significantly cheaper.

Step one, therefore, is to do some homework. Visit piano showrooms, look at new pianos and their prices, talk to the sales people and read Chapter 4. (Much of it, especially the sections on testing a piano, will be equally relevant to used pianos, except that you may have to accept a lower pass rate than when testing brand new instruments.) Don't go any further until you can *relate the price of any used piano to the cost of a new one of broadly the same type*.

Step two – if you haven't persuaded yourself to buy new – is to work out a sensible budget to spend on a used piano. Few people do this with any logic or information to guide them. Many just think of a small number and expect pianos to materialise at that price. In the real world there are four cost headings to consider:

■ The negotiated price of the piano.
■ The cost of moving and tuning it, if neither is included

in the deal. Ringing a couple of piano tuners should give you an accurate estimate of the local cost of both.
■ The cost of essential repairs or refurbishment. This is impossible for a non-expert to predict. Most used pianos need some work, and it's common for the cost to exceed the value of the instrument. My final heading is therefore the most important:
■ The cost of professional advice. Get any prospective purchase checked over by a piano technician, or let him or her find a choice of suitable instruments for you. The cost will be predictable (just ask) and it could well save you the dismay of a much greater cost later.

In view of all these added costs, *there may be little sense in paying for a used piano more than half the cost of an equivalent new one*. You should therefore consider looking for a used piano similar to a new piano you have seen and liked and would happily have in your home, and priced at less than 50 per cent of the all-in cost of that new piano.

'Less than 50 per cent' does, of course, give you quite a wide margin. Down to zero, in fact (see *Free pianos* on page 66). As we'll see, how far below 50 per cent you can safely go will depend partly on luck but mainly on good judgement.

To keep costs within bounds, you should also have the assurance of a piano technician that the instrument will be good value for money. Professional advice should be regarded not as an extra cost, but as an essential means of reducing your overall cost and risk.

Where to look

Local small ads in papers, shop notice-boards etc

Some genuine bargains can be had here, usually from private sellers who price their pianos to get rid of them quickly rather than hold out for a fat profit. With luck you'll find a well-maintained and regularly played instrument owned by someone who wants it to go to a good home. It should be fairly obvious when this is the case.

More typically though, you'll be faced with a piano that has been neglected for years and has no 'service history'. This means that on top of your removal and retuning costs (assuming the piano is fundamentally sound), you may also have to pay for repairs or refurbishment to give it a new lease of life. See Chapters 6–8 for an indication of what may be needed.

The work involved can easily exceed the asking price, so it's wise to get a professional opinion on the state of the piano before parting with your cash. You might still end up with a bargain, or you might be better off spending more to buy a piano that needs less work.

Small ads to avoid, or approach warily, fall into two categories:

■ The private seller who is really a trader

Shady traders in all sorts of goods love small ads because by masquerading as private sellers they avoid the legal obligations of legitimate trading – such as providing replacements or refunds if goods are faulty. In my experience, over half of the 'piano for sale' small ads I respond to are from traders. Thus, an early research task should be to spend a few weeks observing just how many times the same phone numbers crop up for differently described pianos. (If you detect this kind of abuse, you might consider passing your findings on to your local Trading Standards department.)

Undeclared traders generally operate from home (though not always their own) and sell only one piano at a time, making it harder to spot any deception. One clue is a willingness to deliver the piano. Transporting a piano is a significant undertaking and a private seller who just happens to be willing and able to move a piano is a rarity. To a trader, delivery is part and parcel of getting hold of your money quickly. Another clue is the seller who just happens to have other items for sale, such as a couple of 'spare' piano stools.

Free pianos

Many pianos are given as gifts, but beware – there is no such thing as a free piano. Many of the pianos I condemn have been given away, for reasons that vary from death to redecoration. But the donor's generosity usually stops short of paying to have the piano moved, or inspected to see if it's worth having at all. Sometimes the recipient gets lucky and acquires a gem of a piano, but often he or she ends up wasting time and money simply to remove and dispose of a useless instrument.

Some donors are, one suspects, wily enough to know exactly what they're doing. They have probably heard of the First Law of Piano Transactions, sometimes known as the Rule of Asymmetry. This states quite simply: It is far easier to acquire a piano than to get rid of one.

At current prices it costs around £150 for local removal and perhaps another £100 or so to dispose of it if it turns out to be useless. (Junk is cheaper to move, as it doesn't matter if you drop it.) So if you're offered a 'free' piano, curb your enthusiasm for a bargain and insist on having it inspected first. If you're so cornered that you can't turn the gift down, shop around for a piano expert who can offer you a choice of two good post-inspection deals: one to transport and retune the piano; the other to give it a dignified removal followed by instant disposal if it turns out to be firewood.

 **Moving pianos**

Moving pianos appears to be a huge physical job like shifting building rubble or garden rubbish. It does require some strength, but also great skill. Many people try to DIY and believe that a couple of strong men with a van or a trailer will find it easy. The instrument, the van and the men are likely to bear the scars forever.

▥ When to buy

Before looking for an instrument, consider the time of year. In the UK, pianos tend to sell best from September to Christmas. The cycle follows the school year, because many piano teachers do as well. Children start lessons at school or with a private teacher in September; soon after, if all seems to be working out well, parents start looking for an instrument. It dawns only gradually how complicated this is, so the piano often ends up being a Christmas present.

The market is very flat for most of the rest of the year. This means that if you can buy some time between January and August, you should stand a much better chance of a bargain, or at least better value for money. A further benefit is that many of the rogue traders won't be so active in these quieter times. They'll be on the beach in Spain.

The risk is high that any piano bought this way will be worth far less than you pay for it, even after haggling. You'll have no legal comeback if anything goes wrong, and with such traders things often do go wrong. Some, for example, will pick up pianos condemned as beyond economic repair and learn just enough technical patter to persuade first-time buyers that they're getting something 'with potential'.

If you suspect that your private seller is a trader, say that you won't make a decision without a professional opinion and valuation from your own piano expert. If the seller then says anything at all calculated to dissuade you – such as dropping the price to encourage an immediate sale – your suspicions have been confirmed and you should not buy that piano.

■ The private seller who hasn't a clue about piano values

This seller thinks that pianos are appreciating assets like houses or Rembrandts, rather than depreciating assets like cars or washing machines. There is some basis for believing that an instrument with a long life expectancy should hold a decent price, but not enough to justify the sort of reasoning I often come across: 'If it cost £1,200 thirty years ago, it's got to be worth at least £2,000 by now.' No it hasn't. For much less than £2,000 you can buy a new piano. The counter-argument tends to be: 'Maybe you can, but I bet it won't be the quality of this one'. I agree. Modern new pianos are *much* better quality than comparable new pianos built thirty years ago.

The seller's piano may be worth having, but agreeing a realistic price may be difficult. One solution is for buyer and seller to agree to accept an independent valuation, but if it gets to that stage you have to question whether it's worth the bother.

Piano dealers

The good

Most cities and towns have at least one used piano dealer. Some also sell new pianos and offer other services like transport, tuning, repolishing and repair. Often these are long-established businesses with a good reputation, and it's a pleasure to deal with them. Their dedication and professionalism shine through as soon as you enter their showroom and start talking to them.

A *big* advantage is that you can sit down and play showroom pianos for ages, often in acoustically sympathetic spaces – and the more pianos you play, the better your decisions are likely to be. You generally have limited opportunity to play in a private seller's home, while fringe dealers may discourage you from playing at all, for fear you'll discover just how bad their pianos are. (This is why their favourite customer is the parent who can't play at all buying for the child who can't play much.)

Good piano dealers will be safe places to buy from, but like any business they have overheads which have to be reflected in their prices. Each piano they sell has to be bought, shipped to their premises, repaired and refurbished as necessary to bring it up to showroom condition (at least a day's work even for a well-kept piano), and delivered to the customer. This means that even the cheapest used piano will probably have to sell close to our notional upper limit of 50 per cent of the price of a new equivalent.

Indeed, the price of a refurbished piano of good but not great quality will often have to be very close to that of a new piano. However, a quality used piano may be aesthetically more

pleasing than a cheap new one, so selling expensive used pianos is by no means a lost cause.

To sum up, you can expect good advice, good service and a good buying experience from a reputable dealer, though this will all come at a price. If you're prepared to invest more of your own time and effort (with the help of this book, of course) and accept more risk, you can almost certainly buy the equivalent of a dealer's '50 per cent' piano for much less.

The bad and the ugly

Piano dealers on the fringes of the used piano market are a mixed bag. An honourable few will be piano technicians running very small or part-time businesses and eager to prove that they're genuine. In the main, though, it's a sector best avoided until you're confident you can quickly recognise a bad piano – because you'll see lots of them.

Fringe dealers hardly ever sell new pianos, so the less scrupulous will often take advantage of an innocent buyer's ignorance of just how cheap new pianos have become, and overcharge for poor instruments. Some are house clearance merchants who acquire the occasional piano that may or may not be tuneable (they're unlikely to admit knowing either way). A few are outright crooks who sell, for as long as they can get away with it, 'reconditioned' pianos that have had nothing done to them beyond a clean-out and perfunctory polish. Most such pianos will be junk. In all likelihood the dealer hasn't bought them, but has been paid to get rid of them – and *you* are his way of getting rid of them.

Once again, all I can say is: if you must buy in this neck of the woods, get expert, professional advice before parting with your cash. (Literally. Cheques or credit cards are rarely entertained.) And don't expect a guarantee or after-sales promise, even if you get one, to be worth anything.

Auctions

Auction houses

There are specialist auction houses in London which regularly sell only pianos, or only musical instruments. Some regional auctioneers sell pianos, but only occasionally.

As with all auctions, care is needed.

Beware 'ringing'

When there are several pianos for sale in an auction house – particularly a small one – there may well be a 'ring' in operation. This consists of a group of colluding dealers present at the auction, only one of whom bids. By eliminating competition from each other, the dealers keep prices artificially low. After the auction, they get together and have a 'knock-out', sharing out the pianos among themselves and in effect taking the profit that would otherwise have gone to the sellers. Ringing is illegal, but I'm aware of only one successful prosecution for it, and that involved valuable fine art.

If it seems too cheap...

Some auctions are only one step up from car boot sales when it comes to off-loading real junk. I was once hired to tune a Knight K10 in readiness for its sale at auction. Good K10s are fabulous pianos, but because of their design they readily fall over backwards. (Best kept against a wall!) This one might have fallen over once too often, because it had a cracked cast iron frame that would have cost a fortune to repair. After a struggle lasting *four days* I got it roughly in tune, but any piano expert would have known instantly from the sound that this was a piano to avoid. Instead it was bought for a lot of money by a lady who, of course, wasn't an expert. She was beside herself with glee, having been advised to go up to twice the price. It was a sobering moment for me, but almost certainly not as sobering as it was for her when she got the piano home. The moral – beside the one about over-keen young piano technicians being too ready to work for crooks – is that if it seems too cheap, it's probably too dear.

Auction websites

At the time of writing there are few specialist piano or instrument auction websites, and the ones I do know about rarely sell other than top quality, expensive pianos. Such websites, however, have the potential to be fair as there are too many buyers creating too much competition for rings to operate. Use your browser and the search term 'piano auction'.

More general internet auction sites routinely have hundreds of pianos for sale at any given time. Even from the descriptions, most are clearly junk. Many sellers offer some plausible reason for this reluctant sale and can, by great good fortune, provide transport. Many also have other items for sale, like several piano stools. Does all this sound familiar? Yes, these are fringe or undeclared traders, so buying off popular auction sites should be regarded as highly risky.

If a seller is reasonably local, a good test is to request a visit to inspect the piano. Of the few sellers I've approached this way, about half have refused, on the grounds that bidding has already gone past their expectations so why should they put themselves out for me? That tells me all I need to know.

RARE OPPORTUNITY!

☞ 100 ☜
–OF–
T. GILBERT & CO'S
GRAND, PARLOR GRAND AND SQUARE

PIANO FORTES

Must be Sold immediately at Auction Prices!

These Piano Fortes are all made of the best materials, and in the best manner, for the retail trade, and warranted in every particular; thus affording a rare opportunity to those in want of a FIRST CLASS PIANO, to obtain one at A VERY LOW PRICE.

☞ Call at 484 Washington Street,
And Examine these Piano Fortes,
THE PRICES CANNOT FAIL TO SUIT.

F. A. Searle, Steam Job Printer, Journal Building, 118 Washington Street, Boston.

Technical criteria for used pianos

Is it even worth looking at?

It must be an *overstrung* piano with an *underdamper* action (see Chapter 2). Any piano with a straight-strung frame or an overdamper action should be rejected. There are no mitigating circumstances. By rights, all of these should have disappeared long ago but many still circulate.

Is it tuneable?

Even one untuneable string will require a repair, and the cost of having several of them repaired professionally may exceed the value of the piano (see Chapter 8, section C). The only certain way to find out is to put a tuning lever on each of the tuning pins. Any that move too easily are slack and may be untuneable. There are, however, two problems with this test:

■ Only a professional tuner or technician can judge how tight the pins are, *and* leave them in the correct position afterwards.
■ If you're not a professional, the seller is unlikely to let you do it. There is a high risk of breaking strings, easily achieved by amateurs.

So what other clues might there be to the piano's tuneability?

Is it at the correct pitch?

All modern musical instruments are tuned to A 440. This means that a correctly tuned A above middle C vibrates 440 times per second when struck. Less than 440 and it's *flat*, or below pitch. More than 440 and it's *sharp*, or above pitch.

Your task is to find out how close the A above middle C gets to the magic 440 vibrations per second. Your ideal tool for this job is a trained musician. Take one with you (any instrument except drums) and he or she will be able to tell you.

The next best piece of kit is an electronic tuner (see Chapter 10). This will instantly tell you what note it is hearing and whether it is sharp or flat. Electronic tuners are now inexpensive and extremely accurate. Though many professional tuners can manage without them, most now carry one because so many professional customers use them to check the human tuner's accuracy!

If you have a yearning for traditional ways, you could use a tuning fork or pitch pipe on any note – but most conveniently middle C, the commonest fork or pipe pitch. It's very simple to do, but you first need to be confident that you have a good musical ear. (And you need to know that young children are often better at this than adults.) This is what you do:

■ First buy or borrow your tuning fork (or pitch pipe).
■ Find middle C – don't set out to do this until you can!
■ Strike your tuning fork (or blow your pipe) and at the same time play C.
■ Are the two sounds exactly the same?
■ If not, are they closer if you play one or more adjacent notes?

If you have to go *up* more than a couple of keys to find an exact match, the piano is seriously flat or below pitch. This is bad news for the piano and a warning that you shouldn't buy it without consulting a tuner – and not one recommended by the seller. A good piano won't go this badly out of tune even if it hasn't been tuned for years. I once had a Bechstein in the workshop that had shared a barn with pigeons for several decades. It was stupendously filthy and all its hammers were broken off. I gave it a new set of hammers, and when I started to tune it I found that, amazingly, it was still in almost perfect tune.

The honky-tonk test

In Chapter 2 I explained that notes can have one, two (bichord) or three (trichord) strings. If the trichord strings are slightly out of tune with each other, they produce a familiar, tinny 'honky-tonk' sound that even pitch-deaf people can recognise. If a piano sounds markedly honky-tonk, there is a good chance that the tuning pins are loose and the instrument either can't be tuned at all, or won't stand in tune for long.

More things to look out for

Even if a piano is roughly up to pitch and reasonably in tune with itself, this is no guarantee that it is fit to buy. Other easily visible evidence includes:

■ Dust on the tuning pins

This may indicate that it hasn't been tuned for years. A recent tuning will have removed dust and will also have left marks on the pins. Be suspicious if the piano appears to have been recently tuned but *still* doesn't sound very good.

■ Corrosion on the strings

Treble strings can still function when they're quite rusty, but bass strings will sound dull and 'wooden'. See Chapter 8, section C. The photo above shows a piano with dull bass strings that will sound as bad as they look.

■ Split soundboard

If under moderate playing you hear growls or rattles coming from deep inside the piano, it may have a split soundboard. This condition is often audible only when certain notes are played, and the growl is the edges of the split touching at certain vibration rates. Splitting most commonly happens

when age shrinks and separates the soundboard's constituent strips of wood, and it happens faster if the piano is close to an active radiator. Palliative treatment may be possible but full repair is difficult without dismantling the piano. See Chapter 8, section D, for more information. See also the photo on page 77. In the meantime, seek professional advice.

■ Split bridge

If you hear a rattle from a note whose string is at the end of a bridge section, the bridge may be split. See the photo on page 78 to see what this typically looks like, and see Chapter 8, section D, for more information. As with a split soundboard, seek professional advice.

▥ Honky-tonk

The honky-tonk sound is often used deliberately for effect, perhaps most famously by the enormously popular Winifred Atwell in the 1950s and '60s. The irony is that while the intention is to replicate the cheery sound of a wrecked, untuneable piano, any pianist attempting to play honky-tonk on a genuinely wrecked, untuneable piano would have a far from cheery time.

For professional honky-tonk performances, a good piano is deliberately tuned so that of each trichord note, one string is very slightly flattened and one very slightly sharpened. For example, the original album sleeve of Keith Emerson's *Honky Tonk Train Blues* showed a battered old straight-strung piano with an overdamper action, no doubt to give the music authentic bar-room credentials. In the

studio, Keith Emerson actually played a specially tuned Steinway grand.

The honky-tonk effect can now be produced by digital processors. On electronic pianos there is usually a honky-tonk option, and any piano can be made to sound like this through 'flange', or slow Leslie speaker effects. (The famously maverick Leslie speaker has a rotating horn that produces a wonderful throbbing tone.)

But nothing can beat the sound of honky-tonk coming out of a real piano. For a tuner it arouses deep, conflicting emotions: it's a terrible thing to do to a piano and an awful waste of a skilled worker's time – rather like asking Michelangelo to emulsion your spare bedroom – yet it produces such a uniquely characterful sound.

Small pianos

Because demand for small pianos has been so large for so long, there is only too ready a market for small used pianos that are simply not fit for purpose. If you must have a small piano and also want to enjoy playing it, seek the advice of a professional because there are so few good ones around.

Ever since the 1940s – roughly the time new houses started having smaller, lower-ceilinged rooms – many manufacturers were tempted to *compress* their pianos to make them ever more pocket-sized. As a result, many pianos made from then until the 1980s suffered such extreme compression that they were never good to begin with and should be avoided now. The Bentley on page 48 is in my view the very limit of successful compression at 39in (1m) high. It has contorted keys to fit under the action and feels stodgy to play, but for all that sounds admirably loud and clear.

Doomed compression innovations included *dropper actions*, where the action is below the keyboard and each key is connected to it with a steel rod. They both sound and feel unpleasant – an irredeemable design disaster.

The worst sins of compression were probably committed by the Eavestaff company (now defunct, though the name survives on some Chinese-made conventional uprights). Most of its Minipiano series have only six octaves (73 keys), and one or two variants have a derisory five. They're attractively small but should be regarded as toys and not serious instruments. The photo top right shows a typical Eavestaff – it looks like a desk until you open it up. The lower photo reveals the dropper rods connecting each key to the action. The short keys and heavy rods make them a chore to play, and they sound dreadful. The already shrunken wrest plank dries out rapidly, so any still around are unlikely to have tight tuning pins. Dismal in every possible way.

Elementary, dear Watson

This has little to do with technicality, but for a clue about the history of a piano look at its keyblocks (the chunks of wood at the end of the keyboard). Are they covered in ugly, dark scars? If so, this is a sure sign that players have left burning cigarettes on them. (The treble end keyblock often suffers most, from right-handed smokers.)

It's also a reasonably sure sign that the piano has spent at least some of its life in a pub or club, where it may have had many players. None of them owned the piano, and probably even the owner wasn't too bothered how it was treated. This lack of respect often extends inside the piano too, so evidence of keyblock burns should prompt you to check the whole instrument extremely thoroughly.

As casual insults to pianos go this is one of the worst, because the marks are often impossible to remove. The piano on the left was painted white and then later had the white gloss and original French polish stripped off, but the evidence of this extremely annoying practice still survives.

Grand pianos

First see my general comments about grands in Chapter 3. The main point is that in terms of sound quality, only a grand at least 5ft long (1.52m) and preferably over 6ft (1.83m) is likely to be significantly better than an upright of comparable quality – but it will, of course, be much bigger and probably more expensive.

As I also pointed out, an undoubted advantage of grands is their double escapement action, even though this can mislead some buyers into believing that the better keyboard feel of even a baby grand makes the whole piano superior to an upright.

That said, in the used market there are still some cheaper baby grands without double escapement actions, examples of which were still being made in the 1950s. Some were as small as 4ft long (1.22m). These piano equivalents of the Shetland pony were also cursed with a mutant action – that of an upright, but with the hammers turned through 90°. It's sometimes called a *simplex* action. These were the ultimate vanity piano because whatever they looked like, they weren't remotely grand in any respect. Avoid them at any price. Don't even have one as a gift, unless you want to keep plants in it.

On the grounds of size alone, few people wanting a home piano will choose a grand. But larger used grands can be fine pianos with usually superior playing quality, and some good bargains can be had by the careful buyer, so neither I nor you (if you have the space) should ignore them completely. And given

Grey imports

Grey imports are new or used pianos imported without the authorisation or approval of the manufacturer or the manufacturer's agent, and they account for many of the instruments sold on auction websites for apparently low prices. The main source of grey imports is South-East Asia, where school and university music departments tend to replace their pianos at fixed intervals.

Some experts question how well these instruments will stand up to a change of climate and to central heating, and for these and other reasons the original manufacturer may refuse to provide any technical support or recognise any guarantee.

My view is that as long as you can play and inspect the piano first, and it's in good condition, you should get an acceptably long life from a grey import. I would not, however, recommend buying one from a website.

Grey imports raise the general point that you should always enquire about the history of any piano you're interested in. If it's obviously fairly new and the seller is vague or unhelpful about its provenance, the chances are high that it's a grey import. But as long as the sale is legal, it's up to you to judge whether or not this matters.

that most players are likely to practise or perform on a grand at least occasionally, some familiarisation may be useful.

For much of the 20th century, German and Austrian grands dominated the world market. The top names to look out for are Bösendorfer and Steinway; in the second division, Bechstein and Blüthner; in the third, makers like Grotrian-Steinweg, Ibach, Lipp, Kaps, Müller, Ritmüller, Rönisch and Schiedmayer. (By comparison, the top UK manufacturer, Broadwood – whose pianos were and are excellent – was ranked behind all of them.)

Not too many years ago, top German grands sold at auction for thousands of pounds in *any* condition. People would buy them, have them rebuilt, and consider the rebuild better than anything available new. (At that time, probably correctly. In the 1960s and beyond, piano manufacturing suffered the same dire quality problems as the European car industry.)

Since then, a growing preference for Japanese grands – principally Yamaha and Kawai – has brought used prices tumbling for all but the top few German makes. Used prices for all other makes are therefore well within the reach of many buyers. Judging by realised auction prices, shabby but playable grands routinely sell for sums well within our '50 per cent of new cost' range. Others can be made playable with relatively little work, so overall it's perfectly possible to buy a big-name grand at fairly modest cost.

You will, though, *definitely* need professional advice, and removal costs for grands are at least twice that of uprights. In fact I think it would be folly for you to buy a used grand without professional assistance, either from an established piano dealer or an independent technician.

Inspecting grands

One of the great things about grand piano inspection is that the vital parts are much more visible than on uprights.

After you've played the piano a while and satisfied yourself that you're interested, do something you wouldn't be able to do when inspecting an upright: ask the seller to remove the action. Or take a technician to do it, perhaps with your help (it's best as a two-person job). Or do it yourself – but first read Chapter 9.

Check the wrest plank

The point of removing the action is so that you can get your head right inside and, with a light or torch, visually inspect the condition of the wrest plank. This is impossible with any upright, even with the action out. Look for cracks in the plank, especially any running between two pins. If you see any, play those notes: they will almost certainly be horribly out of tune. *Reject any piano with this defect*. It will cost more to repair than the piano will be worth. (It's up to you whether you mention this to the seller.)

Wear and tear

With the action out and in the light, it's possible to examine it for wear and tear, moth damage etc as described in Chapter 9.

Lost lyre rod

A common problem with grand pianos is that the lyre rod gets lost along the way. The lyre is the whole pedal sub-assembly hanging down below the piano at the front, and normally held in place by two large thumbscrews. (The name is optimistic. It usually takes tools to undo them.)

The lyre rod is a reinforcing bar angled at about 45° from the back of the pedals to the bottom of the piano. Most pianos have just one rod but some have twin brass rods or wooden rods. The lyre rod's job is to counteract the pushing force applied to the pedals by the pianist's feet. Without the lyre rod, the lyre will appear to work well enough – but only for a while. Sooner or later, leverage on the lyre will cause terrible damage to the woodwork around the thumbscrews. Unless someone spots the problem and replaces the lyre rod long before damage starts, it may be too late. See Chapter 9.

Beware Lindners!

From around 1964 to around 1975, a company called Rippen made pianos in Ireland. Most were badged Lindner, though some were sold as Rippens. They were modern (for the time), small pianos and were overstrung, underdamped – everything you might want. They didn't sound too bad either, because the soundboard and frame were quite reasonable. But other, highly unusual features made these pianos quite remarkable – for the wrong reasons.

First, Lindners had a welded aluminium frame fabricated from standard industrial box-section tubing – see photos below. This may have been a well-meant innovation intended to reduce manufacturing costs and lighten the piano. Whatever the reason, no one has copied it since.

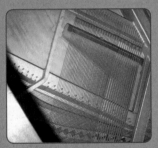

Second, they had only a three-quarter frame – a distinct backward step. (In the photo top right, the black, exposed wood is the wrest plank.) This was perhaps because the usual thin sheath of metal over the wrest plank would have to be cast, which would have defeated the object of making the frame simply and cheaply from off-the-shelf tubing. A full frame might also have been pointless, as aluminium has far less strength than cast iron and so would have provided little support to the wrest plank.

Third – and worst – they had plastic keys. Not wood covered in plastic, like most modern pianos, but keys made entirely of hollow, three-sided plastic channel – see right. These flimsy keys break and are more or less impossible to repair. The keyboard also has a plastic flange connecting it to the action, and this breaks easily too – often because technicians don't realise that they unclip from the rail.

The reputation of Lindners plummeted when stories started circulating within the trade of terminal faults developing after about ten years from new. There were rumours in the 1970s that someone was making conventional keyboards for them, but I could never confirm this. It would probably have been uneconomic anyway.

Despite my distaste for Lindners, they're worth a detour because they contained the germ of a good idea. They were significantly lighter than conventional small uprights at a time when electronic pianos were starting to appear. Had Lindners been better, they might have become popular among bands, as they were no heavier than a Hammond organ and thus reasonably portable – at least, if you had two roadies.

The sad truth though is that they were awful, and so you should turn your face resolutely against them. There are some US websites advertising products for repairing pianos with plastic parts, but Lindners are really not worth tackling.

Rippen/Lindner also made grands, again using aluminium and plastic. I have only ever seen one and that was enough. The likelihood is that few sold and even fewer survive.

Twenty-minute checklist

If you want to find a good used piano, you must to be prepared to look at lots and reject most of them. Based on what you now know, here's a routine for examining pianos quickly wherever you find them.

The whole exercise may not take you exactly 20 minutes, but it will reduce the time you need to spend on pianos that are wrong for you or worth far less than their vendors think or want.

To be really efficient and scarily impressive, practise the hands-on bits on a 'tame' instrument until you can rattle through the whole cycle as though you were born in a piano.

Five-minute check

External inspection

- Do the casework and general appearance make a good first impression? Could you live with this piano?
- Does the keyboard look and feel good? Poor condition isn't necessarily fatal but some jobs – for example, replacing ivory or celluloid key coverings – can be expensive.
- Check the make. Don't be fooled by a transfer on the fallboard naming a major maker, or an invented maker like 'Steinbech'. Full name decals or alphabet transfer strips can be bought from piano supply houses, who sell them in good faith. Top names are either in brass inlay on the fallboard, or cast into the frame near the top treble end and easily visible when you lift the lid. On grands, there may be a decal on the soundboard.
- Is the keyboard level? Kneel and check. A dip in the middle is a symptom of keybed wear, uneven key height a symptom of moth attack.

Quick internal (lid up) inspection

- You need to see an overstrung frame. If it's straight strung, close the lid and go home.
- You need to see an underdamper action. If it has an overdamper or 'squirrel cage' action, don't even think about buying it.
- Check that the top portion of the frame is not a capping piece. If it is, this is a three-quarter frame piano. Refuse it even as a gift.
- Is the wrest plank exposed around the tuning pins? If so, search thoroughly for splits in the wood, especially between pins, and reject the piano if you find any. Even if you don't find any, it's unlikely to be a good buy.
- Look for chalk applied to the head of one or more tuning pins. Many tuners do this to mark pins they know to be loose. This is an instant clue to the state of the piano – the more pins chalked, the worse it is. (Though no chalk doesn't necessarily mean no loose pins!)
- Is the inside very dirty? Serious question mark. Does it smell, as in things rotting or mouldering? Even more serious question mark.

🎹 Questions to ask before any inspection

- What make is it? If it's a Lindner, pull out now. Do likewise if it's a very small piano like an Eavestaff, with the action under the keyboard. (If in doubt, ask for its full height and number of keys. If it's under 38in (965 mm) tall or has fewer than 85 keys – that is, less than a full keyboard – don't go near it.)
- How old is it?
- What is its general condition and history of ownership?
- When was it last tuned?
- What is the serial number? This is important because knowing the manufacturer and serial number enables you to date the piano yourself. (See *How old is that piano?*)

An obscure make doesn't necessarily write the piano off; more important is the way the vendor deals with your questions. Warning signs that an alleged private seller may be a sneaky trader include evasiveness, vagueness or a big difference between the stated age and actual age of the instrument.

If you're happy to go and see the piano, equip yourself with an electronic tuner or tuning fork and a decent torch. Warn the vendor that you may want to inspect the piano internally, so can they please ensure that it's not covered in ornaments, and that it will be okay for you to lift the lid, remove the front board and generally see it undressed. You may also wish to move it away from a wall. All this saves time and makes them aware that you're serious. It also helps assuage the dismay some owners clearly feel when you start taking liberties with their pride and joy.

If the vendor is unable to do any of the physical stuff, get their permission to do it yourself. Also let them know if you intend bringing someone else with you. This isn't just common courtesy; in the case of owners who are elderly or live alone, it gives them the opportunity to have someone with them too. (The other side of this coin is that if you're selling a piano – or anything of significant value – from your home and feel at all vulnerable, don't be alone when prospective buyers turn up.)

Once in the presence of the piano, start with the basic checks that determine whether it's worth staying for as long as 20 minutes.

Quick inspection of grands

The same as for uprights but with these variations:

- Look at the pedal assembly. A glance will tell you if the lyre rod is missing. If it is, crawl under the piano and inspect the wood round the retaining bolts of the lyre. Work the lyre *gently* back and forth. If it moves more than an inch (25mm) and makes groaning and creaking noises, the rod may have been absent for some time. Damage is highly likely and will be expensive to repair. If damage has not yet occurred, fitting a rod may spare the piano this fate.
- Ask the vendor to remove the music desk and raise the lid. (Safety first: if you're invited to do it, *check that the hinge pins are in place*, then fold the front section over the back before raising it.)
- You need to see a double escapement or 'roller' action, visible only with the fallboard removed. Look in across the keyboard. If you see a simplex action (right), leave. This is basically an upright that has fallen over. If you see something like below, with its distinctive row of 'cotton reel' capstans, stay.

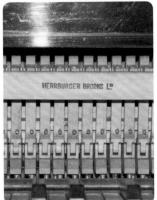

Quick musical try-out

- Is it below pitch? Try it against an electronic tuner or tuning fork.
- Is it terribly honky-tonk? If it is *and* it's below pitch, reject it, as it's unlikely that it will tune and stay in tune.

Vendor credibility

- If the piano is offered as a private sale, do you now believe the vendor to be (a) genuine or (b) a plain-clothed dealer?
- If the piano is being sold by a dealer, does the business clearly specialise in and care about pianos?

If the signs are promising enough to keep you interested, move on to the next phase of your examination.

Fifteen-minute check
Environment

- If you can be sure that the piano has been in its present location for some time, what sort of environment is it? Hot? Cold? Damp? Abusive?
- Will the environment you intend to provide be significantly different – cold and damp to hot and dry, for example? If so, the shock to the piano's system could mean a lot of remedial work within weeks.

Further internal inspection

- Ask the vendor either to remove the front board or let you do it. If this can't be done for any reason, head for the door.
- Find and check the serial number. Is it the same number the seller gave you on the phone?
- Is there any rust on the treble strings? If so, does it affect the sound? Treble strings can stand a surprising amount of corrosion but there are limits, and lots of corrosion is a bad sign generally.
- Corrosion of the bass strings is a different matter. Are there any dark blueish deposits on the copper-wound strings? If so, how do the bass notes sound? If they're dull or 'tubby', this is a serious problem.
- Look closely at the soundboard. Are there any splits, or any suspicious signs that splits may have been disguised?

- Look inside from the *back* of the piano. (Ask to have any cloth covering removed.) You should now see large areas of the soundboard. Look for splits, or separations along its constituent strips of wood. If you see either, reject the piano. If there are significant separations – as, for example, above – the piano is almost certainly doomed.

■ Remove the bottom board and look for splits in the bridges (see right). If you see any, reject the piano – this is terminal.

■ Using your torch, hunt all round the piano for traces of woodworm. Look for fresh, fine sawdust and clusters of perfectly round holes about $\frac{1}{16}$in (1.5mm) across. Look under the keybed, all around the case, everywhere inside and outside the piano. Woodworm can be treated but not in your home, as commercial killers emit toxic fumes until they have dried out and anything sold as safe for domestic use won't work.

■ Examine all felt and other fabrics for evidence of moth attack, or of clumsy attempts to conceal it. Nameboard tape is immediately visible between the keys and the wooden strip running across them. Any munching will be obvious, and likely to be replicated throughout the piano – so be suspicious if the nameboard tape looks brand new. Again, moth can be treated but the cost and effort of repairing chewed components may make the piano an uneconomic buy.

Variations for grands

All the above except those that apply specifically to uprights, but also:

■ In an older grand there may be too much dust on the soundboard for you to see any splits, so crawl under the piano and look up. You will now see large, clean areas of soundboard. First look for any separation of the long wooden strips. Then, if possible, put a light on *above* the piano. With the lid still up, look for any chinks of light showing through. Wherever you see one, the soundboard is split. (There may be large bolts through the soundboard and into the frame. The circular holes around these may leak light but that's okay.)

The action

A badly worn action can instantly turn a cheap piano into an expensive one, so check carefully for any of these problems:

■ Are the hammers badly cut by the strings, or flattened off? (On a grand, you'll see the hammers only if you look down through the frame with the music desk removed. Use your torch.)

■ Inspect the balance hammers – easily seen with the front off. Are the leather coverings worn? (Compare them with the less-used coverings at the extremities of the piano, which are usually thicker.) Severe wear often indicates that the piano has spent a long time in a damp environment.

■ Inspect the action tapes. Are any broken off or dilapidated? A new set is cheap enough but professional fitting won't be.

■ Do any hammers wobble from side to side during playing, or when pressed lightly sideways?

■ Listen for clacking noises as keys are released, especially if the piano shows any sign of moth. This indicates that the felt cushions (not visible) have been eaten or have dropped off.

■ Do any notes carry on after the keys are released? If so, dampers and springs are suspect. Do the dampers line up with the strings, especially on a grand?

Performance

■ Subjectively, does the piano respond well to the way you play?

■ Does it still respond well if you take it to its *fff* and *ppp* limits?

■ Does it *feel* right? Are you truly comfortable, physically and emotionally, with this instrument?

■ If you want to replace an existing piano, is this one a big improvement?

If the piano passes all these tests – in other words, you like it and there are no obvious signs of a need for substantial repairs – and is *no more than* about half the price of a comparable new piano, it may be a worthwhile buy.

Professional opinion

If you like a particular piano but want a second opinion, arrange to go back with a technician. Additional tests that only a technician can do, or do quickly, include:

■ Tuning pin tension.

■ Wear on keybed felt.

■ Wear on key bushings (front rail and balance rail).

■ Interpreting noises – of buzzing bass strings, and of split bridges and soundboards even when these are not visually apparent.

■ Integrity of the instrument (basically, spotting fakery of various kinds).

■ Removing the action and keyframe of grands to inspect them for wear and tear.

■ Inspecting the notches or 'rollers' on grands.

If there are no fatal faults but some work is necessary, get a quote from the technician that includes moving the piano (perhaps twice – to and from a workshop). Add the quote, plus another ten per cent or so for contingencies, to the price of the piano to get a true purchase cost.

Is it still an attractive proposition compared with a new piano? If it only makes sense at much less than the asking price, don't be afraid to offer the lower price *and stick to it.* If the seller won't negotiate, there will always be other pianos and more amenable vendors.

How old is that piano?

Serial numbers

Almost all pianos carry a serial number somewhere inside. It may be difficult to find but it's most commonly in the top treble end and you'll probably have to remove the frontboard to reveal it. If the maker is well known within the piano industry – and most are – that number can usually be matched to a year of manufacture in a database of serial numbers. This is the best evidence you can get of the true age of a piano; you should never accept a private seller's estimate of age without confirming it for yourself. It's difficult for the uninitiated to date a piano even approximately simply by looking at it, and plenty of sellers will swear on holy relics that their piano is 30–50 years younger than its real age.

The most comprehensive published source of serial number data is the *Pierce Piano Atlas*, which lists over 7,000 piano makes worldwide and has entries dating back well over a century. (For example, it lists Broadwoods from 1820.) If you find the price of a new copy off-putting, there are usually plenty of used copies of earlier editions for sale. There are also regional databases covering just the UK, Europe, USA etc, and many databases on the internet. See *Further reading* for more information.

Now that the industry has far fewer makers, nearly all post-1970 pianos will be listed. Therefore, if a maker isn't listed, you immediately know that you're looking either at a very old piano from a lesser maker, or at a modern piano from an extremely obscure maker – and these days, that's likely to mean an instrument of doubtful quality.

Other evidence of age

Though it hardly fits well with the notion of a 20-minute check, it can be highly satisfying to date a piano from internal and external clues, and many technicians can date pianos surprisingly accurately this way. For example:

- It was, and still is, common industry practice to write dates in pencil on the sides of some keys – most usually on A1.
- Makers' labels with a variety of information, often including a date, can frequently be found under the bottom few keys.
- The 'great makes' routinely won prizes in national and international competitions, and these were often proudly commemorated on the frames of their pianos. The year of the last award may indicate a date of manufacture

(alternatively, the firm may have gone bust or been taken over, or simply stopped winning prizes). In the photo below left the last award cast into the frame is 1908, and Pierce dates it as 1908. (This is the most decorated upright piano frame I have ever seen – breathtakingly detailed, and highly informative about the manufacturer's industry status.)

- Design fashion dates some pianos reasonably well. For example, a sloping front is characteristic of uprights from the 1940s and 1950s.

However, some information can mislead. For example:

- The sloping front characteristic of 1940s and 1950s uprights can also be found on much earlier pianos 'modernised' in the 1940s and 1950s.
- Iron frames may have foundry data cast into them, but any date or number shown won't necessarily relate to the piano itself.
- Other misleading numbers can include a dealer's stock number, often stamped into the wood inside one end of the instrument.

On old pianos like the one above, one still occasionally finds no maker's name, no serial number, no pencil marks – nothing. My approach to dating this is as follows:

- It has a mahogany case and square legs – a typical English design from around 1920, though only abundant from the late 1920s to the 1940s.
- But it has an exposed wrest plank, which suggests an earlier rather than a later date – probably early 1920s.
- It has 85 rather than 88 keys – again pointing to an earlier rather than a later date.

Thus, despite a complete absence of anything other than circumstantial evidence, I'm confident enough that this piano dates from the early 1920s.

PART 2

Looking after your piano

Though pianos have been hugely popular for over 150 years, this book is perhaps the first to suggest that a typical owner can realistically tackle even quite advanced maintenance, repair and tuning tasks.

The following chapters explain what you can do to keep your instrument in peak playing condition, extend its working life by decades – and perhaps discover that within it lurks a much better piano, just waiting to be unleashed!

CHAPTER 6

Easy care and maintenance

The routine, day-to-day care that a piano needs, and the safety precautions that you *must* take. Your piano's basic requirements are few and simple. Meeting them will do a great deal both to extend its working life and increase the pleasure you get from it.

Health and safety

All pianos are large, heavy, non-fixed objects, so this is where care and maintenance really ought to start. A lot of my workshop jobs are expensive repairs arising from easily avoidable accidents. Human casualties are repaired elsewhere, sometimes even more expensively.

Upright pianos

- The most popular direction for an upright to fall is backwards, so wherever possible, keep it against a wall.
- *Never* position an upright away from a wall in any place where children are left unsupervised.
- If an upright can't be kept against a wall, have it fitted with purpose-designed angle brackets at the rear (as shown below). The castors are transferred from the piano to the ends of the brackets. This effectively widens the piano's wheelbase, making it much more difficult to push over (see page 24).
- If an upright needs to be moved around regularly, it should be fitted either with larger castors rated for the piano's weight, or – better – a purpose-designed piano cradle. A piano technician should be able to source and fit one for you.
- *Never* pin a decorative cloth over the back of the piano unless you're absolutely sure it can't slip off and drag on the floor. If it does and the piano is pushed backwards, it will flip over without warning as soon as the trailing edge of the cloth winds itself up in the castors. (If this sounds unlikely, believe me, it happens.)

Alarmingly, I find these safety guidelines most often ignored in schools. Contrary to its stable appearance, an upright tilted as little as 5° from vertical can topple over, and this often happens when it is being 'wrestled' to move it just a few feet. Overbalancing can also happen if children climb on an upright or even lean against it. At several hundredweight, a piano falling backwards can easily kill or seriously injure a child. Nor will it improve anything else that gets in its way.

A secondary risk is that a single fall may crack the cast iron frame, which will scrap the instrument.

Grand pianos

- If a grand is to be moved often, it should have an A-frame fitted that connects each leg and has easy-glide castors. Some of these frames bolt on and the piano's original castors are removed. Others have a small cradle in which the piano castors sit. Frames are not attractive but they're much better than a piano with a broken leg.

- If you don't have a frame, move your grand as little as possible. Any move, however small, should be at least a three-person task, and as much as possible of the piano's weight should be taken by the movers in order to lessen the load on the castors. Piano castors can only do so much. Unless the piano is at least partially lifted, any resistance from their being on a carpet, or at the wrong starting angle, or dirty or corroded, may risk breaking a leg off. The piano may then collapse, causing serious injury or damage.
- Forwards and backwards motion is generally easier than sideways.
- Never, ever, raise the lid without first checking that the hinge pins are securely in place. The lid will have either two or three hinges. Each is in two parts, held together by a brass rod with usually a 70° or 80° bend in it, and with about half an inch (13mm) projecting so that it can be pulled out – see the photo on page 85. Sometimes these hinge pins come out easily;

🎹 Easy dismantling

Front board

The front board is usually held in by two fasteners, one at each end. In older pianos these are metal sprung clips. They pull in tighter as the catch is squeezed shut, so that the front board can't rattle (see below). In more modern pianos a plastic or wooden latch swivels around a dowel, or a dowel peg fits tightly into a plastic socket. It can take some force to remove and refit the fasteners, but this is perfectly normal. The bottom of the board will either have dowel pegs, or be seated in a groove. Either way, you must lift the board vertically before you pull it away from the piano.

Place the front board flat on the floor, on an old blanket or similar. Check the safety of any delicate parts; on older pianos there is a sometimes a thin, protruding moulding that will easily snap off.

Fallboard

Close the keyboard lid. Put one hand inside the piano and grasp the back of the fallboard at its centre. (Mind your knuckles don't graze on the action tape stirrups). Place the other hand at roughly the same place on the front of the fallboard. Pull up, then outwards – see below. Place the fallboard safely on the floor, as with the front board. In some pianos, the key strip is separate and held in by two screws (see lower photo) and is, I think, a superior arrangement.

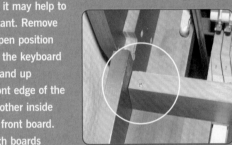

In some uprights, the front board and fallboard are all in one. This can be a heavy unit, so it may help to have an assistant. Remove these in the open position – that is, with the keyboard lid up – one hand up against the front edge of the fallboard, the other inside the top of the front board.

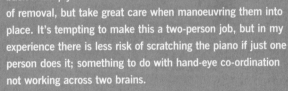

Putting both boards back is simply the reverse of removal, but take great care when manoeuvring them into place. It's tempting to make this a two-person job, but in my experience there is less risk of scratching the piano if just one person does it; something to do with hand-eye co-ordination not working across two brains.

sometimes they have to be coaxed out with pliers. (Watch the French polish! Look at the damage done to this piano.) The point is that nothing other than friction keeps them in. They can be a magnet to inquisitive children, so I've seen plenty of school pianos where the hinge pins were either missing or almost out. They can also work loose if the lid is raised and lowered frequently. The lid can weigh 60lb (27kg) or more, so you don't want it suddenly taking leave of the piano, especially if there are people standing immediately behind it.

■ Grand piano lids are in two sections. Never, ever raise the lid without first folding the front section back over the rear section. If you fail to do this, the front section's substantial weight will only be supported by the tiny screws in the long brass hinge connecting it to the rear section. Sooner rather than later the front section will tear itself free, resulting in injury maybe, expensive repair certainly.

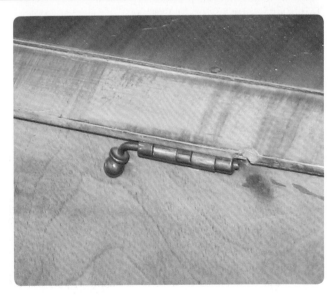

Environment

Generally speaking, most environments that are comfortable for humans will be comfortable for pianos. But:

■ Turn down the central heating

Pianos don't like the levels of central heating some humans seem to need. Central heating accelerates the natural tendency of wood to shrink, and of old glue to deteriorate. If you can keep your piano's space cooler than the rest of the house, it will last significantly longer. If the piano is in a room that is only used for practice, fit a thermostatic valve to the radiator and keep it at its lowest setting, or turn the radiator off when no one is there.

■ Avoid direct sunlight

Direct sunlight will damage or at least fade the case, causing 'Chinese writing' to appear. It may also overheat the interior of the piano. The chemicals used to colour French polish, which is how older pianos were finished, are nitrates and therefore light sensitive. Often a piano left in bright sunlight will fade to a variety of shades. Some modern finishes have more ultra-violet resistance, but even so they're not immune.

■ Avoid damp

Cold won't harm a piano in any way, but prolonged exposure to damp will. The first casualty is likely to be the centre pins – the joints in the action. These will corrode and seize up and replacement is very costly. (See Chapter 8, section B, for how to deal with this.) Monitor your piano's space. If there is evidence of damp affecting anything nearby, the piano will be suffering too.

Damp also causes the strings to corrode. Treble strings may still function with a surprising amount of rust on them, but copper-wound bass strings will not. They will go 'tubby', sounding very dull. See Chapter 8, section C, for possible remedies.

Alarming things can happen when a piano that has lived for a long time in a damp, cold environment is moved to a drier, hotter one. I once moved and refurbished a piano donated to an old people's home. It was a beautiful early 1920s Steck upright, but within months of being transplanted from the front room of an unheated, unoccupied house into a comparative inferno (28°C or 85°F of dry heat) the glue joints were falling apart, reducing the piano almost to kit form.

Cleaning your piano

Clean the case as part of normal housework, but be careful with aerosol polishes as the propellant (not the polish) may dissolve a lacquer finish. Spray the polish on to a duster first.

From time to time, clean the keyboard. If you feel bold enough, remove the front board and fallboard (see *Easy dismantling*), and the key strip if it is separate (it may be held in by two screws). You can then polish right up to the end of the keys without any hindrance from the nameboard tape – the felt strip running between the casework and the keys.

It's quite traditional, if never specifically recommended, to use that well-known general-purpose cleaner and lubricant *saliva* to clean stubborn spots off the keys. Apply it with a slightly moistened, lint-free soft cloth (basically, anything that doesn't shed tiny particles).

Alternatively, a tiny trace of window cleaner may help with stubborn marks, but put it on to the cloth, not directly on to the keyboard. Do *not* use a thick glass cleaner but a thin, aerosol glass cleaner. And do *not* allow any liquid to run down the sides of the keys. Use another cloth to dry off and polish.

If you have removed the keystrip, you can lift each key an inch or so (25mm) proud of those next to it to clean it more thoroughly. But you won't be able to clean the sides of the keys without removing the keyboard, and these can be quite grubby in an old or frequently played piano. In the photo below, showing some of the dirtiest keysides I've ever seen, note the way the celluloid wraps around the odd-shaped key front, and the two rivets through the front of each key. This is evidence

of *tropicalisation* – special measures to make the piano suitable for hot climates. The key coverings should not drop off even if the glue degrades. The black keys appear to have been 'refreshed' using something less than permanent that has transferred via fingers to the sides of the white keys.

In Chapter 7 I explain how to remove the keyboard, which makes it possible to clean the sides properly. This definitely repays the effort. Considering how little of the sides one can see, cleaning them has an amazing impact on the appearance of the keyboard.

Nameboard tape

The length of wood immediately over the top of the keys will have a strip of coloured felt along it: on the keystrip if the piano has a separate one, or along the edge of the fallboard. This is the *nameboard tape*, and its job is to stop the keys bouncing up against the wood during furious playing. On old pianos it is often dirty and discoloured and is the first place to look for signs of moth attack.

Fitting a new nameboard tape greatly improves the appearance of the keyboard. It doesn't cost much and is easy to replace, though it takes a little skill to get it protruding just the right amount and in a dead straight line. Note how far the old tape protrudes, and judge whether this looks right. Scrape it off with a knife, taking care not to run out over the polished surface. Use fabric glue to attach the new tape. Finally, trim to length: there will usually be two pencil marks showing how far the original went.

🎹 Tuning

Have your piano tuned at least once a year. (Most tuners will say twice a year.) Every piano will be less in tune today than it was yesterday, but rates of pitch loss vary from instrument to instrument and even from string to string. After a year, any piano will benefit from tuning. If it is played a lot, have it tuned more often. The most pragmatic rule is to have it tuned when it sounds out of tune to another musician.

The best time for tuning is autumn, because there is generally more pitch loss in a summer climate than in winter. An autumn tuning will therefore, on average, last longer.

Pianos used for public performance are usually tuned for every event. For a series of major performances a piano will be tuned daily, and the tuner may even have to be on hand in case any tuning is needed during the interval. An important requirement here, of course, is to book the tuner well in advance!

CHAPTER 7

Moderate repair & maintenance

Somewhere between five and thirty years from new – depending on environment, build quality and frequency of use – most pianos will start to need more than just tuning to keep them in good playing condition. Fortunately, many maintenance and repair tasks can be easily carried out at little cost by owners willing to make a small effort.

Tools, materials and labour

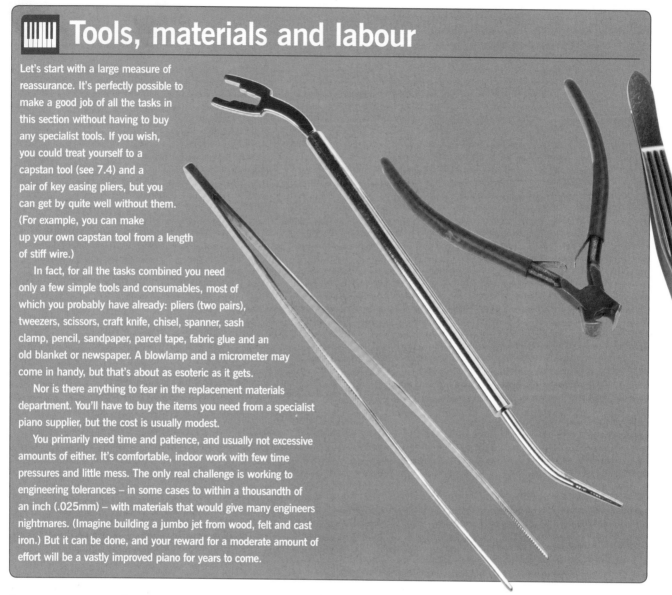

Let's start with a large measure of reassurance. It's perfectly possible to make a good job of all the tasks in this section without having to buy any specialist tools. If you wish, you could treat yourself to a capstan tool (see 7.4) and a pair of key easing pliers, but you can get by quite well without them. (For example, you can make up your own capstan tool from a length of stiff wire.)

In fact, for all the tasks combined you need only a few simple tools and consumables, most of which you probably have already: pliers (two pairs), tweezers, scissors, craft knife, chisel, spanner, sash clamp, pencil, sandpaper, parcel tape, fabric glue and an old blanket or newspaper. A blowlamp and a micrometer may come in handy, but that's about as esoteric as it gets.

Nor is there anything to fear in the replacement materials department. You'll have to buy the items you need from a specialist piano supplier, but the cost is usually modest.

You primarily need time and patience, and usually not excessive amounts of either. It's comfortable, indoor work with few time pressures and little mess. The only real challenge is working to engineering tolerances – in some cases to within a thousandth of an inch (.025mm) – with materials that would give many engineers nightmares. (Imagine building a jumbo jet from wood, felt and cast iron.) But it can be done, and your reward for a moderate amount of effort will be a vastly improved piano for years to come.

Lost motion

The most common early faults in pianos are collectively called lost motion – a gradual slackness in response between the keyboard and the action. It's the equivalent of bicycle brakes drifting out of adjustment. What should happen instantly starts to take longer. The hammer loses its full movement and force, sapping the piano of its vitality.

First, some volume will be lost. Then, as the problem worsens, rapid repetition will become impossible. Finally, the hammers will not 'check' but will bounce on the jack. This is often audible as a rather 'plinky' tone, and notes can even sound twice.

Lost motion has two major causes:
- Compression or shrinkage of the backtouch (LM1).
- Compression of the balance rail washers (LM2).

Correcting them isn't particularly difficult as long as you stick to my sequence of investigations and procedures – LM1 followed by LM2. This matters because the keyboard and action are so interdependent that there is only one reliable sequence of diagnosis. Depart from it, and you risk creating more problems than you started with.

The same problems afflict both grands and uprights, but the remedies are different. In this chapter I'll deal only with uprights; grand piano actions and keyboards are covered in Chapter 9.

LM1: Compression or shrinkage of the backtouch

The backtouch is a thick felt pad running along the back of the keybed (see **7.1**). When at rest, the keys lie on it. The felt gradually compresses and shrinks, and both conditions cause lost motion. Compression tends to be an effect of frequent playing, while shrinkage is the effect of time. Some of the action parts may compress and shrink too, making the problem worse.

To find out if your piano is suffering from backtouch problems:

1 Remove the front board and fallboard (see Chapter 6).

2 Depress *very slowly* any key in the middle of the keyboard, and watch the action.

3 The check – the part covered in green felt in **7.2** – will start to move straight away, as it will be resting on the key.

4 If the check moves a tiny but noticeable distance – ¹⁄₁₆in (1.5mm) or so – before the hammer starts to move, your piano is losing motion.

Now refine your diagnosis:

5 Try the 'lost motion test' on every second or third key, right across the keyboard.

6 If lost motion is much more pronounced in the middle – the most frequently played keys – than at the extremes of treble and bass, the cause is compression. Each affected key will now need separate adjustment, so go to *Fixing compression problems* (below).

7 If lost motion is more or less uniform across the keyboard, the cause is shrinkage – in which case, go to *Fixing shrinkage problems* (page 93).

Fixing compression problems

Pianos have their own internal lost motion adjuster mechanisms. There are four basic types of mechanism, so you first need to identify the one in your piano.

Mechanism 1 (7.3)

Most modern pianos have this type of mechanism, which is also visible on page 57. To make adjustments, the capstan (ringed) is rotated anticlockwise to close up the gap between jack and notch.

The capstan stem may be long or short, depending on the height of the piano. Here it's long, because the keyboard of this large piano is well below the point where the hammers strike the strings. A long stem needs to be held with pliers to avoid bending it while rotating the capstan.

Note that the head of the capstan has a touch of black lead on it. Factory-applied black lead is a highly effective and long-lasting dry lubricant that prevents squeaks and slow movement. It's very rare for more to be needed, even after decades of use. But I keep some on hand, just in case.

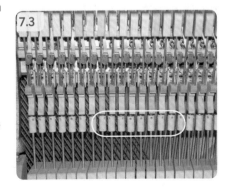

Adjusting the capstan is easy if the piano is relatively new (up to around 15 years old):

1 Insert the pointed end of a capstan tool (**7.4**) through the hole. (You don't need to buy one. You can easily improvise using wire thick enough to fit snugly through the hole.)

7.4

2 Using the capstan tool or wire as a handle, unscrew the mechanism – usually no more than a quarter turn – to take up the lost motion.

3 If the hammer is left forward of its neighbours, you have overdone it and must turn the capstan back very slightly. (If it is overdone by the slightest degree, the piano will slow down. Playing fast will be a problem, as the jack will not return under the notch quickly enough.)

Adjustment may be less easy if the piano is over 15 years old. From roughly that age, the metal screws start corroding into the capstan. (The cause is the acid in the wood of the capstan.) If the capstan is seized up, any turning force may then break the capstan – and if one capstan is seized, they probably all are.

To move them at all, you must remove each affected key separately and hold each capstan in turn with a large pair of pliers. If the piano is cherished, tape felt to the jaws of the pliers. The capstans often move with a cracking sound as the rust breaks away from the wood. This is unsettling but normal.

In a piano more than about 50 years old, the probability of breaking seized capstans is high even for an experienced technician. It's time to start thinking about buying a younger instrument, but if you're really determined, heat the stems with a blowlamp for a few seconds. This may, or may not, be enough to free up the screws. And I suggest that you find out

how many of the capstans will move at all before embarking on the more finicky task of adjusting them individually.

Mechanism 2 (7.5)
Some pianos have this type of mechanism, which is turned by using the jaws of the capstan tool. Otherwise, adjustment is exactly the same as Mechanism 1 – unscrew the mechanism a quarter turn or less.

7.5

Mechanism 3 (7.6 and 7.7)
This mechanism, found only in the cheapest (when new) and most basic pianos, is simply a woodscrew into the key, with a covering of thin felt (called pilot cloth when used for this purpose). The screw head inevitably and quickly wears through the felt. It's then hopeless to try to adjust the screw upwards. Luckily, it isn't difficult to replace the whole felt.

7.6

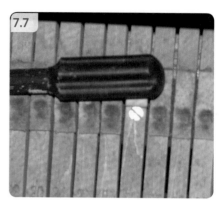
7.7

1 Buy a strip of felt from a supplier (see *Useful contacts*). To get the right thickness, send a piece of the old felt to the supplier. Alternatively, measure it very accurately with a micrometer.

2 Remove the keyboard (Chapter 8), transferring it to a bench or table in sections so that the keys are close together.

3 Clamp the keys firmly together with parcel tape, or with a sash clamp. Scrape off the old felt and glue.

4 Using a fabric adhesive such as Copydex, run a thread of glue along the block of keys and attach the new felt.

5 Do not glue the felt over the screw. It should form a flap over the screw, so that the screw can be adjusted.

6 When the glue is dry, separate the keys by running a scalpel or fine, sharp blade between them. Replace the keyboard.

7 Adjust the screws upwards as necessary. No hammer should be left forward of the others. They should all be just touching the rest rail.

8 Put a finger inside the rest rail near the middle of the piano and pull the rest rail slightly back from the hammers. If the hammers don't move back with the rest rail, your adjustment is correct.

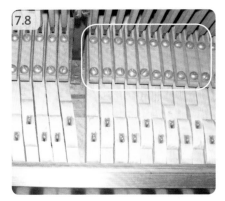

First, though, you have to:

1 Remove the front board, the fallboard and the key strip, as shown in Chapter 8.

2 You must also remove the practice pedal mechanism if one is fitted, as it will prevent access to the tuning pins and action. **7.10** shows a piano with the front and fallboard removed but the practice pedal mechanism still in place. The ends of the mechanism are metal pins pushed into recesses. Simply pulling the bass end out won't free up the mechanism for removal. Instead, undo the screw on the end of the pad that joins it to the end of the operating mechanism, and remove the pad from the bass end – see **7.11** and **7.12**. This makes it possible to remove the treble end – see **7.13**. Be careful how you remove this: it has sharp edges and is awkward to manoeuvre out. As always, be prepared for some other kind of mechanism. For example, in some pianos the pad can be removed without dismantling it, but it's a tight fit.

Mechanism 4 (7.8)

Pray that you don't have this type of mechanism, which is found only in very old pianos such as the Bechstein model 10 in **7.8**. It's essentially a wooden block with two screws through it. The screw nearer the keyboard is a locking screw; the other is the adjuster. To adjust the motion:

1 Loosen the locking screw. Tighten the adjuster screw upwards. You'll see the back part rise, taking up the free play.

2 When there is no more free play, tighten the locking screw again.

3 But tightening the locking screw moves the adjustment, so you have to do it all again!

Be warned: this is frustrating to get right and requires the patience of a saint. It's a process of two steps forward, one step back – as infuriating as adjusting the tappets in an old-fashioned car or motorbike engine, where locking the adjuster slightly alters the tappet setting. (Some of Bechstein's older grands, such as the model B, have the same mechanism but adjustment is an even more wretched experience because the screw heads are completely covered by the action.)

Even worse, if now rare, **7.9** shows that this Bechstein has 'stickers', extra pieces connecting each key to the whippen (the bottom part of the action). Stickers are needed in pianos that are exceptionally tall – but because each key

is now joined up to its own action part, it will take a technician hours to remove the action instead of the ten seconds needed for most pianos. This is not the Bechstein model 10's most endearing feature.

Fixing shrinkage problems

When lost motion is caused by shrinkage of the backtouch felt, there will be little point using the piano's internal keyboard adjustment mechanism. This is because shrinkage tends to affect all keys to the same degree. Rather than adjust every key by exactly the same amount, it makes more sense either to replace or raise the backtouch felt. This one operation fixes the problem in all 88 keys.

Removing the action

This should take only a few minutes. Have a flat work surface ready that won't easily mark, as the steel bottoms of the action posts may be sharp. (In **7.14** I'm running risks for a quick adjustment!) Keep children and pets out of the way.

The action is held in by two or three bolts connecting the frame of the piano to the action posts. Most modern pianos have two action posts – one at each end – but some have three and the mighty 1915 Steinway shown in **7.15** has four – and just look at the size of the pressure bars!

1 Undo the knurled nuts on the action bolts – possibly with pliers if they haven't been off for a long time. (Finger-tight is enough when you put them back.)

2 Examine the pedal mechanism at the bass end. Can the action be pulled out without anything fouling it? In most pianos there shouldn't be a problem; the pedal rods come up to the levers on the end of the action and when the action is removed, they simply come away.

3 But pedal mechanisms like that in **7.16** must be disconnected before the action can be removed. Pull the lever up far enough, and the prong will drop out. Don't lose the rubber liner from the hole, or the mechanism will clank forever more. (If you do lose it or it wasn't there anyway, you can improvise a liner from felt. See *Pedal adjustment – Variant pedal mechanisms*.)

4 For all pianos, check that there are no other connections. For example, some pianos have a small tie bar (**7.17**), a bracket near the middle of the piano from the keybed to the action. If it's there, disconnect it.

5 Pull the action back a little, until the lugs are clear of the bolts.

7.14

7.17

7.15

7.18

7.16

7.19

6 Hold the action with both hands firmly gripping the rest rail – the wooden cross-member against which the hammers rest (**7.19**).

7 Pull the action up and out of the piano. It isn't too heavy – 20lb (9kg) or so – but is an awkward shape to deal with. If the piano has three action posts, manoeuvre carefully around the bolt for the middle post, as a damper can easily be ripped off on the way – see **7.18**. This Rogers also has a fly damper (circled). **7.20** shows how the last few dampers in an overstrung upright are shortened. To make up for this deficiency, some piano makers include one or more of these

extra little fly dampers attached to the existing one. They're fairly ineffective but have lots of snagging potential.

8 Put the action straight down on your work surface. It's then fairly easy to remove the keyboard.

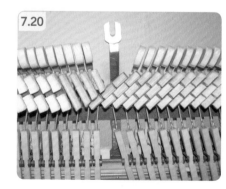

7.20

Removing the keyboard

This too should take only a few minutes.

1 Close the top lid of the piano and cover it with a thick protective pad of folded blanket or newspaper.

2 Starting from the treble end, carefully remove two or three keys. For the first few inches it will be difficult to get your fingers in around them, but they soon come out in handfuls. Remove them carefully so as not to damage the bushing cloth in the balance rail holes.

3 Place the keyboard on the padded top of the piano.

4 Keep the keys in order. Each key is number stamped clearly – until they all tumble into a big heap on the floor, when suddenly the numbers are not so clear. As a precaution, before removing them draw a diagonal pencil line on the wooden part of the keys where they disappear under the keystrip. Then, if the keys get mixed up, you can quickly sort them into approximate sequence by reconstructing the pencil line – at which point the key numbers miraculously become clear again.

7.21 shows a 1974 Kemble with the keyboard removed. Now you can examine the condition of the backtouch felt. If it is worn where the keys touch, or has moth damage, it needs replacing. Cut a small segment from the thickest part and send it to a parts supplier for the nearest match.

Replacing the backtouch felt is always the better option, but if the backtouch felt is in generally good condition it will be possible to raise it. See *Raising the backtouch felt* (page 96).

Replacing the backtouch felt

For this job, set aside a day and assume that if all goes smoothly you'll only need about half of it.

1 Remove the old backtouch felt. On some pianos it peels off readily, leaving a few traces that are easily scraped off. On other pianos the glue has set like concrete and the felt has to be carefully chiselled off – but not with a hammer! Every particle has to come off, and it may be difficult to get into the corners.

2 It's acceptable to sand the now exposed backtouch rail flat and smooth, but remove as little wood as possible.

7.22

3 Drop the new felt in dry – that is, without glue.

4 Put a black key and a white key from each octave into the piano. (I tend to put C and C# of three or four octaves in the middle of the piano, and a couple of keys nearer the end.)

5 Put the action back into the piano. (The reverse of removal.)

6 Hold each end of the felt strip and, by waggling it under tension from side to side, slide it gradually backwards up the slope of the keyframe. (Yes, the back of the keyframe slopes – this may not be obvious at first glance.)

7 At some point the felt will just start to lift the hammers off the rest rail – see **7.22**.

8 Reverse slightly, until the felt is as close as it can get to raising the hammers without actually doing so. Straighten up the felt while doing this.

9 Mark the final position very precisely with a pencil line. Remove the felt Remove the action.

10 Run a thin line of latex-based adhesive along the backtouch rail and drop in the felt. (A product such as Copydex is fine. Avoid 'instant grab' adhesives, which may give you too little time for any readjustment.)

7.21

11 Check the line of felt and your pencil line minutely to ensure that the new felt is in exactly the right position. Trim the ends of the felt to size and shape.

The next steps need to be worked through fairly swiftly, so that any readjustment can be done before the glue sets. You've got five to ten minutes or so before it goes 'stringy', but it will still stick for some minutes longer.

12 Replace the keyboard and action. Depress very slowly any key in the middle of the keyboard, and watch the action.

13 If the check – the part covered in green felt identified in **7.2** – and the hammer start moving at almost the same moment, you have cured your lost motion problem. In this photo the balance hammer – the leather covered part facing the check – is joined to the hammer, so watch closely the gap between check and balance hammer. There should be just the tiniest lag between the check moving and the balance hammer moving.

14 With the keys at rest, any hammers that are lifted slightly can now be adjusted downwards using your piano's capstan adjustment mechanism (see *Fixing compression problems – Mechanism 1*). The capstans will now be unlikely (one hopes) to move for some considerable time since they are being tightened up – that is, screwed up further into the wood of the key – rather than undone.

15 If at step 13 the check moves $1/_{16}$in (1.5mm) or so before the hammer starts to move, you still have lost motion…

16 …in which case, take the keyboard out again and adjust the new felt strip further backwards in order to raise it. You'll have no option but

7.23

to hurry, as the glue will be setting. This is why it's so important to position the felt accurately before glueing it.

Raising the backtouch felt

I would always recommend replacing the backtouch felt, but if the existing felt is still in good condition along its whole length, you can try raising it enough to take up the slack in the motion (see **7.23**). I must stress, though, that if there is *any* sign of compression or moth damage, it will be false economy not to replace it.

Whichever of the following options you try, the procedure for adjusting the felt or tape to the right height is exactly as described in *Replacing the backtouch felt* (step 4 onwards).

- In some pianos, only one edge of the backtouch felt is glued down. A length of nameboard tape or thin felt can then be slipped underneath to raise or 'shim' it to the right thickness.
- Even if the felt is completely glued down, it's worth using a sharp knife to see if you can work one edge free enough to insert a strip of tape.

- If the felt can't be freed, try running nameboard tape across the top of the old felt. Don't glue it yet. Insert it as described in *Replacing the backtouch felt* (step 4 onwards), with two keys of each octave in situ.
- Slide the tape from side to side and backwards up the rail slope until it just touches the bottom of the keys. When you have found the correct position, lightly glue it down with a latex-based adhesive such as Copydex.

All these remedies leave the keys resting on a much narrower piece of material than before. While this isn't ideal, it may cure a minor lost motion problem for many years, and the piano will sound and feel just as good as it would with full-width felt.

Raising the backtouch felt does, however, fall into the category of cheap fix rather than proper repair – perfectly acceptable if you intend to keep the piano for your own use, but more questionable if you intend to sell it. I must therefore repeat the point made earlier: wherever possible, a complete replacement of the backtouch felt is a much better option all round.

LM2: Compression of the balance rail washers

The balance rail washer is the fulcrum on which the key moves – see **7.20, 7.21 and 7.24**. It's a tiny, frail component that has to do a lot of work. Being made of felt, it gradually compresses and wears out, often assisted by moth attack. As the washers fail, the piano will:

- Lose volume.
- Start to feel and sound dull or 'mushy'.
- Cease to repeat rapidly.

As the condition worsens, the hammers will bounce on the jacks and may even play twice.

Diagnosis

1 To diagnose balance rail washer compression, kneel on the floor about 4–5ft (1.2–1.5m) from the piano and look at the keys. Are they level? If the washers are compressed, there will be a noticeable sag in the middle of the keyboard, where the keys are used more. This means that the keys in the middle will have lost keystroke. The standard keystroke is $^3/_8$in to $^7/_{16}$in (9.52 to 11.62mm), though most professional pianists favour $^7/_{16}$. This standard keystroke is magnified into hammer movement of $1^7/_8$ to 2in (47 to 50mm). Therefore, the loss of a tiny

amount of keystroke has a much greater effect on hammer stroke, and thus on the performance of the piano.

2 Now do a quick check for an uncommon but serious problem that may make any further work pointless. Old pianos kept in damp environments tend to be most at risk. Look for distinctive little piles of dust in the keybed under the action – especially in the middle of the piano. This indicates that the buckskin on the balance hammers or the green felt on the checks – often both – is worn and crumbling. **7.25** shows these components. If those materials are much thicker – that is, less worn – at the bass and treble extremes of the keybed, the problem is confirmed. The hammer will be coming to rest 'in check' further back than it should and so the piano will not repeat rapidly, even with everything else set up correctly.

The pattern of wear reflects the way the piano is played. If the most-played notes are badly affected, there may be no point doing any further work on the instrument. In theory, all the worn leather and felt can be replaced. In practice, an old piano this far gone is usually beyond worthwhile repair, even if you do the work yourself. It might be a suitable candidate for a rebuild, but the older the

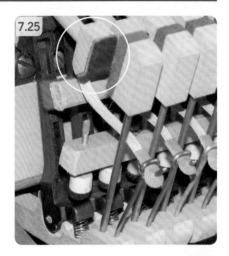

7.25

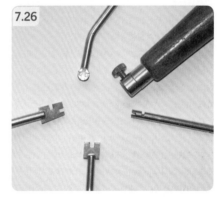

7.26

piano, the greater the likelihood that this isn't its only serious problem. Time to think about replacing it!

3 Another early warning check, but with no serious implications. Look along the action, at the backcheck wires and checks – the wires supporting the green felt covered checks in **7.25** They should all be in a dead straight line. If several wires are bent to the same slightly curved profile, some misguided person has done it deliberately to 'improve' the piano by faking the correct keystroke. What they have actually done is treat a symptom of lost motion rather than the cause. You will have to undo their handiwork, using one of the special tools shown in **7.26**. This shows the three most commonly used bending tools, and their shared handle.

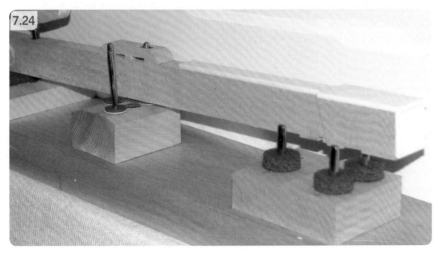

7.24

Remedy

Assuming you don't find the dreaded piles of leather and felt dust, your task is to:

- Replace the worn washers with new washers of the correct original size.
- Then level the keyboard to produce a correct and uniform keystroke.

Your first problem is working out the correct original size. Life would be simpler if piano components were standardised or colour-coded, but they're not. Absolutely nothing on a piano is standard, including balance rail washers. Precise measurement is the only solution.

Finding the right washer size

The relatively unworked washers at the extreme bass and treble ends will be closest to the original size. Measurement based on one of these may be your only hope of finding the size you need – and even then, you have to allow for the possibility that it may have shrunk.

1 Buy paper washers in several thicknesses. They're available in sizes from 12-thousandths of an inch (0.3mm) down to 3-thousandths of an inch (0.075mm), enabling one to make a precision job of levelling the keyboard. Remove the action. Remove the keyboard.

2 Find a balance rail washer that looks in good condition.

3 Put just this key back in, then refit the action.

4 Confirm by measuring that this trial key has $^7/_{16}$in (11.62mm) of keystroke.

5 Confirm that the note is playing correctly. When struck hard and held, the hammer should stop half an inch (12.5mm) from the strings.

6 If it's further away than this, shim it up by placing thin paper washers under the balance rail washer until the note plays correctly.

7 Remove the action and key, and measure the thickness of the old washer plus any paper shims.

8 Remove one white and one black key in each octave and shim the old balance rail washer up to this new thickness. Check that these trial notes work correctly, or nearly so. If the hammers are all ending too far back, shim your trial keys up a little more. (The black keys may well require less shimming than the white.)

9 The thickness that emerges as generally the best is the size of washer that you now need to buy.

Take your time over all the shimming and measuring, because if the replacements you buy are even a tiny fraction too thick, they can't be used. It doesn't matter so much if they're a little too thin, because they can be shimmed up with paper washers, but it's worth experiencing the smugness that comes from getting the size exactly right.

Old paper shims

When removing the old washers from an old piano, a bad sign is finding lots of old paper shims from the last time the keyboard was levelled, possibly decades ago. A worse sign is finding a different thickness number on each shim. This usually means that fitting new washers won't on its own finish the job, and that you too will have to make time-consuming fine adjustments with paper washers.

You might ask: 'How about leaving the old paper shims in place?' Smart question, but this won't work, because time will have wrought other changes. Old shims were also rarely made to precise thicknesses – many were just punchings from old newspapers – and so will be an unreliable guide to what size

of new washer you need. When labour was relatively cheaper than materials, workers could be given junk shims and just had to work harder and longer to do the job. Nowadays, it's cheaper to give the workers better materials.

Fitting the new washers

1 Remove the action. Remove the keyboard. Remove the old balance rail washers. (Drop them in the keybed and then vacuum them out.)

2 Insert the new balance rail washers. Refit the keyboard. Refit the action.

3 The piano should be greatly improved at once. When the keys are struck firmly and held down, the hammers should stop at the correct distance – half an inch (12.5mm) – away from the strings.

4 Get down on your knees again and visually check the level of the keyboard. You want to see a perfectly flat line, with no sagging or upstanding keys.

Sometimes, and especially when it's a well-made instrument, the piano will now work correctly with very little further adjustment. If this happens, consider yourself lucky!

At other times – especially if the old washers were abundantly shimmed – the keyboard remains obstinately not level. Playing several different keys reveals that some hammers end up too close to the strings, and others too far away. You may now be facing several hours' work to level the keyboard!

Levelling the keyboard

1 Find a few keys in the middle of the piano that work correctly – that is, after being struck hard and held down the hammers stop at the correct distance of half an inch (12.5mm) from the strings. You're now going to level the keyboard to these keys.

2 Lay a straight edge – or simply cut a length of wood that you know to be straight – across the white keys from the wooden keyblocks at each end as a visual guide. It needs to be just touching the white keys that you have judged to be correct. (If you must, you can buy a key-levelling device from a piano supply house – you set the height and it slides along the keyslip. But a homemade straight edge is just as good.)

3 Kneel in front of the piano and raise the sagged white keys by dropping thin paper washers *on top of* the balance rail felt washers. This is for speed – see step 6 below. Tweezers will be a considerable help in fitting the washers. (A pair of surgical tweezers is my most used tool over the last 35 years.)

4 Keep doing this until there is no sign of sagging and all the keys are level relative to your straight edge.

5 Now level the black keys in the same way, by finding several in the middle that are working correctly and levelling to them. A straight edge is essential here, as the gaps between the black keys make it harder to judge whether they're level.

6 Once you're happy that the keyboard is fully level, take the keyboard out and go along putting all the new shims *under* the new washers. Refit the keyboard and action.

7 Check the length of the keystroke. If every hammer stops half an inch (12.5mm) from the string, the piano is playing correctly and your work is done.

Adjusting the keystroke

8 If on some keys there is now too much keystroke (the hammer ends up too close to the string), reduce it by shimming the front rail with paper washers. They go under the green felt buffer washer – see **7.24**. For this you'll need an assortment of front rail paper washers, which are much larger than balance rail washers. They're also thicker, because shimming the balance rail by a small amount has a large effect on the hammer, whereas shimming the front rail by a large amount has only a small effect.

Possible additional work

Neither of the following two conditions is common, but they're not so uncommon that I can ignore them.

9a If some hammers in the middle of the piano are stopping too far back from the strings but those at the ends are functioning correctly, the probable cause is worn leather or felt on the balance hammer. To confirm this, check that they have the same keystroke as the ones functioning correctly. (See also *Diagnosis* step 2 on page 97 for a visual check.) A small amount of wear can be compensated for by using the regulating tool shown in **7.26** to bend the affected checks forward slightly until the hammers come to rest half an inch (12.5mm) from the strings. It won't look pretty but it will keep an old piano playing a while longer.

9b If some of the backcheck wires were already bent forward (*Diagnosis* step 3), they will need bending back a little because you have now fixed the problem the person who did the bending didn't bother to fix earlier! Again, use the regulating tool shown in **7.26** to bend the check wires back until the hammers end up half an inch (12.5mm) from the strings after being played firmly.

Moth attack

Piano felt offers moths a sumptuous banquet in relaxed surroundings. When moth damage is as severe as in **7.27 and 7.28**, the piano won't play correctly and the instrument will probably be infested with moth eggs. The usual immediate evidence of moth attack is all of these:

■ A moth-eaten nameboard tape, **7.29**.
■ A highly uneven keyboard – some keys high, some low.
■ Some keys seem to go down further than others.
■ Notes play irregularly – some quieter, some louder.

7.27

7.28

7.29

Removing the keyboard will reveal backtouch, balance rail and front rail partially eaten, as shown in **7.27**. The only remedy is to replace all of the keybed felt and all washers. So:

1 Remove the keyboard. Strip out all keybed felt: the backtouch, balance rail and all balance rail and front rail washers.

2 Vacuum out all dust and moth eggs (tiny spheres the same colour as the felt they've been raised on). Replace the backtouch and balance rail washers as described earlier.

3 Fit new front rail washers. Finding the right washer size for the front rail should be easier than for the balance rail. Because they're bigger and bulkier, there's usually enough left to measure somewhere.

4 Adjust the keystroke if needed. (See *Adjusting the keystroke* above.) This should be easy with new front rail washers fitted.

5 When everything is working correctly, remove the keyboard again and treat the keybed woodwork and new felt with an aerosol mothproofer. Spray lightly to avoid over-wetting. Don't spray the action even if there is evidence of moth in the hammers. See Chapter 8, section B, for how to spray the hammers.

6 Allow the mothproofer to dry thoroughly before putting the keyboard back in.

7 Don't put mothballs inside the piano – the chemicals will start corroding its metal parts.

The cost of materials for the keybed is modest, and working with all-new components makes fitting and adjustment much quicker. For interest, in **7.27** the small piece of red felt poking out from under the next key is not proper piano repair material. It has been crudely cut from (at a guess) an old hat. Someone put this under just the most moth-eaten keys, left the old washers in place infested with moth eggs, and sold the piano as 'reconditioned'. This is blatant fraud, and an example of what some of those at the murky end of the used piano trade regularly get away with.

Pedal adjustment

Over time, the pedals of a piano gradually go out of regulation. This tends to happen so slowly that many owners don't notice that the pedals no longer do very much. Inexplicably, many tuners don't bother to draw their attention to it. As a result, I regularly see pianos with pedals that quite obviously haven't been adjusted for decades, if ever.

The following adjustment procedures are for upright pianos only. Solving pedal problems in a grand piano is more complicated, so I tackle it separately in Chapter 9.

Soft pedal

The soft pedal (the one on the left) is a half-blow mechanism in most modern uprights – that is, it shifts the hammers halfway towards the strings so that they can't get up to full speed and therefore can't generate full volume.

In all fairness, I ought to point out that the half-blow mechanism is of little use even at its best. Being out of regulation only makes it more ineffective, so if you're happy to live without a functioning soft pedal, you can skip this section.

To test a suspect soft pedal:

1 Look inside the piano at the hammers and depress the pedal.

2 Just after the pedal starts to go down, the hammers should all start to move forward.

3 If the pedal has to go down halfway or more before the hammers move, the pedal is out of regulation.

4 Remove the front board and fallboard.

5 To find the pedal mechanism, look into the works at the bass end. In most pianos the pedals operate a vertical wooden rod with a felt buffer on the top. The most obvious one is usually the soft pedal.

6 Depress the soft pedal. The rod will rise, pushing up a steel arm that pushes the rest rail forward.

7 If there is a gap between the felt buffer and the steel arm (see **7.30**) the pedal needs adjustment.

To adjust the soft pedal:

1 Remove the bottom board. Look for a long bolt sticking up out of the pedal mechanism. There will be a nut on the top of it, and a front rail felt buffer washer –see **7.31**.

2 Tighten the nut, and the gap at the other end of the mechanism (in **7.30**) will start to close up. If the nut is stiff with rust, grip the bolt with pliers and use a spanner on the nut.

3 If the nut is badly seized, do not use force as this may cause damage. Instead, insert a felt buffer on top of the vertical rod, filling the gap between the

7.31

rod and the pedal arm. A front rail washer will often do the trick. Apply a dab of latex-based adhesive such as Copydex to hold it in place. (The gap shown in **7.30** is too large for this remedy, so the bolt had to be moved.)

Sustain pedal

The sustain pedal (the one on the right) raises all the dampers simultaneously, as described in Chapter 3. The diagnosis for a loss of regulation is almost the same as for the soft pedal:

1 Look inside the piano at the dampers and depress the pedal.

2 Just after the pedal starts to go down, the dampers should all lift together.

3 If the pedal has to go down halfway or more before the dampers lift, it is out of regulation.

4 Look again into the works at the bass end. The sustain pedal rod is usually hidden behind the soft pedal mechanism. If there is a gap between the rod and the arm, the mechanism needs adjusting.

5 To adjust the sustain pedal, copy steps 1–3 for adjusting the soft pedal. However, do not adjust every last bit of free play out of the sustain, as some of the notes will then not die rapidly enough when the pedal is released. There should be just a tiny amount of free play. To test your adjustment, play with the pedal depressed for several modulations, producing a cacophony, then release the pedal. If it all dies instantly, your adjustment is correct. If any notes hang on for more than a fraction of a second, it isn't – so readjust as necessary.

Variant pedal mechanisms

On the soft and sustain pedal mechanisms of some pianos, especially from the 1980s onwards, there is a prong on the top of the vertical pole that goes through a hole in the steel lever – see

7.30

7.16. (Note that this piano has just a hint of lost motion – a small gap between the pedal lever and the felt washer.)

Pianos with this type of fitting are usually recent enough for the pedal adjuster to work; it's usually a thumbscrew, as in **7.32**. If for any reason the thumbscrew doesn't move, a second washer can be slipped over the prong, under the lever. Two further points about this type of mechanism:

1 Disconnect it whenever you remove the action, or risk breaking the vertical pole.

2 There should be a rubber bush in the hole in the steel lever. These are easy to dislodge. If the bush is missing, there will be a clanking noise whenever the pedal is depressed. It's definitely worth replacing the bush, but for some reason they're hard to get hold of from suppliers. A simple and acceptable alternative is to make your own bush out of felt, and glue it in place.

Third (practice) pedal

Where present, the practice pedal brings down a long felt pad between the

7.32

hammers and the strings, greatly reducing the volume. A common fault is that as the pedal drifts out of regulation, the felt fouls the top of the hammers. This slows the piano down and makes fast playing difficult. This is the main cause of a slow action in newer pianos.

In most pianos, the activation mechanism is at the bass end but there is also a swivel or idler at the treble end. Over time the two ends may lose unison and it may become impossible for the whole felt pad to descend evenly right across the piano.

You can adjust the pedal with a mechanism just above the pedal itself. It usually has a screw that works a normal thread one way and a left-hand thread the other.

Sometimes this only partially remedies the problem. If the felt pad still isn't descending evenly, take a pair of very sharp scissors and neatly trim off just enough of the felt (usually towards the bass end) to enable the pad to clear the hammers. This never feels quite the right thing to do but there is no other practical solution.

Rattles and buzzes

As noted in Chapter 5, about one upright in four – new or used – has at least one bass string with a loose copper winding. It happens to some grands too, though less frequently because of the generally higher level of quality control during manufacture. It can be heard as a metallic buzz.

Assuming you have identified the defective string, you can try these remedies:

1 Ideally, take out the action. If you don't want to do that, make sure throughout the following process that you don't snag any action parts with loose string.

2 Slacken the affected string by turning the tuning pin half a turn (180°) anticlockwise. Hold the string tight while undoing the pin. That way you won't lose the neat winding, or let the slack ride up around the pin.

3 Note which way the copper is wound round the core – clockwise or anticlockwise – because you're soon going to tighten the string by twisting it in that direction.

4 Rummage into the depths of the piano and find the bottom end of the problem string. Still holding the string

tightly and without letting it twist or turn, ease the eye of the pin forward until it is just free of the hitch pin. (The string may come away from the bridge too, but that's okay – see **7.34**, showing the bass hitch pins, and the close-up in **7.33**. If the strings have a felt tape through them like this one, don't just rip through it – unravel it.)

5 Now simply twist the string half a turn (180°) in the direction that the copper is wound onto it, and slip the eye back over the hitch pin. The string will now be tighter – with luck, tight enough to stop the buzzing.

6 If for any reason you had to let go of the string, did it just hang there, or did it of its own accord twist half a turn in the opposite direction to the copper winding? If the latter, someone must already have tightened that string half a turn. No matter – just give it *two* half-turns before replacing it on the hitch pin, to tighten it some more. The guiding principle is that you always give the string a half-turn more than it had to begin with.

7 Put the string back through the pins on the bridge. Check that it runs in the same direction as those next to it.

8 Retune the string by tightening up the tuning pin.

9 If the string still buzzes, repeat the whole sequence to give it another half turn. It may now suddenly become quite badly behaved, so you may need to use two pairs of pliers – one to hold the string, the other to twist it. The alternative is painful grooves in your fingers.

10 If the string still buzzes, the game is up: this remedy has failed. You then have an executive choice.

You can elect to do nothing, and live with the buzz. This is the option I recommend to most customers. Few owners notice the buzz in the first place, so ignoring it shouldn't take much effort. The reason for this apparently defeatist advice is that, as will shortly be revealed, the next cure for a buzzing bass string may leave you with a piano that is harmonically at war with itself. An almost inaudibly buzzing string is a minor irritation by comparison.

The more radical choice is to replace the buzzing string by removing it and sending it to a supplier for a duplicate. (See Chapter 8, section C, for how to replace strings.) But unfortunately, simply replacing the string isn't the end of it. These are the problems you will be up against:

■ In an old piano, and even some newer ones, if the new string is even slightly different from its partner in the bichord – for example in elasticity – then the new and old strings will each have a different harmonic structure. Their main harmonics may not coincide, in which case the two strings will 'beat' with each other. This effect will be noticeable during playing and it is impossible to tune it away. (See Chapter 10 for more

on this.) I therefore recommend that you order and replace both strings of that bichord. Even then, your problems won't be over.

■ New strings, or old strings once removed from the hitch pin, persistently lose pitch and will probably be the most out-of-tune strings for several tunings.

■ When new strings are fitted to an older piano, they sound different. Possibly better, probably louder, but definitely different. When a scale is played, they stand out like an acoustic sore thumb.

The blunt truth is that you can rarely win by replacing just one or two bass strings on an ageing piano. The risk that it will blight your instrument is high, and even the most skilled technician won't be able to do anything about it – which is why I recommend the 'grin and bear it' option.

The blunter truth is that if all piano manufacturers fitted better bass strings, they wouldn't buzz in the first place. The best bass strings use hexagonal rather than circular core wire. This enables the soft copper winding to grip more tightly, which stops it loosening. But this superior quality comes at an added cost, which most piano manufacturers obviously consider too high.

Things sticking

A common and frustrating problem is miscellaneous things sticking. Usually the causes are easily remedied, but sometimes they are serious and expensive to fix. The most stubborn of these are dealt with in Chapter 8. Here I look only at the more minor problems.

Whatever it is that may be sticking, it's vital to identify the problem correctly before trying to fix it. I could fill a warehouse with pianos I've seen on which owners have tried what they assumed was a harmless, universal remedy, only to find that it had zero effect on the problem but lots of unwanted effect on other parts of the instrument.

Perhaps most important of all: resist any urge to whip out the oilcan. Never, never, *never* use lubricants in pianos to try to free things up. That includes lubricants that are not oil, such as powdered graphite, silicones, polishes, petroleum jelly, even washing-up liquid. Anything that works wonders on engines, locks, zips, rusty lawnmowers etc will ruin a piano. There are one or two exceptions, but I'll tell you when these are allowable.

Nor should you waggle things around, thump or otherwise abuse them in an attempt to free them up. I guarantee that it won't work!

Problem: A key sticks down

A key, once played, is reluctant to play again. The key itself may be trying to stick down, or it may resume its correct position but the note doesn't play again, or doesn't play soon enough. Something is wrong, but it isn't something obvious.

In most properly functioning uprights, the keys default into the correct position and will not remain depressed even with the action removed from the piano. They are, however, finely balanced, so that if the hammer is sticking forward the key will indeed remain depressed. Or, if something else is making the key stick

down, the hammer will be left forward. The symptoms are the same whatever the cause.

To identify the cause:

1 Remove the front board and fallboard. Play the offending note until it sticks.

2 Push the action parts back to the rest position. Does this release the key? If yes, the key is likely to be the problem.

3 With the key in its correct rest position, flick the bottom of the action forward to mimic playing the note.

4 Does the hammer stick forward? If yes, the hammer/action is likely to be the problem. If no, the key is even more likely to be the problem.

If the action is suspect, there is a fairly serious recentring problem which is dealt with in Chapter 8, section B. If the problem is the key itself, remedies are much more straightforward.

A key often sticks because it is binding on a key next to it. On most pianos this is easy to remedy, as it's possible to remove keys with the action in place – though you'll need to be careful to avoid knocking the felt off the capstan, or snagging the key on some other part of the action.

In only a tiny minority of models does the action have to be removed to take keys out. (Examples include the Bechstein model 10 in **7.8**, in which 'stickers' link the whippen to the back end of the key.) If you're unlucky enough to own such a piano, the next procedure will require enormous patience, as the affected keys will have to be disconnected individually from the action.

For the majority:

5 Remove the key immediately to the right of the sticking key.

6 Play the sticking key. If it no longer sticks, it has been binding on the key to the right. (You may be able to hear a faint scraping noise.) If it still sticks, remove the key immediately to the left of the sticking key.

7 Play the sticking key again. Does it stick now? If yes, it has been binding on the key to the left.

8 Inspect the two binding keys for wood swarf (particles left from working) or any foreign matter down the sides, such as congealed liquids. Remove anything you find.

9 Try to find the binding point visually and sand a little wood from any suspect places. Use only ultra-fine flour grade sandpaper, available from trade suppliers or some DIY shops.

Problem: Key still sticking

Is the key sticking even with the two adjacent keys removed? If so, suspicion falls on the key bushings or front rail pin.

Each key has two holes – one running right through it for the balance rail pin, the other concealed underneath for the front rail pin. **7.24, 7.35, 7.36 and 7.37** show a section of keybed with two keys removed and one in place. This key is then shown top and bottom, off the rail. Each hole has a pair of felt

7.35

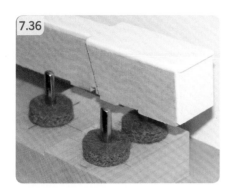

7.36

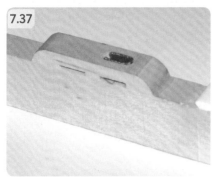

7.37

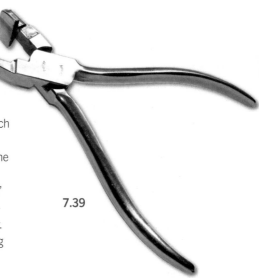

7.39

2 Remove the key, turn it over and inspect the bottom bushing for the front rail pin. Blow out any dust or foreign matter.

3 Inspect the front rail pin, over which the key rests – see **7.36** again. These pins are called 'cricket bats' in the UK because that's what they vaguely resemble. The round-sectioned 'handle' is forced into the wood, while the oval-sectioned 'blade' protrudes into the key. Sometimes these turn slightly, widening their aspect and making the key tight.

4 If the pin is not square to the keybed, turn it until it is. There is a special key-spacer tool for this in the multi-tool kit (**7.26**), but any pliers will do if you protect the jaws with cloth so that no metal swarf is raised.

5 If the pin is not the problem, give each of the four bushings a squeeze to reduce its size slightly. To do this you ideally need special pliers (**7.39**) with a larger jaw on one side to spread the load so that the key is not damaged. In their absence, carefully insert a suitably sized screwdriver and even more carefully lever it against the bushing. You're trying to squeeze just the felt: if you hear a creak, you're hurting the wood.

6 Try the key back in the piano after each squeeze. Not all four bushings may need a squeeze.

Problem: Black key sticking

If a black key sticks down until one of the white keys next to it is played, the black key is catching on the back edge of a white key covering. Using a small file, lightly trim a little white plastic off the edge just ahead of the black key. Keep the shape of the key square and put the smooth side of the file up against the side of the key, as in **7.40**. (I recently did this to two sticking black keys on a 30-year old Bentley. The problem had almost certainly existed from new and no one had bothered to fix it. It took all of 30 seconds.)

bushings to prevent the pins rubbing against the wood, making a total of four bushings you need to inspect. So:

1 On the top of the key, inspect the felt bushing in the hole where the balance rail pin peeps out. Is it worn? (Bushings are especially prone to wear in the part of the keybed where the keys 'dogleg': see the white keys to the left of the break in **7.38**.)

7.38

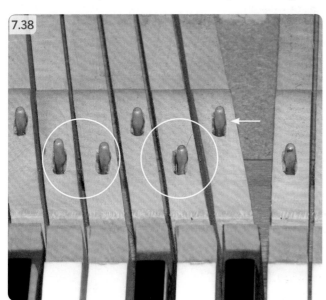

7.40

Miscellaneous symptoms

Problem: Key doesn't stick but note doesn't play

Sometimes, the key and hammer return to their rest positions but the note won't play. It feels spongy and the hammer doesn't go forward. (If more than one or two keys are affected, the following remedy may be inappropriate, and you should instead see Chapter 8, section B.)

1 Look first at the little coil spring under the jack. This is visible in **7.25** and at 'K' on page 37 photo. Its job is to return the jack to the rest position. To see if there is a problem, compare it with the coil springs on keys that don't have a problem.

2 It may have become dislodged. With patience, you may be able to ease it back into position with tweezers.

3 If it works but seems slow or weak, it can be repaired by fitting a larger coil spring. You can use patience and tweezers again, or you can remove the whole affected piece (the whippen) out of the action. The good news is that this is gives you enough space to fit the new spring in seconds. The bad news is that removing the whippen is a task for Chapter 8, so try the tweezers first.

Problem: Clacking noise from key

You play a note, and there is a very distinctive wooden 'clack' when the key is released. This happens when a small felt cushion behind the jack (shown in my model in **7.41**, and in a real piano in **7.42**) has gone missing, possibly because the glue has failed but probably because it has been eaten by moths. The cushion is there to give the jack a soft landing when it is pushed back by the spring. The now hard landing produces the clacking noise.

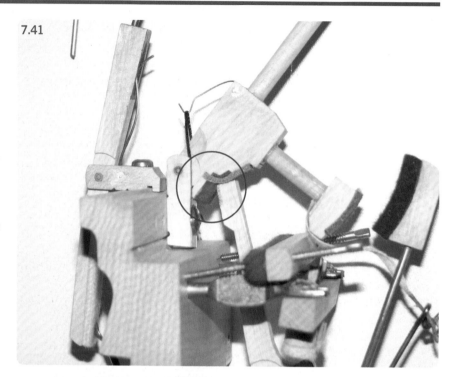

7.41

7.42

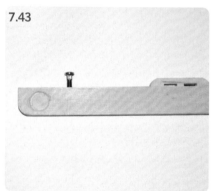

7.43

This is admittedly a very rare problem, but I include it because if moths are making a meal of your piano, you may have it to look forward to. If several notes are affected, you will have to dismantle the action and replace all of the cushions.

If there are only one or two affected notes, you can try gluing in new felt cushions using long tweezers, latex-based adhesive and your best keyhole surgery technique. But it's risky, because other parts around here are delicate. If you find you can't do it, see Chapter 8, section B.

Problem: Thudding sound from key

A thudding sound from a key nearly always signals a loose key weight. These are usually circular, as in **7.43** (the grey circle), and can be tightened by splaying them out.

1 Remove the affected key from the piano. Place it on its side on a workbench with the weight resting on something metal and solid.

Cleaning inside the piano

Opening up a piano for maintenance and repair also creates opportunities to clean inside it. But before you breezily stick a vacuum cleaner nozzle into every recess, read this.

The inside of an upright piano is a dark and sheltered environment, generally not on anyone's list of things to clean. As a result it can accumulate a surprising amount of dirt and debris. Moth eggs, insects, mouse droppings and sometimes the mouse itself are common finds in older pianos. Birds and hamsters are not unknown, and dog hair crops up with puzzling regularity – I have yet to witness it finding its way in.

You should therefore treat an older upright as a biological hazard before attempting to clean inside it for the first time – possibly the piano's first time ever. (This applies even if a vendor claims to have cleaned it. 'Clean' is capable of wide interpretation.) I routinely wear goggles, a facemask and gloves, and recommend that you do too.

For cleaning purposes, grand pianos have a plus side in that most of their interior is far more accessible and well off the floor; and a minus side in that if they spend a lot of time with the lid up, they collect more dirt.

Pianos of any type which were around in the days of open fires need handling with particular care, as they may contain an undisturbed layer of soot. I vividly remember using an old vacuum cleaner to scour out the keybed of a piano that had come from a coal-mining area. Within seconds the workshop was in darkness and I thought the lights had failed. Peeling my caked goggles off, I realised that ultra-fine soot had gone straight through the vacuum cleaner bag and filled the workshop with clouds of black carbon particles. It took an hour to settle – everywhere.

So always check the inside of your piano for any type of particulate layer, as it could prove difficult to contain during removal. It might even be toxic. I often find a white powder once used to kill moths, which contained the now illegal chemical DDT. Asbestos is also a possibility in old pianos from areas where the lethal stuff was once manufactured. If in doubt, consider having the piano inspected by a firm of cleaning specialists.

When it comes to cleaning any piano, it's best not to use either a vacuum cleaner or a duster, except for the keybed. Suction can easily remove damper felt and other felt components, while a duster can turn the dampers out of line and even put the piano out of tune if you're tempted to feed it through and behind the strings.

The best way to clean the inside of a piano is to blow dust and debris out with a compressor, and this is really a workshop or outdoor job. If it's any consolation, a moderate amount of dust in your piano won't be harmful and won't affect its playing functions. Only if there is a lot of dirt in the action is there likely to be a problem worth attacking with a compressor.

2 Using a hammer and a wide-tipped nail punch, hit the top of the weight. This forces it to expand.

Photo **7.5** shows another type of key weight: a lead lump in the end of the key. This is known as a sandwich weight, and it has to be glued.

1 Take it out – or if it's tight, just ease it forward a little.

2 Put or work a dab of glue behind it. (A glue gun is quick and effective.)

3 Push it rapidly back into place. Remove any excess glue.

Problem: Metallic rattle

A growling noise from a particular note or notes sometimes indicates a split in the soundboard. A metallic noise from a single note may indicate a split bridge. If the affected string is the last one over the end of one of the bridges (see **7.44**), you have a serious problem. I discuss what can be done about it in Chapter 8, section D.

7.44

CHAPTER 8

Advanced repair & maintenance

As pianos age, problems affect more of their working parts. Diagnosing and fixing these problems quickly is definitely the province of the piano technician. But if you can stand having your piano out of action for a while, tackling more challenging maintenance and repair work is by no means out of the question. I consider upright pianos here, and grands in Chapter 9.

A: THE KEYBOARD

As long as the keyboard is correctly laid and levelled and regulated to the action (Chapter 7) – in other words, generally functioning as it should – it's possible to tackle more advanced keyboard problems. These tend to arise either in older pianos from wear and tear, or in younger instruments from abuse.

Discoloured or damaged key coverings

Ivory key coverings

As I described in Chapter 2, nearly all pianos made before about 1914 had white key coverings of real ivory. Thereafter, ivory was progressively replaced by synthetics. Only very expensive pianos had one-piece ivory; in most the ivory is in two sections, which join at what looks like a thin pencil line just in front of the black keys. **8a.1** shows old keys in poor condition – one has lost its covering completely – and about to be replaced. One key is turned on its side, showing how dirty the sides can become.

Most pianos with an ivory keyboard are now too old to be functional, but I still occasionally find playable examples. The coverings are often stained yellow in the middle, by perspiration from players' fingers. To clean and whiten an ivory keyboard in reasonable condition:

1 Remove the keyboard. Polish the white keys using just a damp cloth with a hint of glass cleaner (aerosol only – and sprayed onto the cloth, not directly onto the keys). Do not wet any of the wood beneath the covering.

2 More stubborn staining can be tackled by polishing the ivory on a bench polisher. You can improvise one by holding an electric drill in a vice and mounting a cotton cloth buffing wheel in the chuck. The following steps assume you're using a polisher.

3 Buy an abrasive buffing compound commonly called 'soap', because that's what it looks like (see *Useful contacts, Buffing products*). It's colour-coded: white is the most gentle and is usually adequate for piano keys. Tougher

stains may require brown, but you must use a different buffing wheel for the brown and go back to white for finishing.

4 Hold the 'soap' against the rotating buffing wheel, so that a trace of compound transfers to the wheel.

5 Now hold each ivory in turn *very gently* against the buffing wheel, until you get the hang of the technique and its effects. The transformation can be dramatic, but the job needs a steady hand to avoid damaging the ivory. And do not hold the work too firmly against the wheel: the covering may fly off as friction heat melts the animal glue used to stick the ivory to the wooden key. (Heat also makes this technique entirely unsuitable for celluloid or plastic key coverings, which will start to melt.)

6 Health and safety advice: You'll need eye protection, and ear protection isn't a bad idea either. Gloves shouldn't be worn close to rotating machinery, so your hands will get filthy and be at some risk from the rotating wheel.

This is about as far as most owners can reasonably go in reconditioning ivory key coverings. If the above technique doesn't give you a set of sparkling and even ivories, your only alternative is to strip off the ivories and replace them with coverings of more modern (and

8a.1

legal) material. But don't even think of this unless you're confident the piano will remain in good playing condition for at least several more years.

Though it's possible to renovate and replace ivory coverings, this is extremely difficult to do well and so only justified as part of a major restoration of an instrument of special interest – and that's beyond the scope of this manual.

To remove ivory, all you need is enough heat to melt the old animal glue – an ordinary clothes iron will do, turned up high. The smell is awful as the ivory starts to singe, but the covering will eventually come loose. Be warned, though, that my experience is very mixed: sometimes the coverings drop off easily and cleanly, leaving a flat surface for working on; sometimes every square millimetre is a battle. This is why you need first to ask yourself if it's worth it!

Repairing celluloid and plastic keys

Most 20th-century pianos had celluloid coverings on the white keys. Now they're mostly plastic, though celluloid is still used. If you have a number of damaged keys you have to decide whether you can live with a slightly odd repair, because unless your piano is still in production it's unlikely you'll be able to match the originals. Some makers, such as Yamaha and Kawai, are excellent at providing spare parts. Many others could do much better, though to be fair a lot of the problem may be due to language difficulties.

One possibility if you have a few damaged key coverings and can only find odd replacements is to move existing coverings and confine the new ones to the extremities of the keyboard, where they may be less noticeable. Usual practice is to put them at the bass end, but treble does just as well. Apart from a few unique coverings – bottom A 1, top C on an 88-note keyboard and top A on an 85 – all are interchangeable among octaves. (NB: D, G and A may look similar but are different. D is symmetrical but G and A are not.)

8a.2

Plastic white key coverings are inexpensive and ready shaped. Celluloid is available both ready shaped and in sheets. However, on modern pianos the key covering material is much thicker than on older pianos, which can make matching difficult. (Some technicians keep old key coverings and may be able to help.) If only a few keys are damaged and the piano isn't valuable enough to merit complete recovering, this is what you do:

1 Remove one damaged key and secure it in a padded vice. (If the key is doglegged, grip it by the front portion only.) The top of the key needs to stand just proud of the vice jaws.

2 Start to remove the covering with a very sharp thin-bladed knife. It may be easy or it may be difficult. (Sometimes, one has to improvise a technique. I once had a particularly stubborn keyboard where the celluloid was softer than the glue. After some trial and error I found that by heating a thin blade almost to red hot, I could cut through the glue like butter.)

3 Make a judgment about how easily the covering came off, because this may affect your next decision: whether to swap key coverings around so that the new coverings can be relegated to the extremities. If it was a brutal affair ending in gouged wood, the chances are they'll all be like that so settle for just replacing the damaged coverings.

4 Having made your decision, remove the requisite number of keys from the keyboard and take off the coverings. Dispose carefully of old celluloid key coverings: they're highly combustible – for which reason celluloid can't be carried in the holds of ships. (When I lived in a house with an open fire, I used the celluloid-covered keys of scrap pianos as firelighters. They were awesomely good.)

5 If the old coverings came off with a struggle, you'll need to sand them – taking care to keep the surfaces dead flat – and fill any holes with wood filler. If you don't, the new coverings may come unstuck or may sound hollow when struck with a fingernail.

6 Sand or file off enough wood to allow for the extra thickness of both new material *and* new glue, as the original animal glues were brushed on hot and very thin. The new key top must end up at exactly the right height – which is why I advised ensuring a level keyboard before you start.

7 Your replacement coverings will almost certainly be too large. Before you glue them, line up the long, straight side of Cs, Es, Fs and Bs. For the others, try to have the excess material sticking out on just one side – see **8a.2**.

8 Apply adhesive to both surfaces – generously to the wood, as it's

8a.3

more absorbent – and leave them to go tacky. Ordinary impact adhesive is fine. There are special glues from piano repair houses for both plastic and celluloid, but you don't need them unless you decide to recover the whole keyboard. For celluloid and ivory, traditional piano glue is used. This is animal based and has to be melted. For keyboard use it's coloured white by mixing in some titanium white.

9 Bring the two surfaces together. Practise this with unglued components, as you only have one chance to get the positioning exactly right.

10 Squeeze key and covering gently together in your vice and leave them like this for a few minutes. (Pad one jaw of the vice and keep the key surface up against this jaw.)

11 Transfer the keys to clamps and leave them for as long as is practicable. (I carry several pairs of quick-release clamps for this job. When I used to do a lot of refurbishment work, I made a clamp from old pedal springs that could hold 20 white keys at a time. I economise on the number of clamps needed by placing two keys together

with a soft pad between the faces and one clamp, as in **8a.3**.)

12 When the glue is dry, hold the keys in turn on their side with just the slightest bit of the wood showing out of the vice and the excess material to be removed protruding above that.

13 Using a fairly fine engineering file (that is, a flat one with one smooth edge), remove the excess plastic or celluloid right down to the wood. File only towards the key so that you're not tending to pull the covering back off. (In **8a.2** the key needs to be turned around in the vice before work starts.)

14 Your vice must be scrupulously clean as well as padded, so blow out all the swarf and filings before each operation. It only takes one speck of debris pressed into the surface of your new shiny key top to mark it forever.

15 Now hold the keys vertically in the vice to shape into the corners. Use the smooth edge of the file so that only one edge at a time is being worked on. Sand them smooth. However, the edges need to be left sharp, so do not chamfer them.

Key front coverings

Do the key front coverings also need replacing? Pray that they don't. New plastic key top coverings are optionally available with integral fronts. This makes them look temptingly neat, but in older pianos the front covering will be quite thin material, and plastic fronts are so much thicker that the keys may not fit in front of the keyslip. For celluloid coverings there is thin material available to replace the fronts, but it has to be cut and shaped, and this procedure adds massively to the labour of the job. Therefore, unless they're unacceptably unsightly, leave the key fronts alone, even if they're an imperfect colour match to the new tops. Your only minor problem then will be getting the right amount of overhang on each key when you glue the covering down. To do this well, make a gauge of the correct thickness to hold against each key front in turn as the covering is applied. I usually find a plastic key covering is about the right thickness. Hold it against the front and bring out the covering until it's exactly in line with the gauge.

Complete white key covering

If you feel up to replacing the coverings of every white key – and the condition or value of the piano justifies it – you broadly follow the same procedure. It just takes a lot longer.

Cleaning white keys

A recommended, if truly laborious and filthy, extra step is to clean every surface of every key using the finest wire wool you can find. It's graded from 5 (very coarse) down through grades 0 to 0000. Go for as many noughts as possible. And mask up: the dust of some woods may be carcinogenic if inhaled.

When cleaning with wire wool, try not to chamfer the corners of the wood. They will have sharp, pristine angles from the day they were machine-cut in the factory, and you should try to preserve these.

In some older pianos the whole key may be very discoloured, while the keys of other pianos seem to age unscathed.

If you think cleaning every surface is overly virtuous, at least clean the sides that are exposed during playing. Some pianos get very dirty and greasy from finger contact, and this can reveal a lot about the pianists' techniques as well as their personal hygiene. **8a.4** shows the before and after of keys being cleaned during recovering, while **8a.5** shows a selection of recovered keys from the same piano.

If it's perfection you're after...

On an older piano, a full set of plastic key coverings may well look too good and too modern – like film star dentistry in your great-grandad's mouth. Repolishing the piano can make the difference a lot less obvious, but my preference, if a piano is worth the expense, is to have new celluloid keyboard coverings fitted by a specialist (see *Useful contacts*). The coverings are applied in sheets and mechanically sliced up when the glue is dry, giving a degree of factory accuracy unattainable in an ordinarily equipped workshop.

Black keys

Generally, black keys are not difficult to clean and a damp cloth with a trace of window cleaner is all you need. Older wooden keys (*not* plastic) can be cleaned on a buffing wheel as described above, though it's a good idea to keep a separate wheel for black keys, as some colouring material may be deposited on it.

A variety of materials has been used for black keys, from hard wood to plastic. Ebony was once used, but no longer. Any wood that may be exposed below the black key covering is normally coloured black. I use black felt-tip pens for this, but only expensive artists' versions that won't transfer any colouring to the players' fingers. If extensive recolouring is necessary, a special black dye can be ordered from piano supply houses.

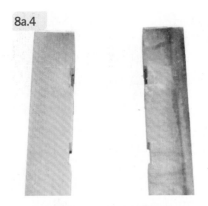

8a.4

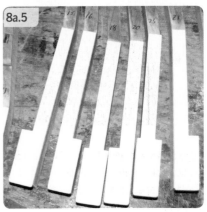

8a.5

Rebushing

This picks up from my dalliance with key bushings in Chapter 7. To recap a little, the balance rail and front rail depend on metal pins which ensure that the keys move only up and down, not side to side. The holes are bushed – that is, lined – with a soft yet hard-wearing felt material so that the keys move smoothly, effortlessly and quietly. These bushings are extremely durable and serious malfunction is due more often to moth or central heating damage than to wear and tear.

But wear may eventually take its toll, particularly on the balance pin hole and especially in keys which have to dogleg around the frame. In **8a.6** the pins and the red key bushing in the balance pin holes can be seen. The keys dogleg to the left, so the wear is to the right of the pin. It's worse in the white keys, because they're a longer lever working against this

bend. The white key bushings are ringed and the first black key bushing to the left of the overstringing break is shown with an arrow.

Eventually, the keys will sag to the left when at rest. To anyone kneeling in front of the piano and looking at the fronts of the keys, this will be visible as a pronounced 'V' between the D and E white keys. Wear in the front bushings can also be felt by holding the front of the key and waggling it from side to side. (Depress the keys to each side to isolate it.) If it moves more than a tiny amount, the bushings are worn.

There are three possible remedies, but I only recommend one of them.

We'll skate over a practice called swaging, which involves splitting the wood round the bushing hole in the hope that the split will partially close the hole. Respectful as I am of most traditional

practices, I hate this one and have never used it. It's brutal and crude, and can't be used on the black keys anyway as there is too little wood around the hole.

Another quick fix I don't recommend is replacing just the bushings to one side of the holes on the balance rail (to the right in the case of **8a.6**) and just over the worst section: say, two octaves. For the front rail, the 'cricket bats' may be

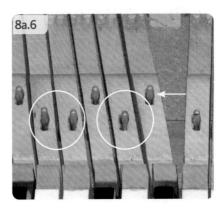

8a.6

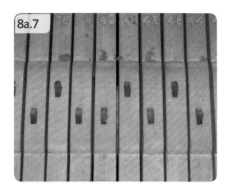

8a.7

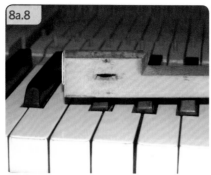

8a.8

be engineered to within thousandths of an inch in felt and wood. If the bushings are too tight, they'll never free up; too loose, and they'll wear out rapidly; just right, and they'll last for decades.

5 In most pianos, there is a small slot in the side of the key from the balance rail hole. Push the cloth through this as in **8a.11**.

6 Glue the bushings in place in the holes and hold them using spring clips or wedges as in **8a.12** (the felt is left extravagantly long for illustrative purposes only). Hold them for about 30 minutes until the glue is dry. (You don't need to use proper piano-maker's glue unless you're doing the whole lot. But if you do it's usually left overnight.) Finally, trim off (**8a.13**) using a scalpel.

twisted slightly to take up the wear. These procedures actually accelerate the wear, so they're acceptable only if the aim is to squeeze a little more life out of a piano before it's either rebushed or scrapped. They are *not* acceptable as a deception to make the piano more saleable. Indeed, it's worth having a technician check for this on a possible used buy.

The only worthwhile remedy is to put new bushes in all the holes.

First, though, check that your piano actually has bushes to replace. In some pianos that were very cheap when new, the balance rail holes weren't bushed at all. When they become enlarged through wear, nothing can be done short of a major programme of creating bigger holes and bushing them – which will usually be unjustifiably expensive. The problem is shown in **8a.7** and **8a.8**; this unfortunate and unlovable instrument is 80 years old and falling to bits through age. Unusually, it is completely unworn throughout and appears to have had very little use. It's therefore a rare instance where the absence of bushings hasn't made a scrap of difference.

At the other end of the scale, in some higher quality pianos the balance rail bushing is on a separate wooden part glued over the hole, as in **8a.9**. But in the great majority of pianos the bushing is glued into the hole itself.

1 To rebush properly, it's vital to get the right-sized bushing cloth, so cut an old bushing out with a sharp knife from the extremes of the piano where wear is least.

2 You also need spring clips or accurately sized wedges to hold the new bushings in place as the glue dries (step 6). Remove the keyboard.

3 Remove the old bushes – apart from the one or two you've removed carefully as a size guide – by scraping them out with a sharp knife, as in **8a.10**. (You can buy an electric bushing cloth remover – like a soldering iron that melts the glue – but I've never found it much use.)

4 Cut the bushing cloth into strips the same width as the old bushings. It's so important to get the size of the bushings exactly right that I recommend that you carry out steps 6 onwards with just a few at first, and see if they're correct after the glue has dried. This is another of those piano jobs that has to

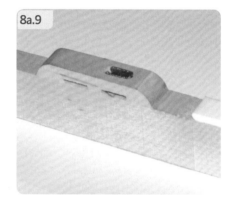

8a.9

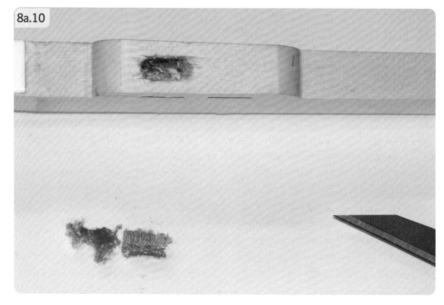

8a.10

8a.11

8a.12

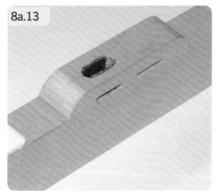

8a.13

7 Before replacing the keyboard, clean the keybed thoroughly. Ideally, use a compressor to blow any dirt out, but this is emphatically a workshop or outdoor job. If you have to work *in situ*, it's enough to use a soft brush with long bristles, and a vacuum cleaner.

8 The balance rail pins and the front rail pins may be lubricated with a touch of silicone spray like WD40 – yes, this really is okay here! But don't get any into the wood. Spray it on a cloth and rub it on. The pins can also be cleaned with a little metal polish if they're rusty, but again, don't get any polish on the surrounding wood. And mask the keybed with old newspaper while you're doing all this. Refit the keyboard.

9 Any tightness can be eased by squeezing the felt using key-easing pliers (see page 105). These are like conventional pliers except that (a) the jaws are parallel as they close on the wood, and (b) one side of the jaw has a bigger surface area than the other, so that the outside of the key isn't damaged: just the felt is squeezed up. But if the wrong size of felt has been used, no amount of squeezing will free them.

Broken keys

Broken keys are rare, but extremely difficult to deal with. The most common cause of breakage is deliberate abuse. Keys usually break across the balance pin hole, leaving too small a surface area at the break for any glue to hold effectively. Nor is it possible to brace the sides or bottom of the key. It may be possible to brace the top of the key by gluing over the break, but a hole must be left over the balance pin. Overall, repair prospects are not good.

The chance of getting a key that fits from a piano dealer's scrap bin is remote. If the piano is still in production, try ordering a replacement key from the manufacturer. Otherwise, the best solution is to get a replacement made – but this is easier said than done. Piano restorers, as opposed to rebuilders, may be able to do it (see *Useful contacts*), but the cost is likely to be substantial. A more economical recourse may be to find someone with woodworking skills and time on their hands. If you find a volunteer, give them the adjacent keys too so that the dimensions can be precise.

In some pianos where doglegging is not very pronounced, it may be possible to swap a key from near one of the ends of the keyboard. You'll almost certainly have to sand some wood off to make it fit. This, though, is a fairly desperate measure.

One lesson from all this is that if you're offered a sale piano in 'excellent condition' but with 'just a couple of broken keys', don't regard it as a minor blemish; it's a reason to walk away.

B: PIANO ACTION REPAIR

There are several possible malfunctions of the action, so I'll deal with them in the order in which they typically occur as a piano ages.

The tapes

Upright pianos have a small linen tape that gives the hammer a tug back when the key is released (**8b.2**). In some pianos the tapes don't do much, but in others it's impossible to play fast if several of them are broken. A visual check should reveal their condition: when new, they're usually white linen with a red tag on the end. If they now look tatty and grubby, and if the tag has come off some of them, they're due for replacement. Compare **8b.2** with **8b.3**, which shows tapes at the end of their life.

Are just a few tapes broken?

If so, it's possible to replace a small number with tapes secured by a small brass clip that goes around the shank of the balance hammer, as in **8b.5**. These clip-on tapes are usually made overlong so that they'll fit any piano. If you need to shorten them a lot, tie a knot near the clip end so that the knot (a) can't be seen from the front of the action and (b) doesn't foul the balance hammer.

As you tie the knot, try not to change the orientation of the tape head or the tape will appear twisted in the stirrup. In **8b.6** the hammer and butt are removed from the action, but with care it's possible to replace tapes without having to remove either the action or any action parts from the piano. You have to:

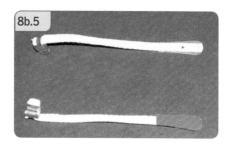
8b.5

1 Get the tape into place, below the balance hammer shank.

2 Push the clip upwards with a screwdriver blade turned on its side.

3 When the tape is attached, thread the head through the stirrup.

8b.2

8b.3

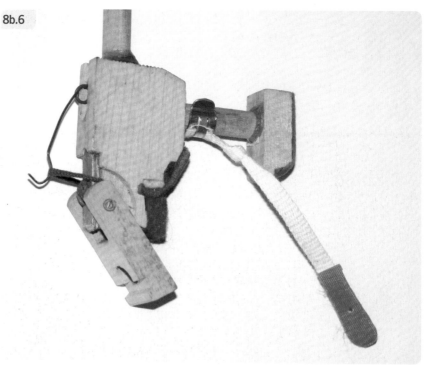
8b.6

8b.7

8b.8

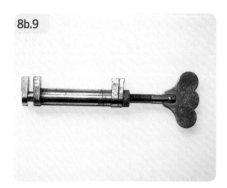

8b.9

It's also important that the replacement has the same working length as the original. You can vary the effective length further, depending on where on the balance hammer shank you place the clip. If it's still too long or too short compared with the ones adjacent to the repair, bend the stirrup backwards or forwards until it has the right length. However, this provides only limited adjustment. If you adjust too many this way, the stirrups will form an irregular line that screams 'amateur repair'. Rather than use fingers, it's better to use a proper wire-bending tool from the multi-tool kit (**8b.7**).

Are quite a lot of tapes broken?

If yes, you can bet that even more will soon follow, so it may be a good time to replace them all. (The tapes on the old Knight in **8b.3** are cracked right across the head, at the retaining hole. Even in this sample of ten, two are broken off.)

In a new piano, factory-fitted tapes are run across the hole in the balance hammer and the shank is forced in on top of it with glue. See **8b.8**. This makes the joint very strong. There is a tool for removing hammers (**8b.9**) which can also force balance hammers off, so if you opt for total replacement, *and the aim is to restore or rebuild the piano*,

this would be the correct path to follow. It would take all day and in an older piano there would be some collateral damage to action parts that would also need repairing – but if it's a quality piano, it's worth the extra labour to do the job properly.

8b.10 shows the hammer extractor being used in reduced length mode to

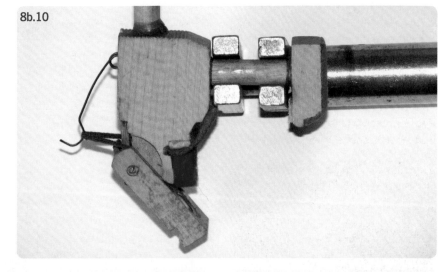

8b.10

🎹 Standing or sitting?

When working on an upright piano action, standing is more practical than sitting because you'll be constantly changing the side you work from. It therefore helps to improvise a narrow workbench (it needn't be much wider than the action) at somewhere between waist and chest height. A folding electronic keyboard stand with a plank of wood across it, like the one here, is favoured by many mobile technicians and will do the job – as long as you keep in mind that this isn't what it was designed for. Something more substantial, like a sturdy workshop bench or large table, is always better if it can be arranged.

🎹 Broken tapes? Don't remove the action yet

An alarming and easy trap to fall into is to remove an action that has some broken tapes. Tapeless and therefore unsupported whippens drop down and the jacks go under the little felt cushion, jamming under the tiny bit of wood to which the cushion is glued – see 8b.4. The dire consequence of this doesn't strike home until you try to put the piano back together: those jacks push the hammers up against the strings, making it difficult or even impossible to get the action back in. And the more desperately you try, the greater the risk of seriously damaging the hammers, hammer butts or jacks.

This happened to me once (and once was enough) long ago, when I played pianos rather than mended them. My attempt at minor improvement suddenly rendered a pub piano unplayable. The solution, which I might not have discovered so quickly had the situation been less dire, is to start with the action nearly in and the hammers lightly up against the strings. Then insert the blade of a screwdriver on its side between the set-off button and the top of the heel of the jack – see 8b.2. Push down on the heel of the jack and the jack jumps back into its rightful position. Repeat for each affected jack.

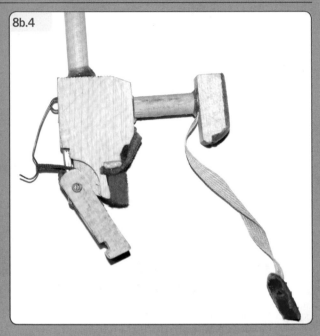

8b.4

---

remove a balance hammer. As the handle is turned, the jaws open up. If the glue on the balance hammer wins the battle and the shank is pulled from the butt, you'll have to saw off the balance hammer, drill out the hole and make and glue in another shank. Tip: put the moving part of the tool up against the part you're trying to remove. Most of the time it will pull this part off and not the other. I have no idea why this happens; just be thankful that it does.

For the majority of older pianos it has become standard practice to use a hot-glue gun to glue the new tapes on to the back of the balance hammers. While this ought to produce a perfectly adequate repair, the work is often done badly and I regularly see cases where new ones have come off and other tuners have repaired *those* with clip-ons.

Clip-on versus glue-on tapes

I take the traditionalist (or stubborn?) view that clip-on repair tapes are fine for occasional breakages but glue-on replacements are better if more than

ten or so tapes are broken. Other technicians clearly see things differently and are happy to replace all the tapes with clip-ons. In truth, the weight of the clip is negligible so my argument against a total clip-on repair is weak. The choice is yours. If you choose glue, the procedure is:

1 Choose your time well. Your best opportunity is if the action is already out of the piano and dismantled for other substantial repairs. It's harder with the hammers in place, though not impossible (put a blob of hot glue on each tape and quickly squeeze it on to the back of the balance hammer with something like my dental tweezers in **8b.11**).

2 **8b.12** shows the original decaying tape head. Order new tapes from a piano supply house.

3 If the action is not to be completely dismantled, remove the rest rail for easier access.

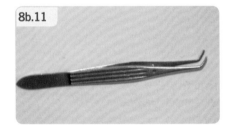

8b.11

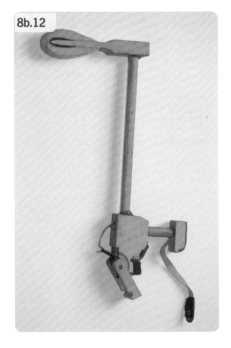

8b.12

8b.13

8b.14

8b.15

8b.16

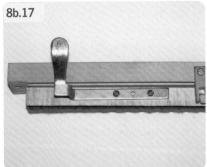

8b.17

Removing the rest rail

In some pianos, the rest rail screws are inserted into the back of the rail and the action has to be removed to get at them. More typical, though, are **8b.13**, **8b.14** and **8b.15**. These show all three rest rail fixing points on this Kemble: the retaining screws are conveniently placed on the front and can be seen at the ends. The bass end screw is shown close up in **8b.16**. **8b.15** shows an additional tie, at the overstringing break gap: you'll need a short screwdriver to get up at it. Manoeuvring the soft pedal operating arm out through the bass end action post can be awkward. If so, remove it before lifting off the rest rail. It's usually attached to the bottom of the rest rail by two or three screws – see **8b.17**. In **8b.18** these screws are visible in another piano. Again, you'll need a short screwdriver to do the job.

4 Identify and mark some tapes to leave on as a guide to correct length. *This is vital.* The action is usually in three or four distinct sections, so leave the end ones on each section.

5 Cut through and remove the rest. **8b.6** shows where the old tape has been trimmed off. (It won't be possible to be so neat if the job is tackled without dismantling the action.)

6 Pull the heads off the stirrups. Large tweezers are best for this.

7 In passing, check the condition of the cushions (see *Cushions* on page 120). If they need work, this is your best opportunity to do it.

8 Estimate the length needed for the replacement tapes by holding a new

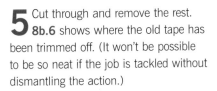

8b.18

tape next to one of the old tapes left in place. Cut the new set for that section to exactly this size.

9 Put a blob of hot glue on the end of each new tape and quickly glue it on to the back of each balance hammer in turn. **8b.19** shows the job under way with the butt removed. If the action is not dismantled, I use my dental tweezers to give each tape a firm pull into position. Be careful not to get glue anywhere else. In particular, don't glue any tapes to the bottom of the balance hammer, where they may interfere with the way the checks contact the balance hammers during playing.

10 Go along the action, attaching each new head to its stirrup. Start from near where old ones were left on and make sure that the new length is as close as possible to the original. Crooked tweezers are perfect for this job.

11 As each whippen is lifted, the jack will jam under the felt cushion as described in the *Broken tapes?* boxout on page 118, so give the heel of the jack a little push down to release it.

12 If any of the new tapes are too long or short, make fine adjustments by bending the stirrups slightly backwards or forwards – see *Are just a few tapes broken?* For best results, use the check bender tool from the multi-tool kit rather than your fingers. Put the rest rail back on. Replace the action.

Cushions

Under each hammer butt, by the leather notch, is a small felt cushion – coloured red in **8b.4** and **8b.12**. This gives the jack a soft landing each time it returns to the notch when a key is released. Cushions usually last the life of the piano, but occasionally one becomes detached or eaten by moths. A sure sign of a missing cushion is a distinctive 'clack' as the key is released.

8b.19

Cushions are normally difficult to access and can only be removed and replaced with tweezers and a steady hand – the piano equivalent of keyhole surgery. But access is much easier when the tapes are being replaced, so that's the ideal time to inspect, repair or replace them as necessary. With the action removed and the old tapes cut, the whippens drop and the cushions are revealed. New cushions need to be cut from felt of exactly the same thickness as the old ones were when the piano was new. The best guide you'll get to this thickness is the least squashed cushions at the extreme bass and treble ends.

Set-off in uprights

Set-off in grands is covered in Chapter 9.

As explained in Chapter 2, the very essence of the piano is the set-off – the mechanism that releases the hammer, allowing it to fly through the air for a specific distance. In an upright, the standard set-off is an eighth of an inch (3.17mm) from the string; in a grand, a sixteenth of an inch (1.59mm). (I often use the grand set-off for uprights used for public performance. This increases the volume out of all proportion to the size of the adjustment. It also increases the risk of breaking a string or hammer, but I seem to get away with it.)

Getting the set-off distance correct is critical. Having it just a fraction too far from the string will greatly reduce the volume and vigour of the piano. Unlike lost motion (Chapter 7), the piano won't *feel* wrong; it will just sound too quiet and be frustrating to play.

1 To establish whether set-off is the problem, hold a hammer with just a little resistance and press the key *gently* down.

2 When the hammer is an eighth of an inch (3.17mm) away from the string, you should hear a little 'clunk' from down inside the action. This is the jack coming out from under the leather notch on the bottom of the hammer butt – see **8b.4**.

3 If you don't hear a definite clunk, there may be insufficient keystroke. Go back to Chapter 7 to see how to check that.

4 If the clunk occurs more than an eighth of an inch (3.17mm) away from the strings and the keystroke is correct, the set-off is too generous and needs adjusting.

5 To find the set-off screw, look for a little felt-covered button mounted on a screw. The screw usually comes up through a mounting rail and curves over into a loop or eye (**8b.20**), though other types are also common – for example **7.25** on page 97.

8b.20

8b.21

8b.22

6 Adjust the set-off screw using the set-off regulating tools from the multi-tool kit. For the loop or eye screw it's the tool with the slot in the end (see page 97). (Most kits have a different tool that fits right over this type of screw, but I find it too prone to breaking off the loop or eye. The tool I recommend may slip off occasionally, but it rarely breaks the screw.) For most other types of set-off screw, use the tool in **8b.21** that also fits the multi-tool kit handle in **8b.7**. This has to go right down into the works, past the balance hammer. To move the set-off nearer the string, turn the adjuster anticlockwise; to move it further from the string, adjust clockwise.

In an older piano, these screw adjusters may be corroded and seized. If the first few you try break off, there's trouble ahead. It may be possible to obtain a new rail and new adjusters, but the old one will have to be copied exactly and the new adjusters mounted on the new rail. It will be a very time-consuming job, so this is another of those moments where you might have to consider saying goodbye to the piano.

Sometimes the set-off for just one or two notes has to be adjusted, but it's more typical for most or all to need correcting. If this is the case, you'll have to remove the hammer rest rail as detailed in *Clip-on versus glue-on tapes* (page 118). **8b.22** shows the job in progress with the tool right down in the works: it would be more or less impossible with the rest rail on.

From now on, an experienced technician can adjust the set-off on most pianos by eye. You'll have to use the much more accurate but quite simple method used by professionals to regulate a high quality piano.

7 Arm yourself with a strip of wood exactly an eighth of an inch (3.17mm) thick and about 12in (300mm) long. An old-fashioned school-issue wooden ruler is conveniently close. If all else fails, pay a joinery shop to machine one for you.

8 Temporarily attach the strip of wood to the strings in front of the hammers you're working on. (I usually work on about one octave at a time.)

9 Screw each of the set-off buttons anticlockwise just a little bit too

far, so that when the note is played the hammer blocks against the wood, as in **8b.23**. Hold the key under gentle pressure so that the hammer stays in this blocked position.

10 Screw the button slowly clockwise. When the exact correct position is reached, the hammer will drop back a little off the wood.

11 Repeat steps 9 and 10 across the whole compass and you'll end up with a uniform, correct set-off on every hammer.

8b.23

Damper regulation

In Chapter 7 I explained how to set up the keyboard correctly. In this chapter we have regulated (a) the action and (b) the set-off. The next task may be to regulate the dampers – I stress 'may' because most pianos get through their life without it.

I stress, too, that *the keybed must be set up correctly*, because if there is insufficient keystroke the dampers won't be raised enough and it'll be a lost cause trying to regulate them. In other words, it's no good trying to fix faulty dampers until everything else in the action is known to be working correctly.

8b.24 and **8b.25** show that when a key is depressed, the damper is lifted from the string by a small steel damper spoon on the end of the whippen. The spoons usually function well but may need adjustment if:

■ Extensive work has been done on the keybed or action.
■ There is a felt or leather pad on the damper against which the spoon pushes. These pads may be worn – most usually in the middle of the keyboard. Pads in poor condition should be replaced; it's pointless wasting time regulating the spoons to deteriorating pads, and replacement is easy – it can be done without removing the dampers. That said, severe pad wear is often a sign that the whole action is badly worn, which, of course, brings the condition of the piano into serious question.

But most usually, dampers need regulating because constant use has bent the damper spoon back a little so that

the damper can't lift sufficiently for the full vibration of the strings. The cure is to bend the spoon very slightly *towards* the damper until the damper works correctly. (Bend the spoon *away* from the damper if a damper has too much movement or is not damping at rest.)

You must remove the action to get access, so carrying out and checking several damper adjustments is irksome. You also need to use the general bender from the multi-tool kit – but at the same time you need to hold the whippen steady with a pair of pliers or an adjustable wrench of some kind, so that when you bend the spoon you don't exert any load on the whippen flange. (Some multi-tool kits include a tool that goes right under the action and on to the spoon, but I've never enjoyed much success with it. It's

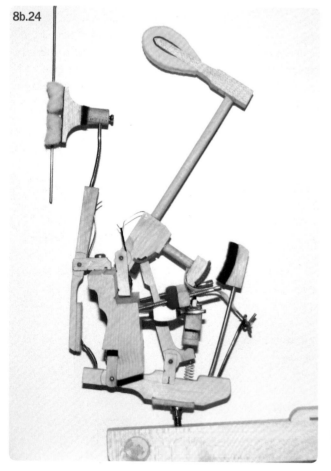

8b.24

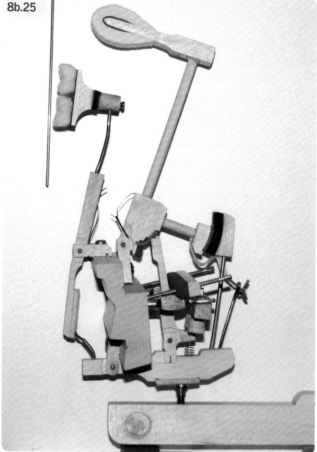

8b.25

8b.26

8b.27

a bit like painting the back of your door through the letter-box.)

8b.26 shows the damper being held so that the spoon is exposed. (It's normally up against the felt pad on the back of the damper.) The circular metal rod above the spoon is the sustain pedal mechanism. This moves forward when the pedal is depressed, lifting all the dampers at once.

If no more than around five dampers need adjusting:

1 Remove the action. Bend the spoon a little the correct way: towards the damper for more lift; away from the damper for less lift.

2 Put the action back in and try the affected notes. The dampers should start to lift just before the key is halfway down and just before the hammer is halfway through its travel – that is, when it has moved around three-quarters of an inch (19mm) from the rest rail.

3 The dampers should all be uniform. At full stroke, no damper should lift back far enough to (a) foul against the next one (in the bass section) or (b) press too hard against the slap rail, the felt covered wooden strip running right through the action that prevents excessive damper travel. If you have over- or underdone it, try the sequence again.

If more than about five dampers need adjusting:

1 Remove the action from the piano. Examine the line formed by the dampers. If it is highly irregular, some of the damper head stems may have been deliberately bent in an unwise attempt to improve their performance.

2 To fix this, go along the action with a straight edge (a steel rule is good for this) and push *gently* against an octave or so of the wooden damper bodies, near where the damper wires exit. Just take up a little tension in the springs.

3 Now that the wooden parts of the dampers are in a straight line, the damper heads should be too. If they're not, line them up using a bending tool (**8b.7**) on the stem.

4 Try the action back in the piano to ensure that the dampers line up to the strings. If they do, you can go ahead and regulate the spoons.

The procedure for this is:

5 Find and make a note of a damper in each octave (or a sample across the compass) that works correctly, or adjust one in each octave until it's correct. Be aware that this may require several removals of the action.

6 With the action in the piano, measure precisely the distance from some fixed point on the damper to some fixed point on the rest rail. For example, in **8b.27** it's precisely 2½in (63.5mm)

from the head of the damper screw to the red layer in the rest rail. You'll need to take two measurements because there are two lines of dampers, as overstringing requires the bass dampers to be set back a little from the rest. You'll need these measurements at step 10.

7 Remove the action and place it on a flat work surface. The whippens will now hang down, suspended on their bridle tapes. All the dampers will move forward until they have made contact with the damper spoons.

8 Do the dampers that were working correctly form a different line from the rest? If so, all the others need adjusting until they form the same line as the 'correct' dampers.

9 Find a damper that was working correctly and raise its whippen with a finger. The damper will start to lift. When the hammer has moved three-quarters of an inch (19mm) from the rest rail, the damper must be exactly the same distance from the rest rail as it was when the action was in the piano. Measure to confirm this.

10 Go along the action, raising each whippen in turn so that the hammer is three-quarters of an inch (19mm) forward. (It helps to make a gauge of some sort – for example, a wooden block – to fit under each whippen in turn to raise it by exactly the right amount.) If the damper is further away from the rest rail than it was at rest in the piano (step 6), bend the spoon slightly *towards* the damper until the damper is just at the rest position. If the damper is closer to the slap rail than it was when at rest in the piano, bend the spoon *away* from the damper.

11 Put the action back in the piano, and confirm by playing that all the dampers now function correctly.

Damper missing strings

One further form of damper regulation may be necessary. Sometimes, just one string of a trichord continues to sound after a note has been played. This happens because the head of the damper has twisted slightly and is only confronting two of the three strings. (This problem is less common in the bichords and monochords: the bichords usually have wedge-shaped dampers that self-centre, and the monochord dampers wrap around the strings – the technical term is 'clip' – and thus also self-centre.)

If just one string of a trichord is still sounding:

1 Undo the retaining screw in the back of the damper head (**8b.28**). The screw is tiny so use a small screwdriver, but it must be long enough to pass between the hammers.

2 Twist the head slightly until the damper faces all three strings.

3 Tighten the screw up again, checking that the damper head doesn't sneak out of alignment as you do so.

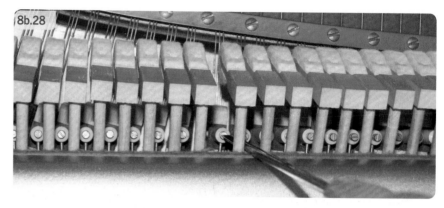

8b.28

4 If the damper has been skewed for some time, it may be grooved. If so, tease the felt up a little with a needle or some tweezers until the grooves have gone.

It's now a good idea to check all the other dampers for tightness. The primary cause of skewing is a loose damper head. If one is loose, others may be about to follow its example.

Replacing damper felt

Modern underdamper action felt doesn't wear out very quickly: it's on a spring and just keeps moving forward to take up any wear. Nonetheless, damper felt can eventually wear out and need replacing.

A more common reason for replacing some damper felts is if spilled liquid has hardened them. The telltale sign of this is buzzing noises on key release. (In many pianos the join in the top lid is conveniently placed right over either the dampers or the hammers, ensuring maximum damage from any spillage.)

Whatever the cause of deterioration, one option is to replace just the felt; you simply slice the old felt heads off with a scalpel and glue new ones on to the wood. The usually better but much more expensive option is a full set of replacement damper heads, *if* a matching set can be found.

Centre pins

All the moving parts of a piano action hinge on tiny nickel centre pins. Each joint has one part that moves while the other is fixed. The moving part has two tiny felt bearings in it, while the fixed part has a hole drilled into it for the centre pin, which is a very tight fit in the wood. **8b.29** shows a hammer flange with the old centre pin removed and a shiny new one ready to replace it in the bearings. It is pointed for easy insertion, and overlong so it can be cropped to size afterwards.

The felt bearings are a remarkable achievement. Correctly put together, they can last for decades and millions of operational cycles; but it takes the judgment of Goldilocks to get them just right. Put them in too tight and the part won't function: it can't free itself up like a metal bearing in a vehicle engine, because none of the felt material can escape. Put them in too loose, and the joint will drop to bits in a few weeks.

Two problems may affect the centre pins as the piano ages:

- The pins may corrode, usually through damp, causing the action gradually to seize up.
- The wood shrinks, losing its tight grip and causing the pins to start coming out. The parts will then rock loose; the hammers may flop around, striking adjacent strings or even dropping out altogether.

Butt plate arrangement

In some higher quality pianos, the hammer flange pin and bearing are held in place with a small screw-on plate called, imaginatively, the butt plate. Recentring this type of joint is much easier than recentring the more common friction-fit or push-in joint (see below), so I'll deal with butt plate joints first.

8b.29

⫿⫿⫿ Warning

Warning 1: On any piano, if you investigate a hammer rocking from side to side and identify the problem as a loose centre pin, it's likely to be sticking out as in 8b.32. Protruding pins often glint from deep down in the works. Do not give in to the huge temptation to put a long screwdriver into the action, lever against the next flange and so force the pin back in. It's 99 per cent certain that this will simply push the felt bearing out of the other end of the hole. And even if you did succeed against these fearful odds, the pin would drop out again within a few days.

Warning 2: Also on any piano, when removing flanges you may sometimes find tiny strips of paper under one edge. Put them back where they were. These are shims, and are there for a reason – most commonly because a hammer has been found to veer off target slightly on its way to the string. For example, a paper shim under the right-hand side of the flange has been put there to correct a hammer veering to the right. (In fact, these shims are a useful remedy for any hinged component not working at precisely the right angle.)

8b.12 shows this kind of hammer assembly from a 1920s Schiedmayer. **8b.30** shows the plate arrangement, while **8b.31**, **8b.32** and **8b.33** show the joint during disassembly. The ends of the old pin are corroded and were preventing the hammer from moving smoothly.

The correct repair for pianos with a butt plate is this:

1 Measure the pin and order a selection of larger pins. See Appendix 1 for a table of pin sizes. Like strings, they're measured in Music Wire Gauge (MWG). Pins in new pianos are commonly MWG gauge 23 and they ascend in half sizes, one thousandth of an inch (0.03mm) at a time to gauge 26.

Piano parts suppliers usually offer a measuring gauge with graduated MWG slots around the outside, and holes up the middle for gauging tuning pins – see **8b.34**. These offer a convenient alternative to a micrometer.

2 Take a new pin, one size up. They're longer than needed and have a point on one end for insertion.

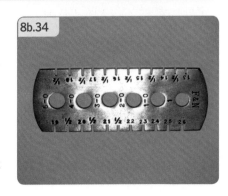
8b.34

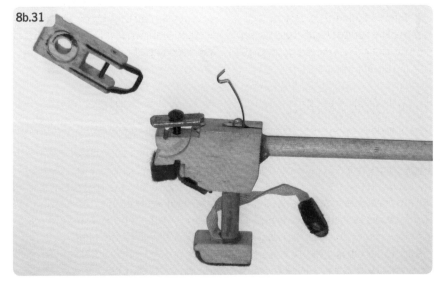
8b.31

8b.30

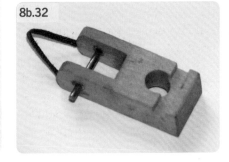
8b.32

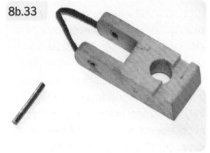
8b.33

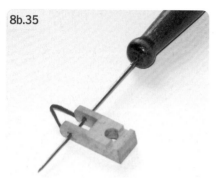

8b.35

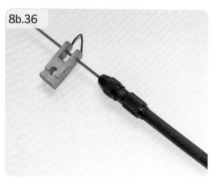

8b.36

8b.37

8b.38

8b.39

3 Try the new pin in the bearing. If it's a loose fit, try one the next size up.

4 When you have a pin that will fit in but is tight, ream the felt bearing out until the pin is a firm (or 'Goldilocks') fit – see **8b.35**. Insert the tiny reamer gradually, revolving it between your fingers. Because its shaft is tapered, insert it to the same depth from both sides of the flange. The resulting hole will still have some taper and its felt will be roughed up – so not good enough yet!

5 Insert a broach (**8b.36**) – a microscopically fine revolving file available in sizes to match the centre pins. Its sides are parallel, so insert it from only one direction. Its job is to firm up the felt and burnish the surface that forms the bearing point. Use the broach, inserting it from the same direction each time, until the pin is a snug trial fit. (Some broaches – usually the ones supplied with their own wooden handle – have a roughened section at the top, near the handle. This may be used instead of the reamer to remove some felt.) Insert the pin.

6 Cut off the excess length of the pin. Use only end-ground cutters (**8b.37**) that cut off flush. Reassemble the joint as shown in **8b.38**.

7 Once reassembled, push the flange away with a finger and let it go. It should spring back to the position in **8b.12** under the tension of the small butt spring. If it doesn't, the pin is too tight so you have more broaching to do.

8 It may take some trial and error to get the pin and its movement just right, but then that's it.

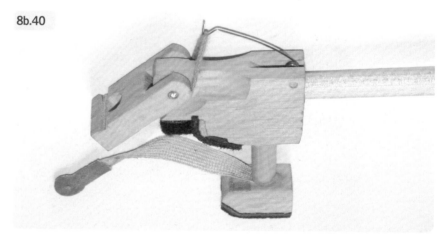

8b.40

If your piano doesn't have butt plates, life won't be quite this simple.

Push-in joints

The screw-on butt plate arrangement is a luxury feature of quality pianos. It is found only on the hammer flange, as this flange does much more work than the others. In most other pianos all the joints, including the hammer flange, are the push-in type shown in **8b.39** and **8b.40**.

The typical action has four centre pin joints per note; that is, one centre pin per moving part on each note. As numbered in **8b.41**, these pins are on: 1 the hammer flange; 2 the whippen flange; 3 the jack itself; and 4 the damper flange.

The recentring procedure – fitting new pins – is the same for all of them. Here it is with illustrations based on recentring a hammer flange:

1 Disassemble the joint using a decentring tool (**8b.42**), which looks suspiciously like a knuckle-duster. **8b.43** and **8b.44** show its working parts: the pointed end is for removing old pins while the other end is for inserting new ones. Disassembly is shown in **8b.45** and the disassembled components in **8b.46**.

2 Find a new pin that will be a tight fit in the hole – see **8b.47**. First try the next size up from the original – see step 1 of *Butt plate arrangement* (above) for

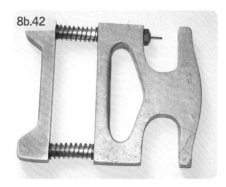

8b.42

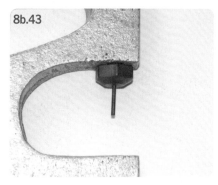

8b.43

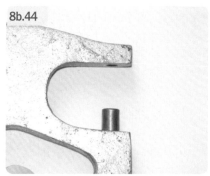

8b.44

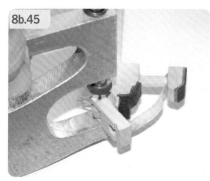

8b.45

8b.46

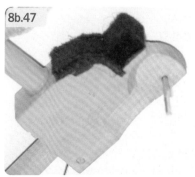

8b.47

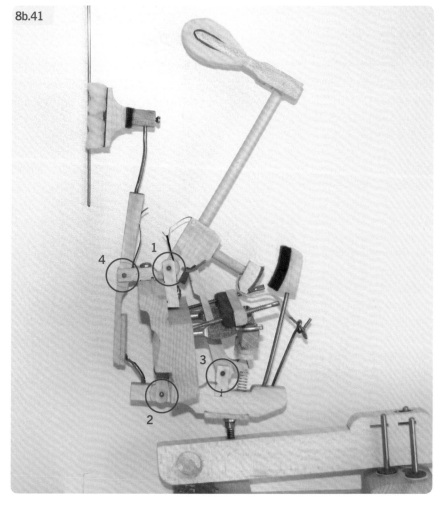

8b.41

sizes. If it won't hold tight in the hole, go one size bigger. Take care over your judgement. You must balance the risk of splitting components by squeezing in too tight a pin against the risk that the job won't be effective for long if the pin is too loose.

3 Ream and broach the felt bearings as in steps 4 and 5 of *Butt plate arrangement* to match the pin you've found to do the job. Once the pin is a cosy fit, you're ready to reassemble the joint.

4 Position the flange in roughly the correct place and hold it up to the light. Amazingly for three such small holes, you can see all the way through them when they line up. Keeping them in this position, insert the pin by hand as far as it will easily go (**8b.48**).

5 Squeeze the pin further into place with the 'blunt' or insertion end of the decentring tool (**8b.49**).

6 With your end cutters, trim off the excess from the centre pin (**8b.50**).

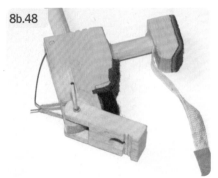
8b.48

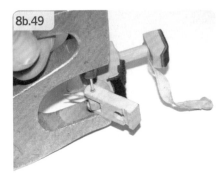
8b.49

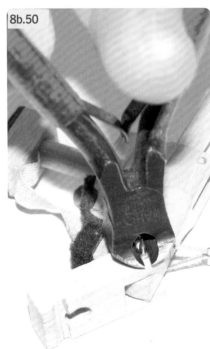
8b.50

Damper spring repair

8b.24 and **8b.25** show a spring behind the damper which (a) holds the damper on the string at rest and (b) returns it to the string when the key is released. When a key is depressed, the spoon on the back of the whippen pushes the bottom of the damper forward, raising the felt damper pad off the string(s) for this note. In the factory, the spring is put in with a piece of cord through it that acts like a centre pin. (Cord is used because it doesn't squeak or rattle. Replacement cord is extremely expensive for what looks like a piece of string. I trust it has superior qualities and that ordinary string would last only ten minutes.)

If this spring doesn't function, the note keeps sounding after it is played until it dies of natural causes. If several do this, or even just one near the middle of the keyboard, the piano is unplayable. If you're lucky, the damper spring has simply become dislodged from the groove in the wood in which it sits, and all you need do is bend it to encourage it to stay

central, and drop it back into place with long tweezers.

But the more usual cause of malfunction is one of these:

- The spring has broken. This is especially likely in a piano showing signs of corrosion.
- The spring has weakened through use and, although intact, no longer kills the sound effectively.
- Replacement springs of only one gauge have been installed. A full set contains three gauges: light for the treble, heavier into the bass, reflecting the extra power needed to stop the vibration of the heavier strings. Bass dampers with treble gauge springs won't function correctly.

The cures are many. Some are quick, effective and cheap but unlikely to last long. One or two are astoundingly fiddly and pointless. It's also quite common to find earlier repairs where the spring

is put in with cocktail sticks or toothpicks rather than the correct cord. This works but is likely to squeak.

In an emergency, this temporary fix works well:

1 Put a rubber band around the wire stem of the damper. Twist it so that it stays there.

2 Loop it around the bottom end of the whippen.

Rather like choosing the perfect stone to throw through a window, a skilled technician will try to match the tension of the rubber band to the spring tension, so that the associated key doesn't feel noticeably different.

There is only one 'proper' cure, but this is unfortunately time-consuming and expensive. It involves recentring the damper flange. If more than five or so springs need replacing, or if it's evident that several have already been replaced,

8b.51

8b.52

8b.53

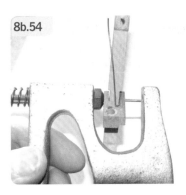

8b.54

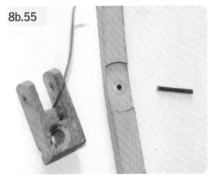

8b.55

8b.56

8b.57

8b.58

the piano will be plagued with spring problems for the foreseeable future. In that case, you might as well fit a full set of new springs, as replacing them one or two at a time is more fiddly and takes longer than it's worth. Once you get into the swing of it, replacing them all at one go can be done quite quickly. The correct repair, for one or all of them, is:

1 Remove the action and place it on a bench. Remove the damper from the action. You need a long screwdriver with a small blade for this (**8b.51**), and access to the damper screws in the middle of the action is difficult. **8b.52** shows a damper removed from the piano.

2 Remove the flange, using the decentring tool shown in **8b.42**.

3 **8b.53** and **8b.54** show the old pin being removed from the felt bearing in the flange holes and the wooden centre of the damper arm. **8b.55** shows the disassembled components. Corrosion can be seen on the ends of the old pin, and the hole in the damper body through which the pin must be a tight fit is revealed.

4 Drill the old cord out with a very small drill (**8b.56**).

5 Now pull the old damper spring out. **8b.57** shows the old cord and spring, and debris from the old cord. **8b.58** shows the hole into which the end of the spring is inserted.

8b.59

8b.61

8b.63

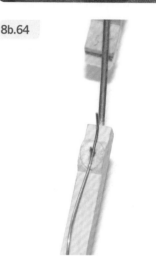

8b.60

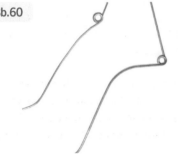

8b.62

8b.64

8b.65

6 Insert the new spring (**8b.59**). New springs are generic and so usually too long: **8b.60** shows a new spring alongside an old one.

7 Fix the spring into place with cord. Make a lead-in on the cord with a small piece of clear adhesive tape (**8b.62**). Trim the cord ends off with a scalpel (**8b.63**). Trim the new spring to length (**8b.61**)

8 Now put a new centre pin in the flange. This is as described in the section above on recentring a hammer flange (see *Push-in joints*).

9 If the new spring is still too long, bend it so that the peak of the bend is in the middle of the felt-lined groove

in the damper body when the flange is pushed up with the finger to its normal operating position at 90° to the damper body (**8b.64**). Where possible, copy the bend profile of the original spring – see *Spring tension adjustment* below. Trim off the surplus (**8b.65**).

10 Try the flange. It should rotate easily, but not rock about sideways. If it now resembles **8b.52** again, it's ready to be returned to the action.

Spring tension adjustment
It's important to leave the piano with an even touch, which you won't get if the springs are left under different tensions. Generally, if the bow shape of

the springs is the same on each damper spring, the touch is likely to be even. If playing suggests that it isn't, you can vary the tension in the springs by bending them slightly.

Seized or slow action

If a piano is kept in a damp environment, the wood around the bearings may expand, squeezing the felt bearing tight. This will slow the piano down, and if advanced can seize up the action completely.

Moving the piano to a very dry environment may free up the action, or you might try one of the proprietary 'easing' products from piano parts suppliers. These contain Teflon and can work extremely well, though I personally

wouldn't use them on a valuable piano, or one worth rebuilding. A tiny drop is put on to the bearings with a small art paintbrush.

But if exposure to damp has been prolonged, you may be fighting a losing battle. Corrosion may have swollen the centre pins so much that they'll never free up. If you don't get any success from either letting the action dry out naturally or using an easing product, the only remaining option is to recentre (put new pins into) the whole action.

It's now time to pace up and down the room for a while, thinking things through.

■ Recentring a very old piano may be uneconomic, or out of the question entirely if the wood has become brittle through shrinkage.

■ Recentring the action is normally done as part of a complete rebuild. Get this far and the whole hog beckons – new strings, tuning pins, soundboard repairs, keys etc. I don't cover full rebuilding in this book because it's a major operation that usually only makes sense if done professionally. By all means recentre the whole action – it's not a particularly complicated job – but you'll end up with a piano that may be an uncomfortable mix of new and old. Will you be happy with it?

■ Be warned that as it involves close to 400 separate pin replacements, recentring ranks as one of the most tedious and dispiriting jobs in the world. Or it certainly seems like that while you're doing it.

If your piano is in very poor condition, with the hammers rocking about, but you're determined to rescue it, consider recentring just the hammer butts over the middle two octaves and playing the piano for some weeks. If the new pins are too tight, the hammers won't play properly and will never free up; if the new pins are too loose, the joints will drop to bits in weeks. If you got it wrong, take the new pins out and replace them with different sizes until the piano plays those notes correctly. When you're confident by trial and error that you've got the hang of recentring, then you can consider tackling the whole action.

If you decide to go ahead:

Dismantling and recentring the whole action

It may help to think of the task ahead as qualitatively the same work you may already have done to replace centre pins in various action joints. The only real difference is that there is now a lot more of it.

It may also help to set aside a few days and do a set quota each day. However you manage your time, don't be tempted to rush the job just to get it over and done with. Aim to get satisfaction from the work, even if enjoyment eludes you.

Removing and dismantling

1 Remove the action and place it on a bench. (If you think it will help, number all the action parts.)

2 Unhitch all the action (bridle) tapes. It's highly likely that an action being recentred will also need retaping. If so, follow the procedure in *Clip-on versus glue-on tapes* (see page 118).

3 Remove the rest rail. See *Set-off in uprights* (page 120).

4 Go along the back of the action, removing the damper screws and thus the dampers – see **8b.51**. Store with care, in order.

5 Go along the back of the action again, removing the now exposed whippen screws and dropping the whippens off (**8b.66**). If the action posts don't raise the action much, you may need to put them on blocks of wood to raise the action enough to provide clearance for the whippens to drop out.

6 Line up the whippens neatly in order. (I keep a number of thin strips of wood at around head height on which I can hang the parts.)

7 Go along the front of the action, removing the hammer butt flange screws and thus the hammers (**8b.67**). Store them so you don't lose them or mix them up.

8 It's almost certain that the whole action will have had the same-sized pins originally, but to be on the safe side check a few on each row. You're now ready for the ordeal of replacing the pins.

Inserting new pins

Assuming you have a large supply of new pins in various sizes, carry out the procedures detailed earlier in *Butt plate arrangement* (page 124) and *Push-in joints* (page 126) for all 330 or so centre pins – three per note, plus usually about 60 damper centre pins.

8b.66

8b.67

Replacing felt bushes

As part of the recentring work, you may have to replace some felt bushes. There are usually two circumstances in which this becomes necessary:

■ The originals are in poor condition, for example after a spillage of liquid into the piano.
■ During extensive recentring, one or two felt bushes may come out or be forced out by clumsy operation of the decentring tool. (Breaking the work into a series of short sessions may help avoid this.)

You can replace the bushes yourself, or buy new flanges with bushes in them; it's a question of balancing cost against time and tedium. If they all need replacement, I'd recommend new flanges.

To replace the bush yourself:

1 Ensure that you've got the right thickness of bushing cloth. (Send a sample to your supplier.)

8b.68

2 Cut a long, narrow strip of bushing cloth as wide as the circumference of the hole.

3 Drill out the old bushing cloth (**8b.68**). Use a drill as close as possible to, but no larger than, the original hole size.

4 Cut the end of the strip to a V shape to help get it through the holes in the part. Thread the strip through the holes.

5 Put glue on the portions of cloth that will form those particular bushes, and pull the cloth so that the glued portions are in the holes. (There are two on each flange. The one in **8b.69** awaits glue.)

6 Insert a centre pin – it should be a tight fit – until the glue is dry. Use a number 23, the smallest common size.

7 When the glue is dry, cut around the centre pin with a scalpel. Remove all the surplus, leaving just the bushes in place. Remove the centre pin.

8 Ream and broach the bushes to the correct size for the pin.

9 Insert the pin and chop off the surplus.

10 Reassemble the joint, as detailed in *Butt plate arrangement* (page 124, step 8 onwards) and *Push-in joints* (page 126, step 4 onwards).

Spring and loop: the Schwander action

8b.40 shows a small spring on the front of the butt attached to a loop that is fixed to the flange. This is a characteristic of the Schwander upright action, by far the most common in Europe and possibly the world. (These springs and loops are not to be confused with spring and loop actions on

8b.69

pianos well over a hundred years old, an example of which may still surface every now and then.)

Schwander spring-and-loops are rarely required to do anything; in most circumstances, the hammers will bounce back from the strings after playing. However, in *very* soft playing with the half-blow pedal depressed, these little springs are needed to bring back the hammer ready for repetition. If some of these springs or loops are broken, such playing may be difficult.

Most pianos get through their lives with the originals intact, but some modern pianos, especially from the 1960s and 1970s, had weak loops which broke easily. This is why used pianos of this period sold by dealers are often described as having new loops.

If you have to do your own repair, it's fairly easy:

1 Order springs and loop cord from a parts suppliers.

2 Press and glue the loops into small grooves on the flange (**8b.31**). Be guided on length by unbroken loops.

3 Mount the springs on bushing cord. This is the same stuff the damper springs are mounted on, and the technique is the same (see steps 8 and 9 in *Damper spring repair*, page 128).

🎹 Centre pin mystery solved

I was once called out to a grand piano in which a large number of hammers were not dropping to their rest position, and the regular tuner didn't know how to fix it. It was obvious to me that it was a centre pin problem, but the piano was well kept and only a few years old, so the puzzle was why anything could be going wrong. Desperately trying to look as though I knew what I was doing, I slid on my back under the instrument, searching for a clue, and immediately felt my shoulders go damp. There was a radiator nearby – actually turned off because of its proximity to the piano – that had been dripping, unnoticed, presumably for months, and wetting a large area of carpet under the piano. A plumber was called and the leak fixed. It was a warm summer, so I advised leaving the windows and patio door open as much as possible. I went back after two weeks and had to recentre only five or six hammer flanges. The rest had dried themselves back to normal. An expensive insurance claim avoided!

Hammers

After many thousands of hours of playing, piano hammers will become badly cut by string contact. The ends will flatten off and there will be one, two or three grooves across the flats. The trichords in the middle of the piano are likely to be in the worst shape, followed by the treble because the hammers are much smaller. The top few treble end hammers may even have their felt cut right through to the wood.

In correct operation the hammer doesn't hit the string squarely; it's still pointing slightly upwards at the point of contact – see page 39. Hammer wear increases the area presented to the strings. This causes the piano's tone to change; and if there is only one regular player, the tone may gradually come to reflect the manner in which he or she plays. If played softly, the hammer brushes the string quite gently. This will

8b.71

8b.70

tend to fluff up the head of the hammer, making it progressively softer. If thumped mercilessly, the hammers flatten off and harden up, making the tone louder and more strident, with more and more harmonics, as a greater area strikes the strings. Experiencing these different tones is one of the more fascinating aspects of being a piano tuner!

Refacing hammers

Hammers can be refaced at least once during their life, to compensate for wear by abrading them back to their 'as new' shape. The main tool here is a stick that comes covered in baby's-bottom grade sandpaper, though I always re-cover them with a more ferocious grade. (I bought ten sticks thirty years ago and still simply re-cover them every so often: see **8b.70**. The green covering is grade P60. Some of my colleagues in the trade wince when they see it, but it shortens the job from a couple of hours to 30 minutes or so with no loss of finesse.)

The basic technique for uprights is to lie the action on its back and *very carefully* sand the hammers back to their original profile. (Grand hammers are already conveniently prostrate, ready for work.) One false move and you can easily break off a hammer or damage a centre pin. And always work towards the strike point, never across it or away from it (**8b.71**). I sand two hammers at a time where I can, but in the overstringing

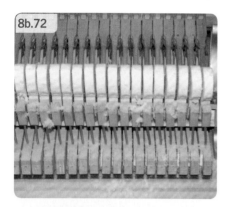

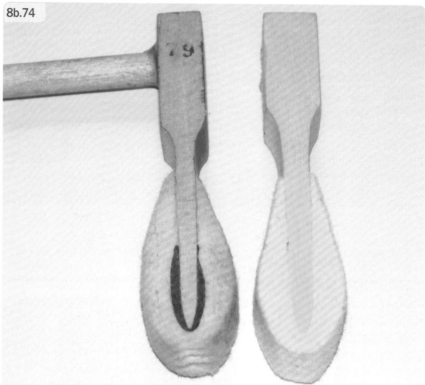

section (bass and lower middle) the angle of the hammers makes it necessary to do each one individually.

Be warned: sanding makes a dusty mess – see **8b.72**. In the home, a vacuum cleaner and brush attachment is the least controversial way of getting rid of it; but in a workshop or outdoors, a much better weapon is a compressor set at 100psi (approx 7 bar, 7kg/cm) to blast the dust out.

As you work along the trichord section of the action, check that each hammer has three grooves in it before you sand it off. If there are only two, or one of the three is perilously close to the edge, the hammer is misaligned. (Irregular spacing between the hammers will usually confirm this.) In **8b.73**, one hammer is striking only two strings and several are striking very close to the edge of the felt.

Perform similar checks on the bichord hammers (look for two grooves) and check that the monochords are striking centrally.

You can realign a hammer by releasing the hammer flange screw and moving the flange a little. In an upright it looks improbable, but you can insert a thin screwdriver under the hammer butt and past the jack to loosen the flange. You may need a torch. Wedge the flange into position with the tip of another screwdriver and tighten it up. Do not hold the hammer itself.

If any hammer is in the correct position at rest – that is, correctly spaced relative to those around it – but not striking correctly, it is veering off to one side instead of going dead ahead. The remedy is to release the flange screw and place a tiny paper shim down the side of the flange to which the hammer is veering. Thus, if it veers to the right, shim the right side of the flange; if it veers to the left, shim the left side of the flange. See also Warning 2 in the *Butt plate arrangement* section (page 124).

Take care to reshape the hammers back to exactly their original shape. I often see poor attempts that have left them too flat or too pointed – usually because the hammers were too far gone to begin with. For example, there is no

point trying to reface hammers in the treble that have been cut right through to the wood; these must be replaced. In **8b.71**, the hammers to the front of the shot have been reshaped. Note how flattened the rest look by comparison. Note too how firmly you must hold the hammer to avoid damaging the centre pin or flange.

8b.74 shows an old hammer and a brand new hammer. The older hammer is noticeably shorter as a result of wear, but has just about enough meat left on it to reshape. Anything worse than this is past it, and indicative of a piano possibly beyond economic repair.

If a lot of felt is removed, as it would be from the old hammer in **8b.74**, hammer travel will be increased by the amount lost from the front of the hammer. Strictly speaking, this has a significant domino effect (all of which is covered in Chapter 7):

- The hammer rest rail needs shimming up with felt to restore the correct travel.
- This causes lost motion, which has to be removed by raising the backtouch.

8b.75

■ The set-off will also be wrong, by the amount of hammer material removed – so this too needs regulating.

■ This will probably result in too little key dip, which must be restored by shimming up the balance rail slightly.

■ The dampers may now be lifting from the strings too soon, so the damper spoons may need regulating.

This is a sobering demonstration of the interdependence of the action and keyboard parts. Make a tiny change to one part, and all the others have to be re-regulated. (There is a similar chain of consequences in a grand.)

However, that is the counsel of perfection. In practice, if the piano is more than about 20 years old and the action is already reasonably well regulated, there is a near-unassailable argument for not bothering with all this consequential adjustment:

■ Hammer reshaping takes 30–40 minutes and usually has a dramatic impact on tone.

■ All the other regulation takes far longer and will probably make little, if any, noticeable difference to the sound or feel of the piano.

The case for doing nothing falls down only if (a) the piano is fairly new but has had a lot of use, making reshaping necessary; or (b) it's particularly valuable (or valued by its owner – not always the same thing). It's then worth putting in the extra hours to do the job correctly. But

note that if hammer wear is substantial, full replacement beckons anyway.

Voicing or needling hammers

It may be possible to tame a strident piano by refacing *and* 'voicing' or 'needling' the hammers. On an older piano it's essential to do both; as I explain below, needling on its own is unlikely to help much.

The basic voicing technique is to soften the hammer by judiciously pricking the felt with a needling tool (**8b.75**). This slightly opens the fibres, and just a small amount of needling will greatly soften the tone of a *new, unused* hammer. It may sound primitive, but it's actually a precision job because it's irreversible: one little pin-prick too many and the hammer is ruined.

To soften the tone of the piano for soft playing, only the very tip or 'crown' of the hammer is needled because this is the only part that hits the string. To soften the hammer for more forceful playing, one must needle further back from the crown because a larger area of the hammer now hits the string.

All new pianos are voiced in the factory to give an even tone across the register. If a piano is too harsh, it can be softened by needling. But this only works well on new hammers. Needling is much less effective on older hammers, though if desperate one might try it because it's

usually harder to ruin an old hammer. An older piano with hard hammers can indeed be needled a great deal. The problem is that it can easily make the tone uneven, leaving some notes harsher than others.

Guidelines for needling are:

■ Only ever use one needle (though see *Virtuoso needling* on the next page and consider the odds).

■ When needling the tip of the hammer in the treble, only a short length of needle should project from the tool. This is because in the treble there may be only a very small amount of immensely compressed felt over the wooden core, and this compression may be lost if the tip of the hammer is needled too deeply. (If ever a hammer felt comes unglued, it swells up rapidly and dramatically into its relaxed state.)

■ When needling in the bass, or further away from the tip, a greater amount of needle can be exposed and plunged into the hammer felt.

■ When testing voicing work, it's important to play with very consistent pressure. Play softly up and down the piano and needle the soft zone of the hammer for any notes that sound harsh compared to the rest. Then do the same for medium and loud playing, needling the appropriate zone (see **8b.76** 'Bass hammer' and **8b.77** 'Treble hammer').

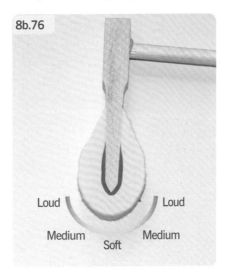

8b.76

Loud · Loud
Medium · Medium
Soft

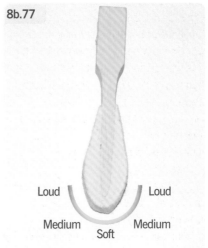

8b.77

Loud · Loud
Medium · Medium
Soft

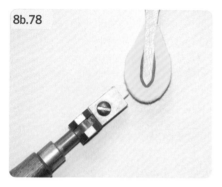

8b.78

8b.79

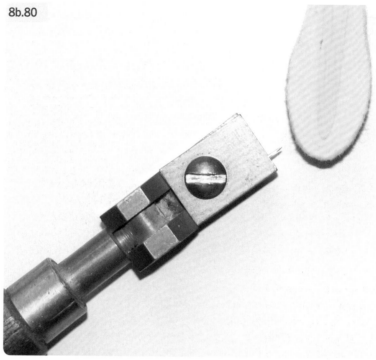

8b.80

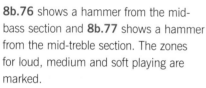

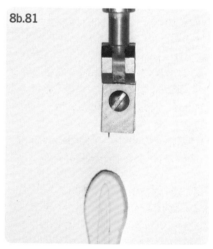

8b.81

8b.76 shows a hammer from the mid-bass section and **8b.77** shows a hammer from the mid-treble section. The zones for loud, medium and soft playing are marked.

8b.78, 8b.79, 8b.80 and **8b.81** show the hammers and the tool with an appropriate length of needle protruding.

Hardening the hammers

Sometimes a piano can be too soft or mushy in tone. There can be many causes of this: most commonly an incorrect set-off, as discussed earlier; or occasionally an incorrectly set up keyboard (Chapter 7 for uprights, Chapter 9 for grands). In a grand – and remotely possibly in an upright – the action may not be correctly located in the case, resulting in the strike line not being at the correct point on the strings.

When all these causes have been eliminated, the likelihood is that the hammers are too soft. A new set is expensive but is the only correct choice if the piano is valuable. If its value doesn't justify the outlay, you might try to harden the hammers to squeeze a little more life out of it.

🎹 Virtuoso needling

When I learned how to needle, every piece of instruction I read counselled that although the hammer needling tool (8b.75) holds up to six needles, only one should ever be inserted. This made the job enormously long and tiring, especially in a grand, as the action had to be put back repeatedly into the piano to test the results. Some years later I watched a TV programme about Bob Glazebrook, then chief technician for Steinway. He was setting up some famous pianist's concert grand. The pianist complained that the instrument seemed a little harsh in 'this area' (hand waving vaguely, indicating about two octaves above middle C). Bob dragged out the action, leaving the back edge resting on the piano and the front edge on his lap. With his left hand and forearm firmly holding down the hammer shanks, and with his right hand clutching a needling tool with three needles bared, he proceeded to batter the hammers in that area like a bad-tempered post office counter clerk.

We live and learn. From that moment on, I greatly speeded up my needling technique – but I still don't have the nerve to adopt Bob's three-needle blitzkrieg.

There is at least one proprietary liquid for hardening hammers (see *Useful contacts*), but in essence all you're doing is applying thin glue. My technique is:

1 Remove the action and lie it on its back. Mask everything – every bit of felt, wood etc – except the hammers with several layers of newspaper.

2 Push more layers of newspaper between the backs of the hammers and the rest rail felt.

3 Spray the hammers gently with clear cellulose lacquer, exactly as sold for vehicle wheels. I use it because it dries very quickly. Spray from the front of the hammers, so that the tip gets most; and on each pass go well beyond the ends before changing direction, or you'll risk putting twice as much lacquer on the end hammers. Two or three passes should be the maximum for a first try.

4 Leave it long enough to dry fully, so that no lacquer is carried into the interior of the piano. Replace the action.

5 Try the piano. Risk a little more lacquer if necessary, and if you dare.

Replacing hammers

If the hammers are badly worn, it may be time to replace them. This would

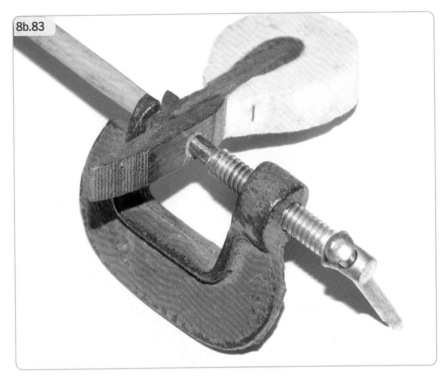
8b.83

normally only be done as a part of a major rebuild, as it's unlikely that a piano with exhausted hammers won't want other work doing too. But it's worth knowing how to do it in case some mishap leaves you needing to replace just one or two hammers (see *Repair of single hammers* on page 138).

Complete repair

The hammers will be in at least three runs: bass section, and treble section with one or maybe two breaks somewhere.

1 Take off the end hammers from each section using a proper hammer extractor (**8b.82**), so that the hammers are complete for your supplier's examination. In a grand the shanks go right through the hammer head, so the extractor *pushes* the shank out (**8b.82** and **8b.83**). In an upright, the extractor forces the hammer off by *expanding* between the butt and the hammer.

2 Clearly indicate the number of each hammer (on it, or on a label). Your No 1 should be A at the bass end.

3 Send these hammers to your parts supplier so he can set up his drilling machine. He needs all of these because all the holes into the hammers to receive the shanks are drilled at slightly different angles because of the overstringing – see **7.20**, which shows the most extreme switch in angles, around the overstringing break. The angle continues to change slightly throughout the treble.

4 When the new hammers arrive, install the end hammers of each section first so that you can line them up and preserve the strike line.

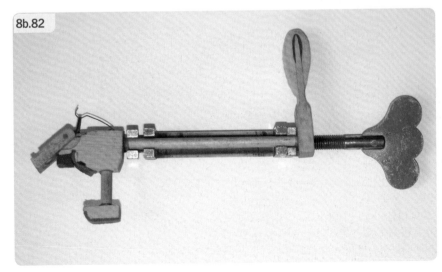
8b.82

8b.84

2 If you have trouble getting at the hammer butt flange screw, disconnect the action tape and take out the whippen flange screw. Drop the whippen off. Access to the hammer flange is now easy. Refer to the photos in *Dismantling and recentring the whole action* (page 131).

3 Hold the broken portion in a vice (mole) wrench and use the hammer extractor in reduced form, as in **8b.84**.

4 No matter how careful you are it's common for a fragment to break off, leaving the rest of the shank in place. If this happens you'll have to saw off the stub, then drill out the hammer head and the butt to the correct size for a new shank. I use an electric drill to put a small pilot hole in first. Then I hand-drill the butt, holding the sides firmly in the vice as they otherwise split easily. An engineer's vice with shallow, padded jaws is better than a carpenter's vice: you don't want to have to take off the butt flange and you want the head of the butt just proud of the vice. Take care not to drill right out through the hammer head, unless you're working on a grand. **8b.85** to **8b.90** show the main operations up to dry-fitting the parts back together.

5 Now chop all the rest off using large wire cutters. It's best to cut the back, behind the shank. Destruction of the hammer doesn't matter, but you want the shank intact.

6 While some technicians trust their eye, I recommend that you run a length of string along the strike line – that is, the tips of the hammers – to get the new hammers into alignment.

7 Now glue on the new hammers, working quickly so that you have enough time to adjust them a little if necessary before the glue dries. When replacing one or two hammers, ordinary woodworking adhesive will be fine. For full replacement use proper piano builder's glue, which comes in small tubs and has to be melted in hot water. It's more tricky to work with than ordinary adhesive but what makes it special is that it retains a degree of flexibility for many years, even decades.

Repair of single hammers

If a hammer has been broken off during playing or through misadventure, repair is trickier.

1 Remove the hammer butt and the broken fragments.

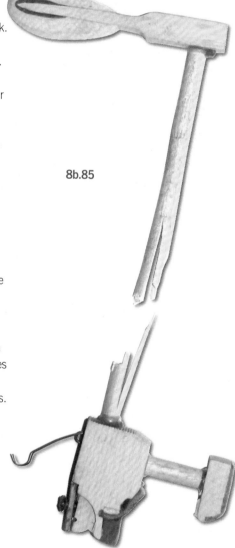

8b.85

5 Shanks don't go into the butts at exact right angles, so copy the ones on either side.

6 Nor do shanks go into the hammers at exact right angles, because of the overstringing. This becomes increasingly marked into the bass. Again, copy the ones on either side.

7 Send a piece of the old shank to a parts supplier for the correct replacements. Shanks come in many diameters, though for an emergency repair you don't need an exact match. You do, however, need exactly the right size drill for the shank you choose to put

8b.86

8b.87

8b.88

8b.89

8b.90

in. It should leave the shank a snug fit in the hammer and the butt.

8 Reassemble dry, check the fit and screw the butt back into the action.

9 Glue the hammer on to the knurled end of the shank. (Most shanks come with knurling on the hammer end to increase grip. If your replacements have no knurling, you can add some by rolling the end of the shank under the edge of a heavy, coarse file.)

10 Trim the shank length down until it just fits. The hammer shank cutting tool shown at **8b.91** makes it possible to remove just a tiny amount off the shank to get the length exactly right. (Hint: a remarkably similar tool called a dog's claw cutter may be bought from a pet shop for about a quarter of the price.)

11 Drop a blob of glue into the hole in the butt and put the shank in.

12 Set the hammer position exactly in line with all the other hammers.

Drawing pins – just say no

A final bit of advice on hammers. I don't have to go far these days without someone telling me about a friend of a friend who got a great novelty sound out of a piano by sticking drawing pins into the hammers. Yes, I know about this; it produces a really plinky sound that some people claim to like. But no, it isn't something you should ever try unless you want to kill your piano. The drawing pins soon work loose and drop out. The hammers are then useless; they make a sound like snowballs hitting the strings. There should be a law against it. Some people claim that (re)hardening the hammers (see above) can rectify this damage, but I'm sceptical.

8b.91

C: STRINGS AND TUNING PINS

Sometimes a string will break. This is most common during tuning and can happen to even the best technician. It can happen during playing too, but this is less common because of the forgiving way the set-off works. (Funnily enough, when it does happen it tends to be when teenagers are home alone.)

In most pianos, each treble string serves twice – going round the hitch pin and back again – so when one wire breaks you lose two strings, either from the same note or from two adjacent notes.

There are two basic types of treble wire: polished and plated. When rebuilding it's best to use the same type throughout, but for odd repairs it really doesn't matter. Polished is more popular than plated but I've never noticed any difference in sound.

If your piano is fitted with agraffes (see Chapter 4, and page 59), fitting the string will be easier than if it has a pressure bar. Nonetheless, fitting new strings on any piano should be fairly straightforward – particularly grands, as you're spared having to work around the keybed. It is, however, important not to snag the dampers when working on a grand; the risk is that the damper wire bends, making the damper less efficient because it isn't working squarely.

Gauge

When ordering a new string, if you don't know the exact gauge send a piece of the broken string to your parts supplier. Piano wire may appear to be the same gauge all the way down to where the wound strings start, but in fact the gauge changes every few notes. Measure the gauge of the wire with a micrometer or a wire gauge like that shown on page 125, and see Appendix 3 for how music wire gauge (MWG) converts into measured sizes.

Some physics here: if a given wire were doubled in length but kept under the same tension, it would produce a note an octave lower. The trouble is that if a piano were strung throughout with the same gauge as the extreme treble, the bottom string would be 20ft (6.5m) or more long. Worse still, its behaviour when the hammer struck it would be very different from a short string; so throughout the compass, the strings are made progressively thicker and the length less than doubled in each octave.

Handling

Piano wire is highly unruly and contrary material. It comes in a coil from which it is eager to spring free – yet the minute you cut a length off and want to work with it in a straight line, it tries to coil itself back up again. It's therefore wise to wear gloves when handling piano wire; some experts worry that substances from the skin have a detrimental effect on wire, but I worry much more about the detrimental effect of wire on my skin. In fact, I keep wire in cans made especially for the job – see **8c.1**.

8c.1

String replacement procedure

8c.2 shows a typical broken string problem. Note that as explained earlier, one break in the wire has caused the loss of a string each from two adjacent trichords.

1 Remove the action from the piano (**8c.3**). Cut the old wire off near the pressure bar (**8c.4**).

2 Measure its gauge, or send a small piece of the broken wire to your piano

8c.2

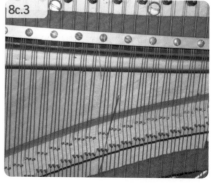

8c.3

8c.4

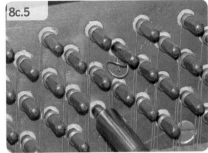

8c.5

8c.6

8c.7

8c.8

8c.9

parts supplier, and buy replacement wire of the correct gauge.

3 Count how many turns of wire there are in the coil around the tuning pin. If for any reason there is no coil left – for example, if the piano came to you with the string already removed – count the turns around the pin next to it.

4 Unscrew (anticlockwise) the tuning pin this exact number of turns (**8c.5**). As you unscrew, the broken ends of the old string will start to lift from the coil.

5 When there is enough to get hold of – it helps to use pliers – uncoil it enough to pull it right off.

6 Cut off a generously calculated length of new wire for the replacement. (If you take your measurement from the broken one, don't forget that it has a bit missing!) Piano wire may be cut with any good quality wire-cutters. Pliers will do only if the cutter is in good condition. The wire is very hard: worn pliers may not produce a clean enough cut to enable you to thread it through the eye of the tuning pin.

7 Put a bend in the wire in the middle, where it will go round the hitch pin (**8c.6**).

8 Feed the top two ends towards and under the pressure bar (**8c.7**). There may well be a cloth tape woven through the tops of the strings to stop sympathetic vibration, and it may not be possible to get the new wire neatly through this. If that's the case, ignore the regular weave pattern. Just get the wire through anyhow, even if it means ripping the cloth.

9 Turn the tuning pin so that you can easily thread the end of the string from below through the eye – the hole in the pin – and start to wind it on clockwise (**8c.8**). I use a T-shaped tuning key for winding on. You'll need to use a screwdriver to help steer the string into a coil: otherwise, it may try to wrap over itself.

10 Hook the bend around the hitch pin and push it into the bridge pins, observing the pattern that the strings form around the two rows of pins (**8c.9**).

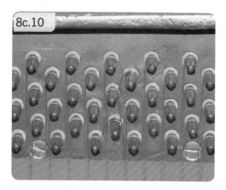

8c.10

8c.11

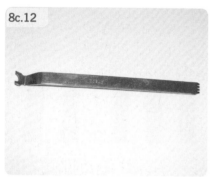

8c.12

11 Take the wire past the tuning pin it is going into by the same number of finger widths on your hand as there are coils around the pins. (Make allowances if you have unusually thin or broad fingers.) Cut off the surplus.

12 While you're working on one end of the string, the other may misbehave. If so, lock it with a mole (vice) wrench.

13 Once you have a turn or two on the first string, repeat step 11 with the other one (**8c.10**). It's important to draw them up evenly because you've fixed the bottom position by putting a bend in the wire round the hitch pin.

14 As each string starts to tighten, check that it is correctly located at the hitch pin and the bridge pins and has not snagged anything, such as adjacent hitch pins.

15 Keep drawing the strings up a little at a time, ensuring that the coil around the pin is squeezed up tightly.

If it isn't tight enough, this string may well be the most out of tune at each tuning for years to come. Once the coil is tight enough to hold itself in position, squeeze the turn into the eye flat against the tuning pin with a pair of pliers (**8c.11**). A tool called a coil lifter can help squeeze the coil (**8c.12** and **8c.13**), but there is often insufficient room in modern pianos to get in to use it. It's also prone to knocking gold paint off the frame, which then looks annoyingly like the legacy of an amateur. (It can happen even to the

8c.13

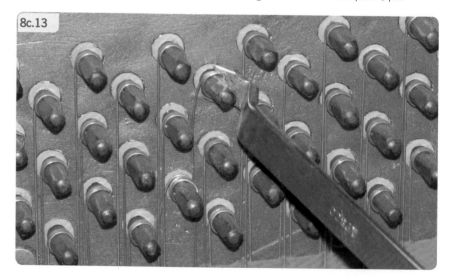

best of us.) So if you use a coil lifter, protect the area around the spot you're going to lever against with cardboard, masking tape or similar. The coil lifter shown in **8c.12** has three slots at the other end: sometimes the trichord strings close up a little and this can be used for spacing them. This is likely to be helpful when fitting a new string.

16 Bring the strings gradually and evenly up to pitch. If you're doing other work on the piano, pull

8c.14

8c.15

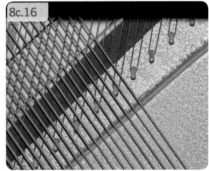

8c.16

them a semitone sharp to stretch them. *Don't sharpen more than this* as it may damage either the strings or the bridge.

17 Push the string right up against the frame with a screwdriver (**8c.14**).

18 Then, slide a screwdriver in behind the string where it goes around the hitch pin, and use it as a lever to give the wire a little jolt to force it tightly up against the pin (**8c.15**). The point of this is to ensure that the string isn't snagging on any 'pimples' on the rough surface of the cast iron frame.

19 Leave the strings for several hours in this condition: ideally, overnight.

20 Finally, tune to the correct pitch (Chapter 10). You'll find that neighbouring strings have gone flat as a result of your work. This is normal, so don't take it personally.

Inaccessible hitch pins
The worst luck you can have is a broken

string with a hitch pin right down behind the bass strings in an overstrung piano. **8c.16** shows the hitch pins for the treble section disappearing down behind the bass overstrung section. The further down you go, the harder it is to get at the pins. There is a special tool for putting such strings on (see *Useful contacts*), but it's usually easier and much cheaper to improvise thus:

1 Buy a length of narrow brass tube from a DIY store.

2 Put a bend in the wire in the middle, where it will go round the hitch pin, and push the double length right through the tube.

3 Get the 'U' end of the wire protruding a little way, push the tube down behind the bass strings and hook the 'U' over the hitch pin.

4 Draw the tube off the wire, keeping the wire under tension so that it doesn't come off the hitch pin. If you can get at the pin, put a mole wrench on it to stop the string escaping.

Alternatively, remove the bass strings that are in the way. Or if you're really, desperately unlucky, you'll have to remove them anyway even if you use the tube method. Undo each tuning pin a little more than half a turn – keeping the string under tension so that the coil stays neat – until there's enough slack to pull the eye off the hitch pin. The problem with removing strings is that when they're put back, they'll tend to flatten rapidly for quite some time.

Replacing a bass string
This is much more straightforward. If you have the old one, send it to a string maker for duplication. But as explained in *Rattles and buzzes* in Chapter 7, if it's a bichord be prepared for the possibility that the new one may not tune to the other string of the pair. If you decide to replace the pair, note that one may be longer from hitch pin to winding, as they're usually arranged in an offset pattern. You need to send both, or the broken one plus the measurements for the other, and give very clear instructions to your piano parts supplier to ensure that you end up with two wires, each of the right length.

Loose tuning pins

During tuning, or when replacing a string, you may find that a pin you're working on is loose in the plank, in which case it will be a good idea to replace it with an oversize pin. However, if a large number – say ten or more – are loose, the piano needs rebuilding. For most uprights this will be uneconomic (which means start looking for a replacement piano), so the following procedure only makes sense if the whole instrument has fewer than around ten loose tuning pins.

Is the wrest plank split?

Even if there are fewer than ten loose pins, you must look for any pattern in them in case the plank is split – and a piano with a split wrest plank is usually beyond economic repair. Even in a modern upright with a bushed frame, splitting is not unknown.

Typical signs of a doomed piano are:

■ Several loose pins close together. This may happen where there is a break in the stringing pattern in the treble section. See **8c.17**. This is a poor design feature: the possible consequences were obvious from day one.

■ Every 'odd' or 'even' bottom pin is loose. This initially puzzling symptom is evidence of a split running sideways along the plank, missing every alternate note because the pins are arranged in an offset pattern (discernible in **8c.17**).

■ Any older upright with an exposed wrest plank must be regarded as suspect, even if few pins are loose. Examine the plank very carefully using a magnifying glass. If you find any splits like **8c.18**, it's a dead piano and you're about to drive a stake through its heart, so save yourself the trouble. (**8c.19** shows the worst splits I've seen. Someone has evidently tried to glue them up and insert new oversize tuning pins. A triumph of optimism over common sense.)

■ On any piano, a truly terrible possibility is that the plank isn't split before you hammer in new pins, but is split afterwards. I've never experienced this but I know it happens, so even now I'm still much happier putting new pins into my own pianos than into someone else's. (I sometimes rehearse what I might say to a customer who has entrusted the family heirloom into my care for improvement…)

Replacing pins

8c.20 shows three pins. The one on the left is battered and rusty and has been removed from an old piano. The one in the middle is nickel-plated for appearance and to prevent rust. The one on the right is the most common: the traditional type, made of blued cast steel.

Replacement tuning pins are hammered in, so the first point to make is that you should only replace pins before you tune the piano. Bashing the piano with a big hammer is not good after tuning.

The second point is that the basic procedure described below for hammering in pins applies only to older uprights

8c.17

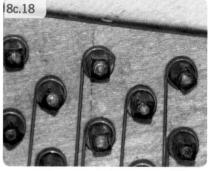
8c.18

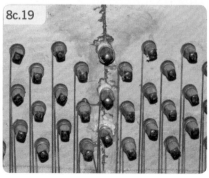
8c.19

8c.20

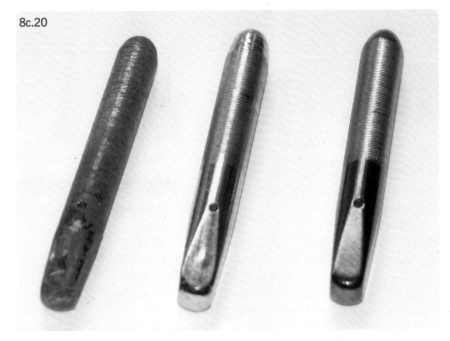

with a substantial wooden frame at the back. Other types of piano need a different approach – see *Variant procedures* below.

Tuning pins have the slightest suggestion of a thread on them, so that they can be extracted – though it takes a large number of turns to remove one. But they are always hammered in by hand, even in a modern factory. Despite the threading, do not be tempted to screw a pin in. This will tend to enlarge the hole, making the pin instantly loose.

I did once screw in a pin in an emergency. A jazz club discovered, minutes before a world famous pianist was due on stage, that its piano had one very loose pin. By the time I arrived, the start of the set was overdue and the audience in no mood to appreciate my dilemma – which was that hammering a new pin in would put the whole piano instantly out of tune. The pin was so loose that I decided to go up two oversizes and screw it in – but at some risk of splitting the plank. It was a long, nervous time getting the pin in, but it worked and the plank didn't split. As predicted, the pin wasn't as tight as it should have been for two sizes up, but it did stay in tune well enough for the performance not to be marred.

Now back to the *correct* procedure!

First remove your pin. For rapid pin extraction, piano parts suppliers stock special tool bits that can be put into a reversible power driver or a carpenter's hand brace. But even when the pin is too loose for tuning stability, powered extraction can generate a great deal of friction, scorching the wood inside the hole. For that reason I recommend slow removal by hand tools only, especially when you're dealing with only a small number of pins.

When the pin is out, measure it with a micrometer or standard measuring gauge (**8b.34**). Pins are available in various lengths and in sizes 0–5, ascending in increments of five thousands of an inch (0.127mm). It's usual to go up one size unless a

8b.34

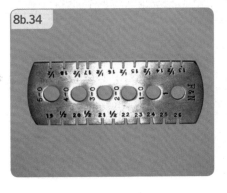

pin was very loose, in which case it's justifiable to go up two sizes.

Alternatively, it may be possible to go up only one size but put a slightly longer pin in. However, trying to hammer a longer pin into a hole not deep enough to take it is dangerous! Push something into the hole and measure to see if a longer pin might fit. In some pianos the hole goes right through the plank; in others it doesn't.

Do not go up two sizes *and* use a longer pin at the same time.

To insert the new pin:

1 First acquire a wrest pin punch: it has a hollowed end (**8c.21** – note the battered end of mine after three decades of work).

2 Hammer in the pin until it's level with the others.

3 Note how many turns of wire the other pins have on them.

4 Turn the new pin anticlockwise that many times.

5 Refit the old string, following the steps in *String replacement procedure* above.

Variant procedures
Grand pianos
For grands there is a completely different procedure, described in Chapter 9. Never hammer tuning pins into a grand without following the correct procedure – you risk wrecking the piano.

8c.21

Modern uprights

How you hammer pins into a modern upright depends on circumstances. Lift the top lid. If there is a cloth running across the top, just over the frame, tear some of it away. Go round the back to see what, if anything, is behind the plank. The point of all this is to find out whether the wrest plank goes right through the piano.

If you find a fairly substantial piece of timber running along behind the plank, it should be safe to use the basic hammering-in procedure. (See **8c.22**. The nine-layered composite is the plank; the thick chunk behind supports it.)

But if the wrest plank goes through the piano (proof: you can see it from the back), do not use the basic hammering-in procedure, as you risk splitting the plank and murdering the piano. Instead, you should:

1 Recruit at least one burly helper. With help, lie the piano on the floor, on its back.

2 Place a chunk of wood directly under the spot you're working

on, to absorb the energy that might otherwise terminate the wrest plank. The chunk needn't be too big; you need to concentrate a lot of support in a small area. Now hammer away.

Pin tightening fluids

Grudgingly, I ought to mention proprietary products available to tighten up tuning pins. Basically, a few drops of liquid are dropped around each pin to soak into the hole. Some fluids soak into the wood, causing it to expand and tighten the pin. Others also contain a substance that makes the tuning pin corrode rapidly, further tightening the pin because rust occupies a larger volume than steel.

Piano technicians in the USA call this expedient 'doping'. In principle there is nothing wrong with it if the piano is of little value and otherwise unusable. But there are few other circumstances where I would consider it justifiable.

- It should never be used to conceal a serious fault from a potential buyer.
- It should never be used on a piano that someone might one day want to rebuild, because when larger pins are eventually put in they won't move

properly in the plank and will be difficult to tune.

- It shouldn't be used on a piano with an exposed plank; it will just swell forwards, forming small cones around the base of each treated pin.

All I can finally say is that pin-tightening fluids can be bought from piano part suppliers.

Wrest pin bushings

Another way of dealing with loose tuning pins is to buy wrest pin bushings (**8c.23**). These are made of soft metal and should not be confused with the wooden bushings fitted in the wrest pin holes of all modern pianos, as shown in **8c.24**.

Wrest pin bushings are almost the length of a standard tuning pin. The procedure is:

1 Remove the tuning pin as explained above. Insert a wrest pin bushing.

2 Hammer the original pin back in. It will now be held tight in the bushing.

3 Proceed from here on as though you've fitted a new, oversize pin.

The main purpose of wrest pin bushings is to make pin remediation less obvious to the casual glance. A new pin always stands out like… well, like a new pin. But new pins are better than old pins, so concealing their use in this way may be construed by some as deception. The procedure is also quite brutal: the force needed to hammer in the bushings is greater than that needed to hammer in an oversized new pin, so the risk of splitting the plank is greater too.

For both these reasons, I dislike wrest pin bushings. I have successfully fitted them on many occasions, but only at the specific request of piano dealers. I would never recommend them to a customer; nor have I ever used them on any of my own pianos.

'Tubby' bass strings

Sometimes, a few bass strings – occasionally a whole section – sound dull and lifeless. In my experience this is always because the copper windings have become heavily corroded, turning a dull blue-grey. There is usually other evidence of the piano having been kept in a damp environment.

To tackle this problem:

1 Remove the front board, bottom board, fallboard and action.

2 Starting with the problem string that is furthest into the bass, detune it by a little more than half a turn. As you do this, keep the winding tight on the pin by pulling at the middle of the string, drawing it into a bow.

3 Pull the string out of the bottom bridge pins and take it off the hitch pin. *Note whether there was a twist in it or not.*

4 Cover the keyboard and the front of the keybed with a large, thick

protective sheet. (Ideally, remove the keyboard too at step 1. Even consider removing the keybed if it's held in with just a small number of screws and no glue.)

5 Pull the string up from behind the keybed and out through the front of the piano.

6 Make a loop of the string – as tight as possible – around the shaft of a long, thick screwdriver.

7 Holding the screwdriver firmly, run the loop up and down the length of the string. You'll probably hear and see dirt and debris falling off it.

8 Run a handful of grade 0 or 1 wire wool up and down the string until it looks like copper again. It will make a terrible mess – hence the protective sheet. Only tackle this in the house if you live alone or with people of a tolerant nature. Otherwise, do it outside on a nice day or in the garage. And clean all the wire wool swarf off thoroughly, as it tends to stick in the windings.

9 Refit the string, giving it half a twist more than it had to start with.

10 Tune it. Does it sound any better? If not, the technique has failed and there is little chance of it working on any of the other strings. (But hope springs eternal, so try one other if you must.)

11 If you have a failure, take off all the affected wound strings. Sometimes only those at the bottom are affected, but if there is an irregular pattern to the problem, replace every wound string, as you won't get satisfactory results by having a mixture of new and old.

12 Get a cost estimate before ordering. Bass strings are not

too expensive but if the piano needs other work as well, repair may not be economic.

13 Send all the monochords and just one bichord of each pair if the bichords are identical, making clear which ones you want two of.

14 If the bichords are of slightly different lengths – because the hitch pins are staggered – either send them all, or convey very clear instructions to the string supplier.

15 While you're at it, check the bass section for loose tuning pins. If you find a few, replace all the pins whose strings you're taking off. Even if they weren't too bad, it's so easy to replace them with the strings off that you might as well do it.

Many experts counsel against leaving a piano with all the bass strings off, claiming that it risks cracking the frame by skewing the load on it. All I can say is that I've done it plenty of times and never known the frame suffer. The belt-and-braces option is to detune all 200-plus treble and bass strings *at the same time*. This has to be done gradually, which means repeatedly going along the piano, releasing the tension a quarter-turn at a time. This is not a task to volunteer for, which is why I choose to live dangerously. But take this as a warning – if you also choose to live dangerously and wreck the piano, don't even consider suing me.

Fitting the new bass strings is fairly easy: make sure that exactly the right amount is trimmed off the lead-in (as described earlier in *String replacement procedure*) and keep the coils tight and neat. Put them all under some tension and bring them up gradually. Then fine-tune them. They're bound to need further tuning soon, but by now you can take this in your stride.

D: THE SOUNDBOARD

Chapter 2 explains the function and construction of the soundboard and bridges, while Chapters 5 and 7 explain how they can cause problems. Now I will tell you how to solve those problems.

As a piano ages, its soundboard is more likely to split. To recap briefly, the soundboard is made from many parallel glued strips of wood, usually spruce, reinforced by ribs running across and behind it. It is crowned slightly towards the strings and has a load of up to half a ton (453kg) imposed upon it by the strings pulling down on the bridges that are attached to it.

All the wood inevitably shrinks, to an extent that varies with age, original build quality and exposure to central heating. Advanced shrinkage causes the strips to start separating, creating what are effectively splits in the soundboard. In serious cases, the strips themselves start to split. Splitting of either kind can be heard as growling noises, usually in sympathetic response to certain notes. This is the sound of the edges of the splits touching each other during what is otherwise normal vibration.

Soundboards can in fact tolerate some splitting and still function well, so a split isn't necessarily the end of the world. The death knell may, however, start tolling if:

- The growling is so obtrusive that the piano is unplayable.
- Tuning is made difficult by movement in the (now) separate parts of the soundboard.
- There is hardly any sound at all as the soundboard loses its structural integrity.

Repair options

Unfortunately, a badly split soundboard is next to impossible to repair economically, especially in an upright. A piano of high value or historic interest may justify being stripped down and completely rebuilt or restored, but for the vast majority it's the end of the road.

What principally thwarts repair is lack of access to the soundboard. In an upright, most of the soundboard is covered by strings and the cast iron frame. A grand permits a little more access – sometimes enough to repair splits, but more often not. In most pianos, access to the bottom of the soundboard (grand) or back of the soundboard (upright) is restricted if the piano has a substantial wooden frame. Therefore, unless the split is in the small accessible portion, major work lies ahead. Any conventional repair should be performed from the string side, and with at least some and more usually all string tension released so that reapplying it squeezes the repair material under enormous force

into the split. For most pianos, all this effort – to which must be added years of much more frequent tuning – simply isn't worthwhile.

There is a glimmer of hope for some modern uprights with no wooden frame, as this allows full access to the back of the soundboard (**8d.1**). 'Proper' repair from the string side still won't be practicable, but I've heard of splits being repaired from the back by releasing some of the string tension in the affected area, then forcing very hard, two-pack vehicle body filler right through the split. This is an unorthodox repair that will probably leave a blister of filler on one or both sides of the soundboard, but there's no reason why it shouldn't work. It could be worth trying as a means of extending the life of a piano if the only other option is to scrap it.

Another unorthodox and decidedly desperate measure is to insert a screw into a split to keep its edges apart and thus stop the growling noise. In theory it

makes the problem worse by wedging the split open, encouraging it to spread, but in practice it can work well. I once did it to a pub piano in an emergency. (Yes, pub pianos do have emergencies.) It got rid of the growl and the piano soldiered on for many more years. Even so, I'd be unhappy to do it again and would only attempt it on an otherwise doomed instrument.

For the record, soundboard splits in grand pianos are repaired during a rebuild (that is, with strings and frame removed) by opening up the crack with a V-shaped

8d.1

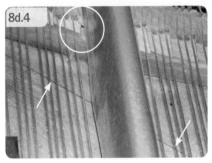

scraping tool, cutting a sliver of similar wood (often from a scrap soundboard) into a V-shaped strip, covering it in glue and hammering it with a mallet into the crack. If the split is irregular, several slivers may need to be inserted. When dry, the repair area is planed and sanded back to shape, and refinished. See *Useful contacts* for more information on soundboard repairs.

8d.2 shows a fairly typical split in a soundboard, and someone's attempt at a repair. When it came to me, this 1940s or '50s Challen was already well past any reasonable life expectancy and of little value. Though the piano tuned and was up to pitch, this split continued up behind the cast iron frame, where it became inaccessible. This was a piano living on borrowed time. Something black can be seen wedged into the split, presumably to keep the edges apart, and perhaps courtesy of whoever put the screws in. It's unlikely that

these two screws so near the edge of the soundboard have had much adverse effect; some makers put screws in near the edge while others don't, so it's a matter of choice. My only criticism is that this venerable English piano at least deserves good old slotted screws rather than anachronistic cross-heads!

8d.4 and **8d.3** show splits in a grand piano soundboard and bridge severe enough to make it an unlikely candidate for rebuilding: this is pretty much the end.

Split bridges

8d.5 shows the upper end of a bass bridge, and a typical bridge problem: the pins holding the strings in place have forced a small split right out to the end. As a result, the string is trying to straighten itself up and has more or less succeeded. When played, this note rattles and makes the instrument unusable. In due course the split will travel to the next pin, and so onwards. **8d.4** shows similar problems in a grand at the break in the treble bridge (ringed) – exactly where we might expect it.

This problem can be solved in two ways:

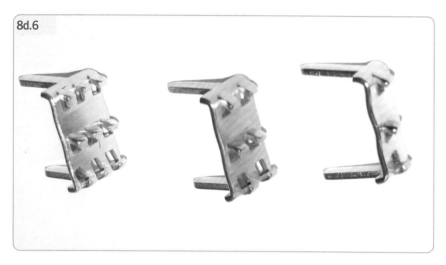

8d.6

at the life left in an instrument, it's worth looking here for clues. In this case, better design would have left a bigger space between the bridge and the frame and more 'meat' on the end of the bridge. This outcome could reasonably have been predicted in the 1920s, when the piano was made – though a more generous view might be that 80 years for a design fault to surface isn't bad going.)

■ Be prepared for a different, usually metallic, tone from the affected notes.

1 Steel bridge cap

If the split hasn't gone far, it's possible to remove the affected strings and take a section off the top of the bridge with a saw and chisel. You then buy from a piano supply house a steel bridge cap with pins built in. Some caps have holes for screws to go right through, while others have projections on the back which mate with guide holes that you have to drill. You then hammer the cap on to the bridge. The type shown in **8d.6** (monochord, bichord and trichord) has these projections. There must be enough wood around the original bridge pins to get the projections in, but once they're correctly located the string load helps keep them in place.

If you opt for the steel cap solution:

■ You must prepare the bridge so that the new part is as close as possible to the same height as the old one, or downbearing will be affected.

■ The bridge must not split further, which makes this repair something of a gamble. **8d.7** shows what to aim for – enough wood to the right of the end pins to make splitting unlikely. Compare this with the minimalist bridge on page 149. (In trying to guess

2 Replacement bridge

An alternative is to remove the whole bridge and get a new one made. This will be expensive and you'll have to send the old bridge to a supply house as a model. The replacement procedure is similar to but easier than that for detached 'shelf' bridges (see below).

8d.7

Separated rib

Sometimes, ribs part company from the back of the soundboard. If the precise spot can be found and accessed from the front, I re-glue and put a screw in, with a large button washer to spread the load (see **8d.8**, a modern plastic example of a button washer).

If the problem affects a larger area,

I drill right through and put thin bolts through both rib and soundboard, with large washers on each side. This may sound brutalist, but I've never known it make any difference to the sound. When doing this repair to a valuable piano made without any screws in the soundboard, I later remove the bolts, pare

down hammer shanks to make them a snug fit, and glue them right through the holes. I then trim the ends and sand and varnish the repair. It looks good and panders to the traditionalist queasiness about 'industrial' fastenings, but in my view it converts a strong repair into a significantly weaker one.

Detached 'shelf' bridges

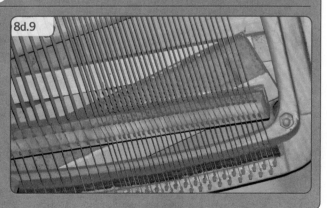

8d.8

In some pianos the bass bridge attaches directly to the soundboard; in others, it attaches to a 'shelf' that in its turn attaches to the soundboard. The shelf in effect moves the point where the bridge contacts the soundboard away from the edge, and the general view is that this improves tonal quality.

Shelves are difficult to photograph, but **8d.7** may help by showing a shelf with screws into it from the front. Most are screwed from the back or glued invisibly, so this is very unusual but serves our purpose by showing the line (indicated by the four screws) where the shelf attaches to the soundboard. The bridge cap over which the strings are stretched is several inches below and the gap increases into the lower bass.

Quite often, shelf bridges become detached. When this happens, none of the bass notes will work at all; the best you'll get out of them is a 'thunk'. Failure is hardly surprising given the load on the shelf, but in my experience the real problem is the use of glue rather than glue plus screws. A piano with a soundboard relying on glue alone is highly susceptible to bridge detachment if it moves from a damp environment to a warm, dry one: the animal glue used until relatively recently simply can't cope. By contrast, I've never known a screwed-in bass bridge to become detached, and I've never been able to tell from the sound whether a bridge or a soundboard has screws in it or not. This tells us that the allegiance of some manufacturers to glue rather than screws may be misplaced. Consequently, whenever I repair a glued bridge that has come adrift, I re-glue *and* insert screws.

In detail, the repair sequence (for which you'll briefly need an assistant) is:

1 Remove all the bass strings (see *'Tubby' bass strings*, page 147). Extract the bridge.

2 Chip off the old glue and sand the old surfaces until reasonably flat.

3 Drill three or four holes right through the soundboard along the attachment line (be guided by **8d.7**), ensuring that there is access to them from the back.

4 Hold the bridge in place and drill small guide holes into the bridge from the back.

5 Select gauge 8 screws of the right length – that is, not so long that they risk distorting or splitting the wood they anchor into.

6 Increase the guide-hole sizes to match the screws chosen. The bridge will be fairly hard wood, usually maple. The holes should be the size of the core of the screws so that only the threads are cutting into the wood. I drill in two stages: a small hole for the threaded portion and a slightly larger hole for the threadless shank.

7 Glue the bridge back in, using piano-maker's glue (see *Useful contacts*).

8 Ask a helper to hold the bridge in place from the front while you put the screws in and tighten them up. Put a large button washer on each screw (see **8d.8**).

9 After leaving the glue overnight to dry, reattach the bass strings.

10 Retune the whole piano. (Removing and refitting the bass strings will almost certainly affect the treble strings too.)

I have never encountered this problem in a grand piano but it can't be ruled out. The procedure would be the same as for an upright, but grands are generally much more straightforward to work on.

Detached bass bridges

Photo 8d.9 shows a 'double jeopardy' situation – a shelf detached from the soundboard, and the bridge cap detached from the shelf. (The exposed clean wood shows where both ought to be.) The whole bass section produced just pathetic scraping noises. No screws were used during construction; had they been, it's unlikely either part would have failed. This piano was beyond economic repair for other reasons, but making good the bridge damage wouldn't have been difficult. Both shelf and bridge cap could have been removed to a workbench, repaired with screws inserted, then replaced as described above. Probably two to three hours' work for a technician.

8d.9

CHAPTER 9

Grand piano maintenance

With one irksome proviso – the need to repeatedly remove and refit the keyframe assembly – most grands are straightforward to repair. Age takes its toll after 30–100 years, but until then only pianos kept in the wrong environment (for example, being slowly baked by a school hall radiator) are likely to be in seriously bad condition. In most cases, surprisingly little work is needed to get an ailing grand playing well.

🎹 A grand piano – or is it?

Grand pianos are usually better made and better looked after than uprights, which means they tend to survive longer. Unfortunately, some owners make a false virtue of the age of their grand pianos, treasuring them when they really ought to chuck them. I'm often called out to tune a grand, only to find a large piece of furniture beyond any hope of resurrection as a serious musical instrument.

Therefore, an important question to answer before doing anything to an older grand has to be: is the piano in good enough *playing* condition to justify any work at all? Consult a tuner or technician, or another player, if you don't know for sure. There is no room for sentiment here. It's pointless dismantling a grand piano if it's going to be impossible to make it sound any better no matter what you do, short of a total rebuild.

Take a note

One of your most useful tools will be a pen and paper. An important first step towards correcting grand piano problems is to note – literally, in writing – what those problems are, precisely which parts of the piano they affect, and what you're going to do about them. Work on a grand isn't to be hurried, which allows scope for forgetting some of the reasons you ever started. And with the action out so often, you may have to rely on written notes for details you can't re-check by playing the piano.

Early diagnosis

Ageing grands share pretty much the same problems as ageing uprights. The procedures for fixing them are similar too. It's just actually doing the work that is different.

The most common problems with grands are compression of the balance rail washers, moth attack, and incorrect action regulation. The procedure for diagnosis is:

Balance rail washers

- Kneel down and look at the keyboard. Does it dip in the middle? If yes, you've got compression of the balance rail washers.
- To confirm the condition, look inside the piano while you play a few keys in the centre of the dip. If you've got washer compression, the hammers will bounce and not come to a definite stop on the backchecks. (If a hammer actually strikes twice, this is called 'blubbering'.)
- Measure the key dip – that is, how far the affected keys go down – using a steel rule. The minimum is $^3/_8$in (9.5mm) but many pianos are $^7/_{16}$in (11mm). Measure it in different parts

of the keyboard, and measure both black key dip and white key dip. Note especially the measurements for keys working correctly, as detailed below in *Action regulation*. It may be that only notes at the extremes of the keyboard are working correctly. *Write down your measurements!*

- Measure the exact distance from the tips of the hammers to the strings by sliding a ruler down between the strings. It will originally have been $1^7/_8$ to 2in (45.7–50.8mm). Note whether they are regular – that is, all the same height – or not.
- Go along checking how each key plays. In fact, play the instrument for some time. Listen for any rattling or clattering, any slowness, any dampers not doing their stuff. *Write down* which keys or regions of the piano have faults.

Moth attack

- If looking at the keyboard from a kneeling position reveals highly irregular key levels, there is almost certainly moth attack. But to confirm this, you'll have to remove all keys and

check the condition of the keybed felt. You can't do this yet (see step 34 below) but it's something to look forward to…

Action regulation

- Sampling across the keyboard, *slowly* depress a few keys in turn.
- Each hammer should rise until it is $^1/_{16}$in (2mm) from the string, then drop back $^1/_{16}$in.
- While sampling and pressing keys very slowly, can you feel the point where the jack is coming out from under the roller? (See the description of how the grand action works in Chapter 2.) At this point, can you hear any scraping noises? If so, more black lead is needed (step 32).
- After a note has been *firmly* played, the hammers should stop $^5/_8$in (15.8mm) from the strings.
- When the key is released a *little* from this position, the hammer should rise a little.
- The damper should start to lift from the string when the hammer is halfway up through its stroke.
- List any keys that don't comply with each of these conditions, as they'll need adjusting.

Beware action regulation misdiagnosis!

■ Do some notes work intermittently or not at all? And does investigation reveal that, as the key is depressed, the backcheck holds the back of the hammer and doesn't let it rise? If so, it's tempting to bend the backcheck back slightly (see **9.1** and **9.2**), and I often work on grands where this has been done. The note may indeed work again, but in all probability the real problem has been missed. The root cause is nearly always some form of lost motion in the action, which can only be cured by following all the regulation procedures below.

Now the fun starts. Compared with an upright, doing anything to the action of a grand is complex. In the first place the action is screwed down to the keyframe, over the top of the keys, so that you can't remove a single key without first removing the whole

keyframe and then taking the action off the keyframe. (For example, if just one slightly low key needs just one paper balance rail shim under it, the job will take even an experienced technician half an hour or more, compared with 20 seconds for an upright.)

Remove the keyframe assembly

1 Have a workbench or table ready to receive the keyframe assembly. (The folding keyboard stand shown in **9.3** does the job well enough and handily exposes the bottom of the action for cleaning. Note that the stand is set slightly higher than the keybed. This will encourage you to lift the assembly enough on removal – step 11 – to avoid scraping the front of the piano and spoiling your day.)

2 Remove the fallboard. It usually has a brass slot called a fall plate at each end (**9.4**), which drops over a steel or brass pin projecting from the casework at each swivel point (**9.5**). (This pin has a slotted head for screwing in and adjustment, and a recessed washer to stop it going too far into the wood.) Pull the fallboard up a little until it comes free, then pull it outwards. However, in some grands – for example Steinways – the

fallboard can't be removed without first removing the keyblocks (step 7): it comes out with them still attached.

3 Take great care not to scratch any polished casework, and place the fallboard on a sound, non-scratch surface. Watch out for spring mechanisms and 'soft fall' mechanisms, especially on modern Yamahas. They're usually at the bass end. Examine the inside of the

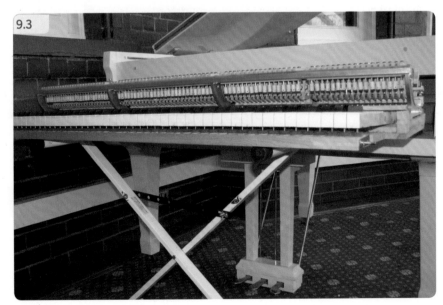

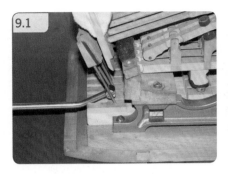

'cheeks' – the casework right next to the fallboard ends – for scratches from earlier removal. Some fallboards are a very tight fit and the piano will bear the scars. If there is such evidence, remove the fittings and sand a little off the fallboard ends to make it a better fit. Make sure you sand just the ends: sanding is fraught because both top and underside of the fallboard are visible and polished, but it's unsatisfactory simply to replace a binding fallboard and leave it until its next cycle of removal damage.

4 Lift the front section of the lid back over the rear section. Safety first: check that the hinge pins are present and fully home *before* raising the lid!

5 Raise the lid on to the highest prop available. (Most older pianos have only one prop but modern ones have two or three at different heights.)

6 Remove the music desk. It usually slides forward and out, but expect some kind of safety mechanism to stop it coming right out too easily. Feel for it; most are overcome by lifting one end vertically. **9.6** shows a typical brass guide rail mechanism (on the right, screwed to the casework) on which the desk slides.

7 Remove the keyblocks, the chunks of wood at the end of the keyboard, just inside the cheeks. Look under the piano. There is usually a huge thumbscrew, or similar fastening, right through the bottom of the keybed into the middle of each keyblock. Check that you're on the correct screw, as there may be several others around there.

8 With the blocks removed, the keyslip will usually drop out, or lift out if it has dowel pegs. The keyslip is normally held in place by a 'snag' (**9.7**) that mates, jigsaw-like, with a cut-out on the keyblock. **9.8** shows the keyslip and snag *in situ* and the treble keyblock

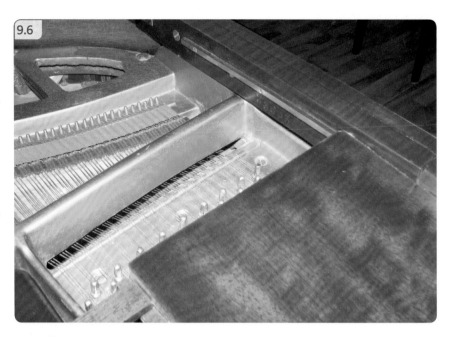

9.6

9.7

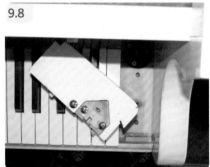

9.8

on its side, waiting to be dropped in, its angled cut-out at bottom right. (Note that some grands have several screws under the front edge of the keybed, going up through it and into the keyslip. These must be removed.)

The keybed will now be exposed, typically as in **9.9**. You'll just about see a steel pin projecting from the end of the keyframe assembly. This and its counterpart at the treble end stop the action from moving backwards and forwards in the piano, but do allow it to move sideways to enable the *una corda* mechanism to operate, if there is one. **9.10** shows a treble end keyblock recessed to fit over the steel pin. The screw into the block limits the movement of the *una corda* mechanism, and the dowel peg correctly locates the block.

9.9

9.10

9.11

case, raise it slightly to avoid damage to the polished surface, especially from any glides (see below). Lifting the assembly is ideally a two-person job; it can be done alone, but it's then harder to hold it balanced.

12 Place the keyframe assembly on your prepared work surface.

13 In the cavity where the keyframe assembly used to be, check that the dampers are working and that all visible screws are tight. **9.16** shows the damper levers and the sustain pedal mechanism. When in the piano, the back ends of the keys fit under the small green baize cushions.

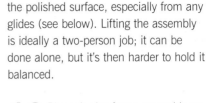
9.14

9 The keyframe of grands without *una corda* may be screwed into the case with two or three screws, usually visible along the front. Remove them. **9.11** shows the keyframe ready to be removed to a workbench.

10 Now check that all the hammers are down in the rest position and that none is raised at all – not even slightly.

Before going any further, beware! About one in five of the grand pianos I see have had repairs to an end hammer that broke off during keyframe removal. Take care that this doesn't happen to you. Grand hammer shanks are much more complicated than upright shanks – see **9.12** and **9.13** – and so have to be replaced rather than repaired. For that reason, a properly equipped technician carries at all times a few new grand hammer shanks and related bits and pieces – flanges,

rollers, spare hammers. **9.14** shows the keyframe assembly coming out, and the removal battle being won.

11 Grab the steel projections and start to manoeuvre the action out. Because this is a big reach for the average-sized person, be careful that you don't spread your hands over the end few keys at either end. If you *even slightly* touch the end keys, their hammers will rise slightly. As the action comes forward, usually taking quite a strong pull, any hammer raised *by the smallest amount* will snap off. There is only the tiniest clearance under the wrest plank and cast iron frame – see **9.15**. As the keyframe assembly goes over the front edge of the

9.12

9.13

9.15

9.16

9.17

9.18

These damper levers move on flanges screwed to a rail behind the felt-edged strip that limits the upward movement of the levers. This is held in place by two large screws with washers under their heads. A technician's worst nightmare is finding just one sticking flange in a piano of this type, because the only way to get to it is to remove all the dampers. No wonder one sometimes finds terrible repairs like **9.17**; in this old Steinway concert grand, someone has attached lead weights to the dampers to push them back down, rather than face such lengthy disassembly for a simple repair. This merits sympathy but not acquittal. It would certainly send the player home more exhausted than usual.

14 The damper wires pass through a felt bushed hole that holds them vertically – see **9.18**. If you find a damper sticking in the up position or going down only slowly, pray that the problem is this bush and not the flange (see immediately above). Bushes are more accessible and are repaired like centre pin bushings (see Chapter 8, section B.)

15 Check that the dampers line up to the strings. To fix the misaligned damper that I assume you can spot in **9.19**, find its damper wire retainer flange (**9.20**) and undo the screw

until the damper head is loose enough to both rotate and move vertically in the flange. Adjust the height and alignment of the damper to match its neighbours and tighten the flange screw back up. Now check the rest, because it's unlikely that just this one is loose.

A cleaning interlude

If the keyframe assembly hasn't left the piano for a long time, there will be lots of accumulated dust and debris in the cavity and in the action itself, as you'll see in several of the photos. In school pianos, crisp bags and petrified sandwich morsels are almost inevitable in the cavity, while pencils are common in the action: a raised fallboard acts as a chute to convey them there.

■ Vacuum it all out but be careful not to suck any felt from its moorings, or any parts from the damper mechanism

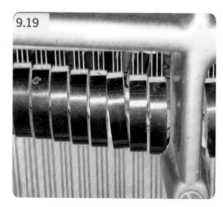

9.19

lurking right at the back of the cavity.
■ Clean the keybed with the finest grade of wire wool available, then vacuum it again.
■ Look out for traces of French chalk or candle grease (used to lubricate the keyframe on pianos with an *una corda* pedal). Clean it off. Sometimes, both chalk and candle grease have been used in the mistaken belief that two lubricants are better than one. Together they form doughy glue – a terrible mess to remove.

Now the activity moves to your work surface.

16 Check that all hammers line up correctly to the strings. Very often they don't. You'll know from the hammer wear: the grooves won't be central. Some trichord hammers may have only two grooves, or a groove right on the edge of

9.20

the hammer that causes lopsided wear as in **9.21**. In this sample of trichord hammers, one is striking only two strings and a number are striking at the very edge of the hammer. This may result in poor sound quality and wear on both the hammer and the flange centre pin and bearing. If all or most of the hammers have grooves too far to the right, the problem is with the *una corda* pedal, so go to step 21.

17 To centralise the hammers, undo the flange screw a little, then move the hammer to the correct

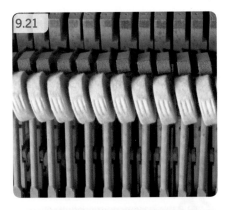

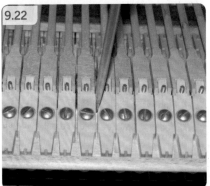

position while tightening the screw back up. (There is a special tool for spacing hammers that I don't use. I simply line up a hammer, then wedge the tip of a second screwdriver between its flange and the flange next door to the right – see **9.22**. The flange will tend to move to the right as its screw is tightened; the second screwdriver prevents this, as long as you first make sure that the flange to the right is itself tight!)

18 You may find that a hammer is evenly spaced at rest but has misaligned grooves on its face. Problem: the hammer is not travelling quite vertically. Solution: put a tiny strip of thin paper under the flange on the side towards which the hammer is veering. This shimming tips the flange up slightly and should correct the motion. (And if you find any shims like this under other flanges, *put them back*; now you know why they're there.)

19 If a great deal of hammer adjustment is necessary, put the keyframe assembly back into the piano when you're done, and observe each hammer closely to ensure that it strikes all strings squarely.

20 Further fine adjustment can be carried out by pulling the keyframe assembly out just far enough

to get at the hammer flange screws – but when returning the keyframe assembly to a piano with an *una corda* mechanism you'll meet resistance from the *una corda* return spring (**9.23**). Keep the assembly square and keep pushing: it will suddenly spring in. Warning: As with removal, do not depress any keys *by even the slightest amount* when returning the keyframe assembly.

The *una corda* pedal (if there is one)

21 With the keyframe assembly back in the piano, check the working of the *una corda* pedal. Depressing it should shift the whole keyframe assembly to the right, so that one less string is struck in both the bichords and trichords. Make sure it slides easily, lubricating with French chalk if necessary. If step 16 brought you straight here, the *una corda* buffer is at fault. This is a strip of felt in the bass end between the keybed and the keyframe assembly, shown in **9.24**. If it has become compressed or moth-eaten, the return spring will push the keyframe assembly too far to the left, causing all the hammers to be out of line. Replace it, or shim it until it maximises the number of hammers striking correctly. The rest can then be aligned as in step 17.

Level the keyboard

As with uprights, this is done by adding or subtracting paper shims under the balance rail washers. With luck and a new set of washers, only a few should need any shimming.

It's customary in grands to anticipate future wear by giving the keyboard a slight crown – that is, leaving the middle key of the piano (E above middle C) very slightly higher than those at the two ends. Levelling is done with a straight edge in two stages: from middle E to the bass end, and from middle E to the treble end. The slopes should be so slight as to be perceptible only to those expecting to see them. The white keys are levelled first, then the black keys.

With the action removed, the natural inclination of the keys in most grand pianos is to flop forward into the down position. To level the keys, you have a choice of method:

■ Weight them at the back so that they are in the 'up' position. You can buy special small weights that clip temporarily on to the backchecks, thus holding the keys up at the front. But I just use old scientific scale weights with a blob of easily releasable adhesive such as Blu-Tack under each. In **9.33**, A1 is weighted so that its front is in the normal playing position. You'll need a lot of weights because half of the whites at a time have to be weighted to carry out the levelling described above.

■ Insert card shims (standard paper shims used for regulation will do) on the front pins under A1 and middle E to wedge them in their correct position *allowing for the crown*, then span a straight edge across the very front of them. Now gently hold down the back end of each unwedged white key in succession. Any key that doesn't touch the straight edge needs paper shims under its balance rail washers until it does. Repeat the procedure three times – for the treble white, the bass black and the treble black keys.

Set the key dip for each key

Once the keyboard is level, the key dip – how far a key moves from up to down – can be checked. Measure the key dip for a wide selection of keys across the keyboard, using a steel rule.

Since the keys have been levelled, and the balance rail washers replaced or shimmed up as part of levelling, they should have approximately the correct key dip. But once you're satisfied that some are correct, you need to ensure that they're all exactly the same as each other. If during early diagnosis (page 154) you were able to work out the original key dip from keys known to be working correctly, stick with that measurement as the 'correct' key dip. But if in doubt, use $7/16$in (11mm) as your 'correct' key dip.

If key dip is uneven, the front rail is implicated, so:

■ If keys are very uneven, replace the front rail washers.

■ If keys are only a little uneven, add or subtract paper washers under the front rail washers until the key dip is even.

In an upright, each individual key can be worked on and tested 'live' – that is, with the action in the piano. On a grand you have to do all the work with the action removed, and the only way to test individual keys is to put the whole lot back together and into the piano and try it. Therefore, for accuracy, speed and consistency I use a key dip gauge, simply a block available in different thicknesses – most commonly $7/16$in (11mm) – that is held on the key. **9.34** shows one in use. The key is depressed and shims are added or subtracted from under the front rail washer until the top of the block is level with the keys on either side. The keys need to be weighted as described in *Level the keyboard* (above), or you can go along holding down the back ends of three adjacent white keys so that their fronts are in the up position. Release the middle one, put the key dip gauge on it and press lightly down.

There is a special tool for the black keys, but I simply measure how far down the ones I know to be correct (from *Early diagnosis*) go, and set the rest to this by measuring each one.

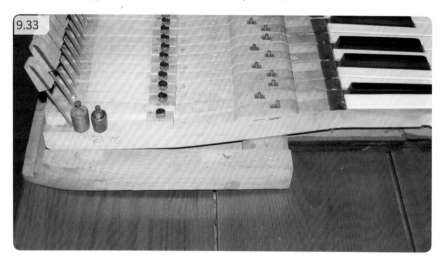

9.33

9.34

Action tasks

1 With the action and keyboard still separated, check the condition of all centre pins. Chapter 8, section D, *Centre pins* explains how to recentre upright action parts. The technique is the same for grands. The typical grand action has five centre pin joints per note. As numbered in **9.35**, these pins are on:

1 The hammer flange.
2 The repetition lever.
3 The jack itself.
4 The whippen flange.
5 The damper lever flange.
6 The damper wire flange.
7 The sostenuto flange (if present – most grands don't have one).
8 The repetition spring bearing.

2 Check that the jacks are central (from side to side) in the whippen. If they're not, you'll have to gently prise them off the flange to which they're glued, and re-glue them – though it may be possible to melt the glue *in situ* just enough with a soldering iron to move it a little, then let the glue reset. **9.36** shows the first four (square, black) jack heads in this piano, revealed by lifting the hammers. **9.37** shows the jack in its correct position.

3 In most grands the repetition spring rides in a slot. Press a few repetition levers up and down and listen for any noise. If the black lead has worn off or the wood is rough, clean both slot and spring. Unfortunately, this can only be done by dismantling the action and removing each whippen, which is a lot of work. For comparison, **9.38** shows a new repetition spring assembly with black lead on it, while **9.39** shows an old one with no black lead and so plenty of squeak potential.

Now put the keyboard and action back together. Once you have correctly set up the keyboard and action, screw the action back on to the keyframe. You can now start regulating the action to the keyboard.

9.36

9.37

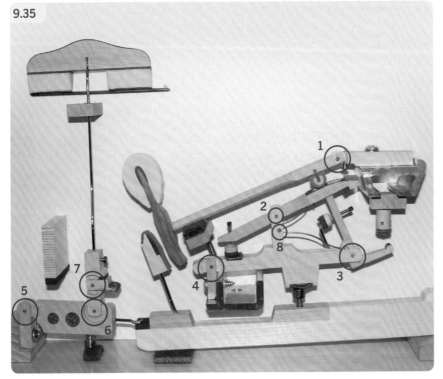

9.35

9.38

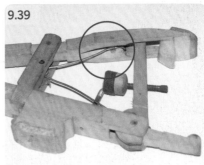

9.39

Regulation

Most grand pianos will, at this point, play perfectly well. The balance rail is the weakest link in the system and likely to be the only thing malfunctioning even after decades of playing. Having put this right, little else should need serious attention – but for the record, we'll now consider every aspect of regulation.

Adjust the jacks

At rest, the jacks *must* point straight at the wooden core of the roller. The leading edge (that is, the hammer side) of the jack should point up the leading edge of the roller core as shown in **9.40**. In **9.41** the repetition lever is held down to expose the top of the jack. Lift all the hammers back, then work along dropping one at a time. This way, each jack can be examined in turn.

■ If any jacks point slightly back, the affected keys will feel spongy or may not go down at all. Worst of all, they may malfunction slightly – but only occasionally and unpredictably.

■ If any point slightly forward, the piano may work but not produce sound at full volume.

■ The position at rest is regulated by means of the screw and felt red button shown in **9.41**.

Adjust the repetition lever

The jack should be just the tiniest amount (0.003in, 0.075mm) below the top of the repetition lever.

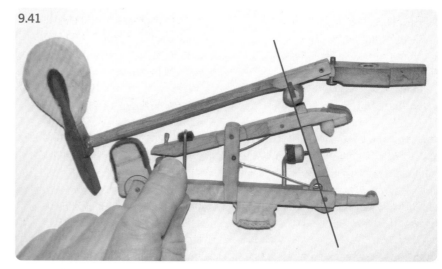

Let-off rack workbench

After regulating the action and putting the whole keyframe assembly back together, there's a good chance you'll have to haul it out again to make minor adjustments to the key level and key dip. This is perhaps the most annoying aspect of working on grand pianos: minor adjustment means major upheaval. The upside is that a grand should need this kind of attention only once in its lifetime after the original factory set-up. This encourages one to be philosophical about it all.

To make work on a grand piano a lot easier, a professional workbench can be bought that has a built-in let-off rack. This is a series of adjustable wooden crosspieces that can be set at precisely the same height as the strings above the action of the piano you're working on. It thus mimics the effect of playing the piano and allows much more adjustment to be carried out without repeatedly installing and removing the keyframe assembly. A free-standing version can be bought that is simply placed behind the hammers on a workbench, but you can make one yourself much more cheaply – see my own in 9.42. Though you can do most of the jobs described here without a let-off rack, work will be easier and your mood much improved if you invest in one or make your own.

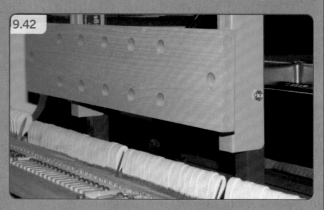

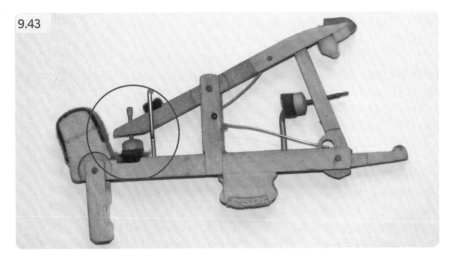

9.43

- If the jack is too high, it won't be able to return under the roller and fast repetition will be impaired.
- If the roller is worn – that is, indented by the jack – there will be lost motion.

The repetition lever can be lowered to compensate for this wear. The most common means of adjustment is a tiny screw at the back of the repetition lever, under a felt-covered button – see **9.43**. Turning the screw clockwise will expose more of the jack, and vice versa. Don't overdo this compensation or the piano will feel spongy. With the hammer at rest, the jack must be able to slide back under the roller. Test it by pushing it out with a finger.

A different type of adjustment is shown in **9.36**. The screw is on top of the lever, identified by its green felt and red leather washers.

Hammer height

The distance from the hammer tips at rest to the strings should be $1^7/_8$–2in (45.7–50.8mm). Different makes differ slightly, so base any work you do on the measurements you took during early diagnosis (page 154). The distance will have increased a little if the hammers have been refaced.

The hammers may already be in a straight line at the correct height, or they may be irregular in height.

1 With the keyframe assembly in the piano, push a ruler down between the strings and note which ones are around the right height.

2 Check that these are playing correctly, but bear in mind that we haven't completed the regulation yet. Remove the keyframe assembly. Back to the workbench.

3 Look for the brass adjustment capstan on the key that pushes the whippen up: the whippens rest on the capstans. **9.44** shows the back end of a single key, the backcheck and the capstan, and **9.40** shows the capstan under the whippen.

4 Adjust the height of all hammers to the correct height for your piano, using a capstan tool. Use a straight edge if you need to, or use a let-off rack lowered down close to the hammers as a straight edge.

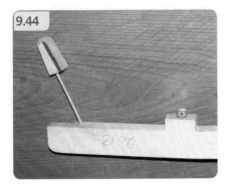

9.44

Hammer rest rail

Next, look at the hammer rest rail (the thick green felt strip in **9.45**). If the felt has been heavily grooved by the hammer shanks, replace it – though it may be possible to give it a new lease of life by moving it along a little so that each shank faces an uncompressed piece of felt.

The hammers at rest should *not* rest on the rest rail! Perverse though this seems, the rest rail functions only as a cushion for the hammers to bounce off during forceful playing. If it has hardened it may become noisy and needs replacing. This is easy: just lift all the hammers and rip it off. Measure it accurately, send off for new felt and replace it using fabric glue.

The shanks at rest should be about $1/_8$ in (3.1mm) above the rest rail. If the height is set correctly but the gap between the rest rail and hammer shanks is too great or too small, replace the felt with the correct size.

All that said, be prepared for differences from my generic description. For example, instead of a rest rail some grands have a small rest pad built into the whippen for each separate hammer – like the Broadwood whippen shown in **9.41**; the hammer rests on the white pad covered with blue-grey felt. Replacing each of these individually will be a lot more time-consuming and fiddly. (If they're uniformly worn, you can try raising them by making small patches of felt to go over the old ones. If they're irregularly worn, you'll have to replace the lot.)

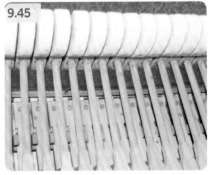

9.45

9.46

Regulate the set-off

The jack should come out from under the roller when the hammer is $\frac{1}{16}$in (1.5mm) away from the string. Set-off is regulated in most grand pianos by means of a bobbin-like wooden capstan that can be worked on with the action in place. **9.46** shows an array of them, but be prepared for other types of adjuster.

Depress each hammer slowly; it should jump at set-off. If set-off is more than $\frac{1}{16}$in (1.5mm), screw the capstan up (clockwise looking from below). If it's less than $\frac{1}{16}$in, screw the capstan down (anticlockwise from below). It should only ever need a tiny adjustment. (If set-off is *uniformly* at more than $\frac{1}{16}$in, the piano may have been deliberately quietened down: for example, if it's a big piano in a small house. If it's *irregularly* incorrect, inspect the condition of the felt on the capstans.)

To do this job with maximum rather than merely acceptable accuracy, you'll need a workbench of the type described in *Let-off rack workbench* (page 164) and shown in **9.42**.

1 Adjust the rack so that the cross spar is exactly $\frac{1}{16}$in (1. 5mm) below where the strings would be.

2 Over-adjust the set-off (turning clockwise) until the hammer blocks against the spar of the bench.

3 Hold the key firmly, but not too hard, with the hammer blocked against the spar. Screw the set-off slowly down (anticlockwise) until the hammer drops off the wood. Repeat for each hammer.

This procedure will give you an extremely accurate and consistent regulation.

Drop screw adjustment

Still on the let-off rack, set the spar back to string height. (Without a let-off rack this is a tedious job, as the action has to be taken out repeatedly to carry out the adjustment.)

1 Slowly depress a key. It should let off at $\frac{1}{16}$in (1.5 mm), then drop back another $\frac{1}{16}$in, thus coming to rest $\frac{1}{8}$in (3mm) from the strings.

2 If it doesn't, adjust the drop screw to the correct setting. This is a highly unusual screw with a slotless domed head that comes right through the hammer butt. It checks upward movement of the repetition lever just before the hammer strikes the strings. When the key is played slowly, it limits how far the hammer drops after set-off. You adjust the 'pointed' end of the screw (**9.47**), which has either a slot that can be worked with a very small screwdriver, or a head that can be worked with the set-off adjuster in the multi-tool kit.

Backcheck adjustment

Backchecks should rarely need adjustment: just enough at some time in their working life to allow for wear. They are felt- or leather-covered wooden blocks mounted on a thick wire on the back ends of the keys. If the hammer has struck the strings and the key is held down, the hammer bounces back and is caught on the backcheck. It is then ready for rapid repetition and is said to be 'in check'.

9.44 shows a single backcheck on a disembodied key, while **9.40** shows how the A1 backcheck relates to its hammer. (This is one of the two end keys – the only ones that can be photographed easily.)

1 With the keyframe assembly either in the piano or in the let-off rack set at correct string height, play each key firmly.

2 The hammers should come to rest ('in check') $\frac{5}{8}$in (16mm) from the strings.

3 Regulate the correct 'in check' distance by using a checkwire bender tool from the multi-kit to bend the backcheck wire. (A problem here is that the hammer must actually strike something to make it check correctly, and this adjustment can't be done with the keyframe in the piano. A let-off rack is therefore essential.)

4 Bend the backcheck wires inward to raise the rest position, outward to lower it. It's important that the backcheck felt and the hammer tail meet in parallel (albeit a curved parallel), presenting a large area to each other. If misalignment results in too small an area of contact, the backcheck will rapidly wear and go out of adjustment; and if the backcheck felt is badly worn, it

9.47

will be impossible to make the piano play smoothly. You may therefore need to adjust the backcheck in two stages: first bend it near the bottom, bringing it forward more than necessary (**9.48**), and then bend the top back a little to preserve this parallel meeting (**9.49**).

5 Verify that the backchecks are straight and line up with the hammers. (In small grands the backchecks may be at acute angles to match the overstringing. Over time they commonly end up fouling the hammers on adjacent notes.)

Repetition springs

1 Play any key so that it checks, then release it very slowly. The hammer should rise just a little. If it doesn't rise, the repetition spring is too weak. If it jumps, the spring is too strong.

2 Pull any malfunctioning spring out of its slot and either bend it slightly to increase or decrease its tension, or use the screw adjuster if it's like the Welmar action in **9.36**. The adjuster is the smallest size of screw visible, just above the small, red felt ringed centre pin that holds the spring in. The spring curls around the centre pin and its end is under the screw, so that as you tighten the screw, the spring tension increases.

Not all springs will be like this. For example, **9.41** shows the spring in a Broadwood. It is mounted on a cord bushing at one end, then goes round a centre pin, and finally into a groove on the jack. The tension in it can be increased or decreased only by bending it with a wire-bending tool from the multi-tool kit.

3 Any broken or corroded springs, or any whose tension can't be raised sufficiently, will have to be replaced. This means dismantling the whole action and recentring each affected spring. If you find a significant number this far gone, it makes sense to replace every spring in the piano, as more will probably soon be in the same condition.

4 When replacing springs into their slots, make sure there is no inadvertent sideways bending that could cause them to become dislodged later.

Keystrip

Most grands have a strip of wood, normally cushioned with felt, running the length of the compass and just visible under the front of the keys – see the bottom of **9.25**. This keystrip is simply to stop keys bouncing up too far during furious playing. It should not quite touch the keys, and is adjusted by slightly tightening or loosening the three or four nuts holding it in place – one of which is visible in **9.25**. There are usually nuts under the strip to set the height, and nuts over the strip to hold it down. Don't tighten it down too much or it will start to depress the keys.

Dampers

When the keyframe assembly is back in the piano:

1 Play each key in turn, watching the dampers. Each damper should start to rise when the key is about half way down. Write a list of any keys where this isn't happening.

2 Remove the keyframe assembly again. Adjust the dampers, depending on the type of damper mechanism in your piano.

There are several different types of damper operating mechanism:

1 Most commonly, the back of the key simply lifts a lever that raises the damper. The wooden contact surfaces between key and lever are usually felt-covered, and thinning of this felt is the most probable cause of a damper rising late, or not far enough. The felt is usually on the damper lever, as in **9.20**, but in some pianos it's on the key. If many dampers are affected, replace all the worn felt with new felt of the correct thickness. If only one or two dampers are affected, remove the felt, glue a paper shim under it, and replace the felt.

2 Some pianos have a screw adjuster, which is much better; in fact, it rarely needs attention. There is usually a felt-covered rail limiting the rise height of the dampers. If the dampers don't reach it, they quiver visibly when a note is played. There are different adjusting mechanisms for these. Some are very difficult to access.

3 And then there are the oddities, too many and too rare to spare space for here. I once worked on a grand with dampers operated by metal spoons, rather like a typical upright mechanism but made of thinner wire than is usual. Years of hard work had gradually bent them until the dampers weren't lifting off the strings and the notes in the middle hardly sounded at all. This was easy to remedy, but the outlook wasn't good: bending them back almost certainly weakened the spoons even more, hastening recurrence of the problem. Eventually, the only option would be to replace the spoons with some made of thicker wire, if any were available.

Regulate the sustain and half-blow pedals

The dampers should start to lift at almost the same instant as the sustain pedal starts to go down. Any free play can be eliminated with the adjuster, a typical example of which is shown in **9.27**.

We have already regulated the *una corda* but some lesser grands may have a half-blow soft pedal, rather like some uprights. When the pedal is depressed, a felt-covered rail, which usually acts as the rest rail as well, lifts the hammers halfway through their stroke. If this is out of adjustment it won't lift them enough. The rail should start to lift just after the pedal starts to go down. If there is a lag, adjustment is needed.

On some grands with this mechanism the keys will, disconcertingly, drop a little when this pedal is depressed. If the key bushings are worn they may wobble as well. This is nothing to worry about; as explained earlier, in most grands the keys at rest tend to dip unless the action is holding them up, so it's simply gravity at work.

Any other business

Lyre rod

A common problem with grand pianos – mentioned in Chapter 5 – is the absence of a lyre rod. (It's most usually mislaid during moving.) The rod is usually brass but may be wood – in which case, it will be a wooden dowel at least half an inch (13mm) thick and so easily replaced.

Most brass lyre rods have plain ends and can also be replaced easily, with brass rod of a suitable diameter – usually $^{3}/_{8}$ – $^{7}/_{16}$in (9.5–11.1mm) – from a DIY store. The length must be absolutely correct, so take great care when measuring: cut it even a tiny bit too short and the rod is scrap. The rod locates in holes and can only be fitted by first loosening the large thumbscrews holding the lyre. As they're tightened back up, the rod is pushed tightly into place.

9.50

Unfortunately, on some pianos the lyre rod is custom-designed and incorporates a hinge or bracket or both. For example, **9.50**, which shows a modern Kawai's double brass lyre rods with hinged brackets on both ends. Replacement may be straightforward if the piano is still a current or supported model; otherwise, ingenuity and orthopaedic surgery may be needed.

The really important thing is that the piano must have a rod. Without this vital flying buttress, the casework will suffer serious damage. The pedals will appear to work satisfactorily, if a little floppily. In fact, the lyre will be acting as a long lever against its own retaining bolts, and energy from the player's foot on the pedals will gradually prise the bolts out of the casework. You may not be aware of this until it's too late, but you'll be all too aware of the resulting repair bill for skilled carpentry.

Replace any broken strings

The procedure for replacing broken strings is the same for grands as for uprights – see Chapter 8, section C.

Replace a few (and only a few!) loose tuning pins

If any tuning pins are loose, fitting oversize replacements is much more challenging than fitting them into an upright. In fact, if a significant number of pins is loose, the piano needs replacing or rebuilding. Therefore, use the following procedure only if you have no more than a handful of loose pins to deal with. Otherwise, don't

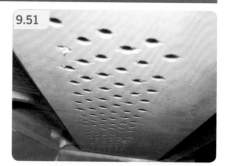
9.51

9.52

bother; instead, get a professional opinion on the state of the piano.

The wrest plank in a grand is suspended under the frame (see **9.51**) and held in place by large screws going through the top of the frame. (For example, in the Steinway model C shown in **9.52** the two large bolts at the front, the screw between the 'C' and the serial number, and the screws just about visible through the dust under the strings, all go through to the plank.) You take out a loose pin just as described for uprights in Chapter 8, section C – but from then on, it's different. If you were to blithely hammer in a new oversize pin you'd most

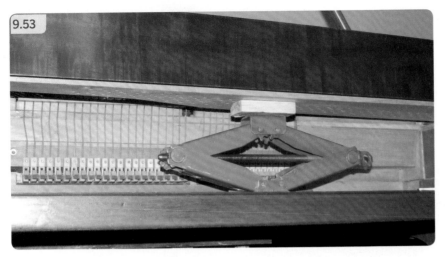

9.53

9.55

likely punch an ugly, splintered volcano shape out of the other side of the plank. You might even split the plank, causing colossal damage.

What you must do instead is position a small (3 x 2in, or 75 x 50mm) but sturdy piece of timber under the area you're working on, and force it up against the bottom of the plank using a vehicle scissors jack, as in **9.53**. This will stop any splintering. You can buy a special tool resembling a scaled-down vehicle bottle jack, but I can't see any advantage over a scissors jack.)

The keybed base in most grand pianos is sturdy enough to take this load. However, during a rebuild I take the belt-and-braces measure of putting a second scissors jack under the keybed, positioned on a couple of beer crates (or milk crates if you prefer). Position a piece of stout timber between jack and keybed to spread the load, then raise this jack until it's about to lift the piano. Thus, any superfluous force applied to the pin goes straight through the piano and into the floor. I then judge it safe to hammer in oversize pins.

How oversize? I explain about pin sizes in Chapter 8, section C. Go up one size unless the original was very loose, in which case try going up two sizes. *Do not use a*

9.54

longer pin in a grand. Using the correct punch – that is, one that fits over the head of the pin (see **9.54**) – hammer the pin home to the same level as those around it. Then turn it back the number of turns of wire you're going to put on it – again as explained in Chapter 8, section C.

From now on the procedure for adjusting tuning pins, and for tuning generally, is the same as for uprights.

Replacing hammers

If the hammers are badly worn they'll have to be replaced; but if the hammers are worn out it's likely that almost all the action parts will be worn out too. Hammer replacement is therefore most likely to be part of a complete rebuild, which is beyond the scope of this book. See the Bibliography if you're interested in rebuilding.

For the record, hammer replacement procedure is similar to that described for uprights in Chapter 8, section B. The main difference is that in grands, the shank comes right through the head of the hammer and can be seen on the top of it. Old hammers are removed by pushing the shank out (if they're going back on) or cutting it off (if they're being replaced). See **9.55**, noting that the tool I use is in fact a modified small G-clamp: the load spreader is removed and a 'U' shape drilled out of the clamp head. The professional tool looks much more sophisticated and is more expensive but does the job no better.

Replacing grand hammers is made quite a lot more complicated than uprights by the need to:

- Precisely align the backchecks and hammers.
- Achieve exactly the right texture on the *back* of the hammers (too smooth and they won't check, too rough and they won't let go).
- (Probably) shape the new hammers to stop them fouling each other during playing.

Detached 'shelf' bridges

Detached 'shelf' bridges (Chapter 8, section D) are a problem that mainly affects uprights. I've never encountered one in a grand piano but it could happen. The procedure would be the same as for an upright, but with less difficulty because the bass bridge of a grand is much more accessible. The only significant difference is:

- When removing bass strings, lift them on to an old blanket or similar so that they can't damage or scratch the soundboard.
- Take extra care not to damage or misalign the dampers.

In larger grands the bass bridge is not a shelf but is screwed or glued (or both) directly on to the soundboard. Bridge detachment is then highly unlikely.

CHAPTER 10

Tuning your own piano

If you have a natural or trained musical ear – and that's a fairly big 'if', as not many people are so lucky – you can tune your own piano. Whether you will want to is a different matter. Taming the occasional delinquent string is easy enough, but taking on over 200 of them at once is much more daunting. Read this chapter and find out how to do it – then view your professional tuner with new respect.

1: How sound behaves in a piano

To tune a piano it helps to understand the basic physics of sound generation. The full story is far more complex but most of it won't help anyone tune a piano.

The source of sound in a piano is a vibrating string stretched over two points which define its playing (or 'speaking') length. One of those points is a wooden bridge that transmits the vibrations into the soundboard, which serves to amplify the sound.

A string hit by a hammer first vibrates back and forth. Then the plane of vibration starts to rotate, changing constantly. Under magnification, it can be seen as a blur.

The rate at which a string vibrates is its *frequency*. This is measured in full cycles backwards and forwards and is expressed as *cycles per second* (cps) or the more modern *hertz* (Hz).

The A above middle C string should have a cps rate of 440. The vibration compresses and stretches the air around the string, and this disturbance causes the membranes in our ears to vibrate at the same 440cps. Our brain then recognises this not just as sound, but as a particular note or pitch.

Sound that we recognise as music is a series of vibrations organised into a rhythmical pattern. Different musical instruments produce sound in different ways, and the method of sound production gives it the 'bar code' that tells us whether we are listening to a flute, harp or trumpet even when they are playing the same note.

Contained in that 'bar code' lie two further characteristics of sound: its dynamics and its harmonic structure.

Dynamics

This determines how we perceive volume. Some instruments, such as the violin or organ, can produce a note of constant volume. But a struck piano string produces an immediately large, percussive sound which then dies rapidly. Most of it has gone after two seconds or so, though if the key remains depressed it may be faintly audible after several more seconds.

Harmonic structure

When we hear a sound of a particular frequency from a piano, it also contains sounds of other frequencies. This is its harmonic structure. We may not be aware that we're getting several frequencies for the price of one, but the piano's sonic largesse can be appreciated when we hear a note with no extra frequencies – a 'mono tone'. Examples are a tuning fork or a TV test signal. Both are 'pure' notes of a single frequency, and while that makes them useful it also makes them characterless and boring – hence 'monotonous'.

How does playing one note result in several frequencies? When a string is struck, it vibrates at the frequency one would expect – for example, 440cps. This is known as its *fundamental* frequency. But vibration also does something one wouldn't expect: it has the effect of subdividing the string into fractions. The string divides into two, and each half produces its own sound an octave above the fundamental. It can also divide into three, four, five or more progressively shorter 'virtual' strings, each with its own sound. We therefore hear a whole family of related sounds when we *think* we're hearing just one. Generally, the longer a string vibrates, the more complex the production of these *overtones* or *harmonics*. This is especially so in the bass of the piano.

A trained ear can just about hear the lowest one or two of these harmonics, but to a normal ear all the harmonics fuse into a single note. We might notice some of the higher harmonics, which are quite discordant – but part of the genius of piano design is that the point where the hammer strikes the string is specifically calculated to mute the discordant harmonics while emphasising the more pleasing ones.

Trichords – three strings for the sound of one

For most of the piano's compass, each note is a trichord comprising three separate strings. This increases the volume of the

note, because when strings of the same frequency are struck in close proximity to each other they tend to release their energy faster – that is, they're louder. But because the energy released by the hammer is the same whether there is one string or three, the increased volume comes at the expense of a note of shorter duration as the energy dissipates more rapidly. Thus, for a given amount of hammer energy, the louder the note, the faster it dies.

So far, so good. But in practice it's difficult to keep three strings at exactly the same frequency. Let's look at what happens when two strings vibrating in close proximity to each other are slightly out of tune. (Why not three strings? Because three becomes much more mathematically complex, and thus harder to explain, than two.) Suppose one string vibrates at 440 and the other at 439cps. This is so close that we still hear just one sound rather than two; but there will be a significant effect on the volume. Here's why.

Beats

During the course of any given second, the strings will be almost perfectly in phase – that is, both will be moving and changing direction in unison, amplifying each other. But half a second later and they will be almost perfectly out of phase – one at the limit of its travel towards us, the other at the limit of its travel away from us. And when they're out of phase *they quieten each other down*.

So for the duration of the note, the sound is repeatedly amplified, then quietened down. What we hear is a throb: the same sound, but getting louder and quieter. These alternations in volume are called *beats* by piano tuners. The beat is at a rate equal to the difference between the vibration rates of the strings. Thus, if one string were vibrating at 440 and another at 438, we would hear two beats per second. At about this beat rate we start to hear 'honky-tonk' – the sound, loved by some and feared by others, of a dreadfully out of tune piano (see Chapter 5).

So to sum up: if all three strings of a trichord vibrate at exactly the same rate, they amplify each other as intended. But if their rates of vibration differ, *however slightly*, beats will be audible and the note will be quieter. The tuner's job is to reduce this beat rate to zero within the trichord.

Sound cancellation

To visualise the *negative wave cancellation* effect of different string vibration rates, put some water in your bath and set one tap dripping. When the drops hit the water, ripples spread across the bath. Now set both taps dripping. Eventually the two drips will coincide – and you'll see that there are no ripples between the drip points. They cancel each other.

Or if you want to save water, connect the red and black terminals of one of your stereo speakers the wrong way round. Sounds coming out of both sides of the stereo will then be perfectly out of phase: as one speaker cone moves forward, the other moves back, and they will quieten each other down. The closer the two speakers are to each other, the more marked this effect will be. Modern sound cancellation devices work on the same principle. Noise from factory machinery can be reduced by having a processor that listens to the sound, finds its pitch and mimics it, but perfectly out of phase. An amplifier and speaker then fire this 'negative' sound back at the machine. The continuous loud noise then becomes a much quieter throb.

2: The theory of equal temperament revisited

In Chapter 1, I explained the historical importance of equal temperament tuning. I now need to develop this a little further.

Imagine an octave of piano keys from C to c, and suppose the lower C vibrates at 100cps. (This note doesn't exist on the piano, but the maths is easier to grasp. The cps of middle C is actually 261.6255. You don't want that, do you?)

According to the fundamental rules of harmony, for two notes to sound 'in tune' the vibration rates starting from the frequency of the lower note are:

1 For an octave, multiply by 2
2 For a minor third, by 1.2
3 For a major third, by 1.25
4 For a fifth, by 1.5

Therefore, starting from C = 100, the c an octave above has a frequency of 200cps according to rule 1.

Tuning in minor thirds using rule 2 ends with the upper c vibrating at 207.36cps – impossibly and offensively sharp. (The calculations, if you want them, are: C=100, D#=120, F#=144, A=172.8, c=207.36.)

And it gets worse. Using rule 3, the upper c vibrates at 195.3125cps (C=100, E = 125, G#=156.25, c=195.31). This will be very flat.

Finally, going the same distance tuning in fifths according to rule 4 – halving the frequency when necessary to keep us within this octave – we end up with an audibly sharp c, vibrating at 202.73cps [$(100*1.5^{12})/2^6$]. Not as bad as the c of rule 2 but audibly vile nonetheless.

Oh dear. Four different harmonic rules, four different versions of c. Anyone prone to despair would give up right here. The fundamental rules of harmony appear to act in anything but harmony.

A major chord like C major is easy to tune. The rule for a major chord is a root, a major third and then a minor third. Tuned using rules 3 and then 2, C major would sound great. Since 1.25*1.2 = 1.5, the major third and then minor third take us up a fifth too, according to rule 4.

A C minor chord can also be tuned: a root, a minor third and a major third. This too would sound very pleasing. Again, the fifth is consistent with these rules.

But a chord like C diminished – C D# F# A c – can't possibly work if the minor thirds are in tune. The octave will be 'out', as the calculation for rule 2 shows. If five string players were asked to play a note each of this chord, only the two playing the Cs – exactly an octave apart – would sound correct. The other three would each have to play slightly flat – and by exactly the same amount – to fit the chord into an octave. It's impossible as a playing proposition, and it would be impossible on a piano too.

If we were to stick solely to simple tunes, we might get by without problems. For example, *One Man Went To Mow* has just two simple chords and a simple melody based on the scale. These notes can all be put in tune with each other and can sound better than equal temperament. But if we want to play anything even mildly complicated, then 'correct' tuning that obeys the rules of harmony will not and cannot work.

The solution, which is purely mathematical and courtesy of Johann Sebastian Bach (see Chapter 1), is to tune each semitone higher than the last by the twelfth root of two. This sounds complicated but it isn't – it's how you calculate a monthly interest rate from an annual one. The only difference is that instead of 12 months in a year we're dealing with the 12 steps in the musical scale.

Once a mathematical formula comes to the rescue, the tuning task becomes relatively straightforward as vibration rates for every note can be calculated and tabulated (see Appendix 2). This system will leave *all* intervals other than the octave slightly out of tune, but *equally* so in every key.

You're now very close to being able to tune your own piano…

3: Essential abilities and equipment

To tune a piano you need these abilities:

1 A reasonable understanding of the theory of equal temperament. (Just supplied above, and in Chapter 1.)

2 The ability to use clumsy-looking tools with the sensitivity of a brain surgeon. (See *Lever technique* below.)

3 Hearing acute enough to distinguish the harmonic components of sound. It's thought that only about 20 per cent of the population can manage this, but that percentage will probably be much higher among the musically trained or inclined.

You'll then need to equip yourself with:

1 A tuning lever

There are several types within a wide range of prices – see *Useful contacts*. If you're prepared to pay for the best, look for something like the lever in **10.1**. It has an extending handle to give more leverage, and interchangeable heads for different-sized pins and different access problems. For example, I work on a grand with a short lever head in the middle, but as I move to the treble end and access becomes more difficult, I switch to a longer lever head to get clearance over the case. Most tuning levers have a star drive giving eight theoretical positions, but a square drive lever, with a fixed head and smaller diameter tool end, may be better for accessing some of the tuning pins in a modern compressed piano. (Some tuners also prefer a square drive for its more positive grip on the pins.)

Lever technique

I can't emphasis enough that while a tuning lever may look as though it's designed to apply massive torque, that isn't what it's for. You must make only *very tiny* and *very careful* movements with it – such small movements, in fact, that you may think you haven't changed anything at all. Rest assured that minute movements of the lever will bring about large changes in pitch. Overdo it even slightly and the string will break. (The first time I ever used a tuning lever, the string broke. Thirty years on and I've broken a total of nine strings.)

To avoid repetitive strain injury it's always recommended that you pull up using your fingers but push the pitch down using your palm – see **10.2** for a grand and **10.3** for an upright. It's tempting to use a short, light tuning lever for speed. It's tempting, too, to grasp the lever tight and to give it small movements while pushing and pulling at the same time. After enduring subacromial decompression and carpal tunnel surgery, my conclusion is that a finger-and-palm technique used with a longer, if heavier, lever has a lot to recommend it. The longer the lever, the less the effort required. I use an expensive extendable model.

Warning: Do not give in to temptation and assume that you can save the expense of a tuning lever by using adjustable spanners, odd sockets etc from your DIY toolbox. Over the years I've done rather well out of repairing people's attempts to cut costs this way: for example, the wrest pin on the left in **10.4** had been assaulted with a makeshift tool. There is nothing like the real thing.

10.1

10.2

10.3

10.4

10.5

one is made of plastic. Plastic Papp's mutes have appeared as a replacement for the earlier nylon ones, and last about three weeks instead of 20 years. Brilliant marketing. Try to get hold of nylon ones if you can.)

3 A tuning fork

Tuning forks are inexpensive and can be bought at most musical instrument stores. Traditionally, the tuner uses just one tuning fork to tune the starting note, usually middle C. Even if you use an electronic tuner it's a good idea to have a tuning fork to check it occasionally.

2 Mutes

Mutes are used to isolate the individual strings of the trichords. In a grand piano, rubber or felt wedges (**10.5**) are pushed in between the strings to be muted and their neighbours on either side, isolating the string in the middle. The wedges usually go in far enough to touch the soundboard, and often leave a neat little row of 'footprints' in the dust on the soundboard or frame as the tuner works across the piano. This provides some idea of when a piano was last tuned: lots of dust but no 'footprints' means a long time ago!

In an upright piano, the cast iron frame prevents wedges from being pushed far enough through the strings.

Instead, a 'Papp's mute' is used. This is like a long pair of tweezers. It is inserted squeezed together, and when released it opens out, touching the strings on either side. Papp's mutes were originally made so that one could be used per trichord, but as modern pianos have become more compressed the strings are now too close together for them to be used singly. Most tuners use two Papp's mutes in the same way that wedges are used in grands (**10.6**). However, at the end of each run of strings there is no adjacent set of strings against which to wedge. There is then no alternative but to use one Papp's mute to isolate the middle string, and this isn't always easy: see **10.7**. (Incidentally, this blue

4 An electronic piano tuner

This is optional if your piano is already in a reasonable state of tune (*Section 6*), but essential if it's well below pitch (*Section 7*). See the *Digital piano tuner: yes or no?* boxout. If you're keen, either buy used or buy one of the cheaper products – perhaps a software-only version to use with your computer – to see how you get on with it. You must understand, though, that no matter what you buy or however much you pay, you will not get the equivalent of a human piano tuner in a box.

10.5

10.6

10.7

Digital piano tuner: yes or no?

While there are plenty of affordable and easy-to-use digital tuners around for guitars and other instruments with only a few strings, these are no use for pianos with over 200 separate strings.

Choice is more limited when it comes to digital piano (or digital chromatic) tuners. This is because they have to do a much more complex job, reflected in equipment that tends to be quite expensive and not easy for the unskilled to use. Electronic piano tuners now come in several formats: as stand-alone hardware, or as software for use with a laptop, handheld or even a mobile phone. (See *Useful contacts*.) But most are designed with the professional tuner in mind, so the big question is: how much benefit will a typical piano owner get from a digital electronic piano tuner?

The broad answer is some, but nowhere near as much as he or she might hope for. From an amateur's point of view, there are perhaps four significant advantages:

- They're good for *starting the job* instead of a tuning fork.
- They're good for *tuning the temperament* (see section 5).
- They're great for *checking the accuracy* of your tuning.
- They're also great for *stabilising a piano rapidly* (see section 7). This is something professional tuners also appreciate; before they came along, few tuners would attempt large increases in pitch in a single session.

Some models claim to be able to *stretch tune* (see section 6), but this is done by a 'cheat' that, while undoubtedly clever, is unlikely to produce as good a result as an experienced human tuner.

Other features tend to benefit only professionals: for example, the ability to store the tunings of many pianos, or switch temperaments (something I've been asked to do only twice in 30 years), or tune two pianos at once, or tune accurately in noisy environments. The longer the features list, the higher the price; and the most expensive tuners can include features that even many professionals don't need.

There's no doubt that for the professional, a digital electronic tuner can improve efficiency – but it isn't a substitute for human skill, and this is what mainly limits its usefulness for amateurs. As digital tuner technology currently stands, someone without a musical ear can't possibly use an electronic tuner to tune a whole piano.

Why not? First, the pitch must be brought close to the correct note before the electronic tuner can do much. This is like employing a short-sighted sheepdog. Second, electronic tuners measure only frequency – and only in the two or three middle octaves do 'correct frequency' and 'in tune' more or less coincide. Outside that narrow zone, each piano has its own characteristics and quirks that mean it can only be tuned accurately by listening to it.

Thus, while an electronic tuner can make part of the job easier and quicker for an amateur, most of it can still only be done properly by a trained human ear.

4: Tuning a few errant notes

Perhaps the easiest way to dip your toe in the water is to have your piano professionally tuned, then wait a few weeks or months until one or two notes start to develop that distinctive honky-tonk jangle that tells you they've started to drift out of tune. Fixing a few isolated notes is much easier than tackling a whole piano, but it will teach you the basic tuning technique and you'll get a good idea of the time and physicality involved.

I'll assume that (1) you've bought or borrowed the necessary hardware; and (2) it's a trichord you're dealing with, as these are the most likely to go out of tune first.

(For bichords it's actually easier – just mentally omit one string from the following.)

This is what you then do:

1 Find the errant trichord. You now have to find which of its three strings needs tuning, so:

2 Using a pair of mutes, isolate the middle string.

3 Play it with the octave below if it's in the treble, or the octave above if it's in the bass. Does it sound out of tune?

4 If it's fine, remove one mute so that you hear two strings (left and middle). Does it sound out of tune?

5 If it's still fine, move the mute so that you now hear the right and middle strings. Does it sound out of tune?

6 Assuming you've actually answered 'yes' at 3, 4 or 5, you have isolated the suspect string. Leave that one *plus one that you think is correct* unmuted.

7 Put the tuning lever on the tuning pin of the suspect string. In an upright piano, angle the lever between twelve o'clock and two o'clock; in a grand, between one o'clock and three o'clock, looking from above the pin. These positions are the best for leaving the pins in a stable condition. Only work outside them when the shape of the casework makes it necessary.

8 Slightly *lower* the pitch by turning the pin anticlockwise.

Safety first! 'Honky' strings are almost always flat because strings don't normally tighten when left alone. So logically, at step 8 you ought surely to *raise* the pitch? No, not if you're smart. A string can indeed become tighter after some types of unusual climate fluctuation, or if the last tuner didn't relax the tension in the pin. So just in case the string is sharp, check by flattening it first. As soon as you hear the note get worse, you can be confident that you're on to the problem.

9 If the note doesn't change, check that you're working on the correct tuning pin. The arrangement of pins is complex and it's easy to make a mistake. Or the string may have stuck to the pressure bar or bridge. Had you tried to sharpen it straight away, you might well have broken it.

10 Start to raise the pitch by turning the pin *very slightly and very slowly* clockwise. Do not turn it by more than a tiny amount.

11 With luck, the pitch will rise almost straight away and the string will sound in tune. If so, your job on that string is done.

12 There is, however, a good chance of overshoot – that is, going too sharp. Gently ease the tuning lever back (anticlockwise). In fact, it's generally good practice to go slightly sharp and then back when tuning an upright, in order to leave it in a stable state.

Pause for reflection

And that's it. You've just tuned your first piano string. Don't be disheartened if it hasn't been quite the smooth, textbook operation you hoped for. Pianos with a mean streak are quite normal. The truth is that while the basic mechanics of tuning are easy enough, every piano has a different 'feel' to it that makes some harder to tune than others.

In some, the tuning pins turn almost too freely; in others, they begrudge any movement at all. Pins may also be 'jumpy' – that is, they turn smoothly but the pitch changes erratically because the

strings can't slide freely over the top bridge and under the pressure bar. For example, in most grands the strings run over a large felt pad just before the tuning pin. This generates a lot of friction, so that when you try to flatten a note, the tuning lever has to move some way before the pitch drops – and then it drops drastically.

It takes a lot of experience to deal efficiently with a massive variety of pianos, and it's this experience that puts professional tuners in a higher league than amateurs. But even if your own piano is one of the tougher nuts to crack, you can tune it if you have patience. In most cases it just takes time – but be prepared for that to mean a large amount of time!

Next steps

If it's some time since your piano was tuned, and you have tuned enough individual strings to feel confident about moving to the next skill level, you can now try tuning the whole instrument.

It's best to think of this as a two-stage operation:

■ You first tune a couple of octaves in the middle of the piano. This is known as 'setting the temperament' or 'laying the scale'.

■ Having checked that you've set the temperament correctly, you then tune the rest of the piano.
So here we go…

5: Setting the temperament

There are several different procedures for tuning. Each tuner has his or her favourite, but they all do the same job in the end. The one we're going to use is my modification of a system devised around 1905 by J. Cree Fischer (see Bibliography) and widely regarded as the easiest for beginners to master.

According to the Fischer system, you need only tune in octaves up and down, and in fifths upwards – because the beat rates are slowest in fifths compared with other intervals.

Whereabouts on the keyboard do you start?

In theory, anywhere. Most tuners choose a sequence and stick to it for speed and efficiency. In practice, the best place for a beginner to start is in the middle, for the pragmatic reason that this is where the readings from an electronic tuner tend to be most reliable.

It's also vital to use a sequence that has built-in checks, as any error needs to be picked up quickly. If it's not, it will have a cumulative effect that could mean

hours of re-work later.

My preference is to start by tuning two mid-keyboard octaves. Other procedures suggest one octave, or one-and-a-half. It really doesn't matter, but I prefer two because it provides more built-in checks.

Tuning those first two octaves is termed 'setting the temperament' or 'laying the scale', and that section of the keyboard is then referred to as 'the temperament'. Setting the temperament correctly is akin to laying the first two or three rows of bathroom tiles; how accurately you do that determines how well the rest will turn out, so it deserves extra care.

Forward planning

- Sections 5 (this one) and 6 assume that your piano is in a relatively good state of tune to begin with. (If you can't remember when it was last tuned, it probably won't be.) This is so that you can quickly grasp how straightforward it is to tune strings that are only slightly flat and present no significant problems.
- Section 7 tells you what to do when there *are* significant problems.
- In both sections I assume that you now know enough about basic tuning lever technique not to need reminders, for example about the importance of making only tiny, careful movements. If you're rusty on any of this, re-read section 4.

Tuning the middle two octaves

Tune middle C

1 Mute off the two outer strings of trichord middle C. Use wedges for a grand, Papp's mutes for an upright.

2 Identify the correct tuning pin for that string. It's easy to get it wrong, so follow it up with your finger.

Now is a good time to give you a piece of advice to bear in mind constantly: if you turn a tuning pin but the pitch doesn't change, *stop turning immediately!* You're probably tightening or slackening one string but listening to another. Simply check that the tuning pin you're turning actually belongs to the string you're working on. The most usual cause of mistaken string identity is a lapse of concentration when you're midway through a tuning session, but it's also possible that someone may have changed a string's position, perhaps to re-use a string that broke near its end.

3a Check the pitch with your electronic tuner or tuning fork. If you're using an electronic tuner, watch the visual display and tune the string (steps 4–6) until it's correct.

3b If you're using a tuning fork, it's usual to use c above middle C to tune middle C. This is because the beat rates will be more noticeable. (Twice as fast, in fact, than if we used a middle C fork.) Strike the fork and hold it somewhere on the inside of the casework, where a mark won't matter.

4 Put the tuning lever on to the tuning pin and start to raise the pitch by turning the pin very slightly and very slowly clockwise. The pitch should rise almost straight away and there will be an audible beat as the correct pitch is approached.

5 If the tuning goes a little sharp, gently ease the lever back. (A justifiable reminder here: it's good practice to go slightly sharp and then back when tuning an upright, as this tends to leave it in a more stable state.)

6 If or when correct, that string is tuned.

7 Staying with the same trichord, remove the left-hand mute and tune the left-hand string to the middle string you've just tuned. You should hear beats as they come closer. The rate should fall and then stop.

8 Now do the same to tune the right-hand string to the middle string. (Swap the mute over, of course.)

9 Now listen to all three strings of that trichord together. When you're satisfied that there are no beats, you have successfully tuned middle C.

Tune the C an octave below middle C

10 Mute one of the strings of C below middle C if it's a bichord, and the two outer strings if it's a trichord.

11 Strike *together* middle C and the C an octave lower.

12 Raise the lower C until it's close to being in tune to the higher one. Again, as it approaches you should hear a beat that diminishes.

13 Sharpen until the beat disappears. If you go too far, the beat will start to reappear.

What you will be hearing now is the interaction of the first *harmonic* of the lower C with the *fundamental* of the higher C. They're *the same note*. The first harmonic of the lower C is only a small fraction of the total volume of sound coming from it, but if you listen carefully you should hear this harmonic interplay.

14 Tune the other string (if a bichord) or the other two strings (if a trichord) to the string you've just tuned. You have now successfully tuned your second C!

Tune the C an octave above middle C

The procedure is more or less the same as for tuning the C an octave below middle C, except that it will definitely be a trichord. Once done, you have tuned all three Cs in the middle of the piano. Time for a tea-break and a small measure of smug self-satisfaction.

Tune the G below middle C

The next phase is to tune round the famous 'cycle of fifths'. The first note in this sequence is G: the first interval other than an octave that you will tackle.

15 Find the trichord G below middle C and mute its outer two strings.

16 Play *lower* C and G together firmly and hold them down.

17 Start to sharpen G.

18 As it comes into tune with C, you'll hear a beat.

19 Eliminate the beat, and the G and lower C will be perfectly in tune.

Now it gets a little complicated. The theory of equal temperament requires the fifths to be *slightly* flat or 'tempered', so:

20 Start to flatten this G. Listen for a beat in the interaction of:

■ The *second* harmonic produced by the lower C, which is the G above middle C, and

■ The *first* harmonic from the G below middle C, which is the same note. (To help you find this harmonic, flick the note G *above* middle C and keep an ear on that sound while listening to C and G being struck together).

The beat rate for this interval is 0.45 per second, or a full beat in just over two seconds. (All the beat rates for fifths in the middle two octaves are given in Appendix 3. They're rounded to two decimal places here.)

Tune the G above middle C

21 This C to G should beat at twice the rate of the fifth an octave below – which from step 20 ought to be 0.90, but is actually 0.89 beats per second. There is a built-in check: the octave should be perfectly in tune, with no beats. If you find it easier to hear the faster beats of the higher fifth middle C to G above, tune this first and *then* the octave below. The two Gs must be left beatless when played together.

Tune D above middle C to G below middle C

22 This should be tuned to remove all beats and then tempered

(slightly flattened) to *around* 1.3 beats per second. There are various methods for timing beats precisely, and there are tables of beat rates in books and on websites. My feeling, though, is that it's better not to make the procedure too scientific. Tuning a piano remains an art. As long as this interval beats at a rate *between* the two intervals C to G that you've just tuned, you can be satisfied – because G to D is more or less halfway between the lower C to G and the higher C to G.

Carry on tuning...

23 After G to D, tune the D an octave below.

24 Now tune that D up to A. The beat rate here is almost exactly one per second (actually 0.994).

25 Tune the fifth D to A an octave above with twice the beat rate.

26 Check that A to A is a beatless octave.

After the next step, you'll be able to play a major chord

27 Tune A below middle C to E above. Once this is done, you acquire an additional check on your accuracy. A to E should beat at 1.1 per second – but you can now play C to E as a major third, which should beat at just over 10 per second. (Don't worry too much if you have trouble hearing this, or judging its beat rate. The more tuning you do, the easier it gets to hear and count beats.)

28 It may be interesting at this point to flatten this interval slightly and tune it beatless. You then hear a perfect major third, possibly for the first time ever. It's a quite soothing and 'round' sound.

29 Now sharpen it to its correct rate of 10 beats per second. If

this is too fast to judge, tune it to the A again. It should be okay as long as you have tempered the fifths correctly so far.

30 Tune this E to the E below as a beatless octave. The third of C below middle C to this E should beat at just over 5 per second and you should be able to hear this even if you can't count it precisely. The note you can hear beating is the fourth harmonic of the C with the third harmonic of the E, which is an E two octaves above. It may help to focus the ear again by flicking this note and trying to keep your ear on it.

31 You can now play the major triad G, C, E in the middle of the piano. You may notice how horrible it is – a revelation that for many is a lifetime first. Indeed, people with a good musical ear who have never tried to tune a piano before may feel that they must have gone wrong because it sounds so unpleasant, even though it's actually correct.

Keep on keeping on

32 Continue tuning in fifths, checking each new note as a major third on the top of a major chord.

33 E to B above middle C beats at 1.11 per second and half that rate in the octave below.

34 B to F# around middle C beats at 0.83 per second.

35 F# to C# around 1.25 beats per second.

36 C# to G# around 0.94 beats per second.

At this point, a new check appears
In addition to being able to try the major triad with the last note as a major third, it's now possible to try the triad C# minor in the position G# C# E, with E as the minor third. Switch between this

chord and G, C, E. In the C major, E is extremely sharp, while in C# minor it's extremely flat – just about as much of each as we can stand. Each new note in the sequence can now be tried in this way. You thus have an extra check on the accuracy of your work so far. It also alerts you to any strings that might have flattened since you worked on them.

37 G# to D# at 1.37 beats per second.

38 D# to A# at 1.05 beats per second in the octave above middle C, and half that rate an octave below.

39 A# to F at 0.78 beats per second.

40 F to C should now be in tune. *If it isn't, something way back has gone wrong and been progressively compounded until it's now badly wrong.* F to C can be nemesis, and is traditionally called 'the wolf' if it howls. Before electronic tuners became readily available, any beginner tuning in fifths and unable to hear the rapid beats in the thirds might get all this way before discovering that all was in vain!

The moment of truth – the ultimate test

Now you can put the accuracy of your work to piano tuning's most sensitive test. Many electronic pianos fail it, even when designed by mathematicians, and it's much more sensitive than an electronic tuner can be. Indeed, I may well be ostracised for letting this trade secret out of the bag.

41 Play middle C to E. Strike it *hard* and listen. It should beat at over 10 beats per second.

42 Now try C to E an octave lower. It should beat at half the rate, or 5 beats per second.

43 Now play chromatically down in major thirds from middle C and E: B and D#, A# and D etc. The beat rate should *slow down* at *every* step.

The same slowing beat effect should be audible with any interval: sixths, tenths etc. Tenths in the bass growl beautifully. But the point is that the beat rate should ideally slow down *at every downward step*. If you move down a semitone and the beat rate speeds up, or doesn't slow, something is wrong.

It may be difficult to trace or fix the cause. The most common culprit is a tuning pin that has slipped since you worked on it; the unisons will therefore be 'out', causing a problem that should at least be fixable. Sometimes you just have to live with a minor imperfection if there is a slight speed-up as you move into wound string territory. Further into the bass there can be problems with heavily wound strings, and where the piano switches from bichord to mono. But if, within tolerable limits, all beats get slower as you move down the piano, you've done a good job.

At this point you deserve another cup of tea before tackling the rest of the piano.

6: Tuning the rest of the piano

Now that you've tuned the middle two octaves, the rest of the piano is tuned in octaves. You should, however, perform frequent checks using other intervals.

For example:

In the treble, try each newly tuned note as a third on the top of a major chord, then as a third on the top of a minor chord. If it's sharp it'll sound horrible as a major third; if it's flat it'll sound horrible as a minor third.

In the bass, try each newly tuned note with the tenth above it, and confirm that the beat rate is declining at each step.

It doesn't matter whether you tune the bass section first or the treble. The bass is my own preference so that's where we'll start, but there's nothing wrong with starting in the treble.

Tuning down the bass

Tune, in octaves, B below middle C to the B below

1 Mute the left-hand string of the bichord.

2 Tune that string beatless to the octave above.

3 Remove the mute and tune the other string to the first.

4 Repeat steps 1–3 chromatically down into the bass.

Unfortunately, the further you go down into the bass, the more you're likely to meet problems. You may, for example, find it harder to hear the fundamental frequency of the lower notes, especially in a small upright piano. Or your ear may be confused by hearing several beating harmonics at once. You may well reach a point where, as you change the pitch, some beats seem to speed up while others seem to slow down. The only practical solution is to stop when you achieve whatever sounds to you to be the best trade-off – though this can be difficult if you don't hear anything that satisfies you!

A more tricky problem is harmonic imperfection in the strings themselves.

Stretching the octaves

As explained in *Harmonic structure* on page 172, strings subdivide harmonically into halves, thirds, quarters etc. The trouble is that piano wire is so stiff and hard, and in the bass section so thick as well, that the *point of inflection* – the stationary point on the string between each part of the harmonic – takes up *some* length, which is effectively subtracted from the playing or 'speaking' length. Thus the halves are less than half the length of the string, the thirds less than a third of the length of the string, and so on. This means that the harmonics are inevitably sharp compared with the fundamental – and the further you go up the harmonic series, the sharper they are. (Though mercifully, the quieter they are too.)

The tuner has to allow for this through a process called 'stretching the octaves'. As the tuner goes down the compass, the bass strings must be left progressively flatter for the first harmonic to sound in tune with the note an octave above.

Electronic tuners are no use whatsoever in this process. Most will simply tell you that the note is flat when it actually sounds correct. On some electronic tuners it's theoretically possible to find the 'stretch' tuning by setting it on the note an octave above

the note you're tuning. The electronic tuner is then 'listening' to that harmonic, and tuning to it is claimed to give you the correct stretch tuning. In my view this is unsatisfactory as it doesn't take into account the many other harmonics present as well.

For the time being, stretching the octaves remains an art rather than a science. Each piano differs in its need for flattening, and different human tuners will make slightly different judgements about how much is appropriate.

Tuning up the treble

Tuning from the middle or temperament octaves towards the treble end is fairly straightforward until, at some point, you run into the treble versions of the hearing and 'stretching' problems you met in the bass: notes sound flat even though your electronic tuner says they're at the correct frequency. The flatness may be even more marked if you actually play a tune.

The problem is partly technical, and partly to do with how human ears work.

Technical first. Even thin piano wire is very stiff compared with, say, guitar strings. The speaking length of the top octave is extremely short – often little more than 2in (50mm) for the top note. The points of inflection in the harmonic

subdivision again 'remove' some of the already short speaking length, making the harmonics sharp.

The human component of the problem is our predisposition to hear upper treble notes or melodies as flat even when the pitch is technically correct. This was unintentionally demonstrated in the 1980s by the first generation of digital electronic pianos. Because they had a comparatively tiny memory capacity, digital economies were made by sampling just one note from a grand piano. The other 87 notes were produced electronically, by multiplying and dividing that one note's frequency. The result was that in the top octave, everything sounded as flat as a pancake. (This intriguing phenomenon is now history. With much greater memory capacity available, all 88 notes are sampled for up to seven seconds, pedal on and pedal off, at up to seven degrees of force from *ppp* to *fff*. And all recent electronic pianos have stretch tuning – sometimes a little too much of it.)

In consequence, there is a need for judicious octave stretching in the treble – perhaps more in pianos used for solo than ensemble performance. I don't believe, however, that there should ever be noticeable beats in the octaves, as this would make them sound worse.

Can pianos sharpen naturally?

Yes, but rarely. The natural tendency is for pianos to flatten as materials give way to huge string loads, so in order to sharpen, the strings have to acquire energy from somewhere. One common source is wet weather; the soundboard absorbs moisture and expands, forcing the bridges up and increasing the tension on the strings. This is always a dilemma for the tuner. If you flatten the piano to the correct pitch, it may go rapidly even flatter when the weather improves. If you leave it sharp, you risk the wrath of the instrumentalists who have to play it. (Soon, if not already, a justifiable get-out will be to shake one's head sadly and blame climate change.)

It's highly unusual to find a piano that has been deliberately tuned

sharp, except through incompetence or malice. There is, however, a historical pitch sharp of A440 called 'orchestral concert pitch', to which a piano may have been raised for a performance of period music. (Other pitches may also just about conceivably be encountered. Before standard pitch was internationally accepted in 1939 – after much heated academic debate that should have been called The Pitch Battles – there were many different pitches which some ensembles, such as brass bands, were reluctant to abandon as it meant scrapping expensive instruments.)

All that said, in the normal run of things you shouldn't find a piano that has become anything other than flat over time.

7: Tuning a piano that is well below pitch

For this, you'll almost certainly need an electronic tuner. A professional tuner could do it without one, but for an amateur it would be extremely difficult.

If your tuning fork or electronic tuner says that your middle C string is so flat that it may even register as a sharp B, you have one of Sherlock Holmes's three-pipe problems. You have to decide:

- Will it come up to pitch at all?
- If yes, will it come up in a single tuning session?

- If yes again, will it come up and be stable enough to use?

Age is certainly a factor; the older the piano, the less likely it is that a single tuning will be enough to keep it in tune. But perhaps the key question is: What is the piano going to be used for?

- If it's to be used solo and the player won't mind or notice whether it's up to pitch, it can be raised a little now and raised more later, perhaps over

several subsequent tunings. We'll call this option A.

- If it's going to accompany a singer or other instruments, or be used with Internet or CD/DVD instructional material, you don't have much choice. Short of dumping it for another piano, you'll *have* to bring it up to pitch. We'll call this option B.

Option A is the better choice if you're not in a hurry, as a piano raised drastically in pitch at one go will drop rapidly out of tune. The argument for option B, apart from desperation, is that a piano below pitch sounds dull and lifeless and has much less volume than a piano at the correct pitch.

Unfortunately, you may have to make your decision without knowing the piano's true condition, which may not emerge until you have set most of the temperament. It's impossible to predict how pianos left untuned for many years will handle a drastic increase in pitch. Some will be fine, others not. If you decide to gamble on option B and lose, notes you worked on earlier may plunge flat again even while you're still working on the temperament. You'll then have no alternative but to start all over again and may be forced to settle for option A.

If your piano hasn't been tuned for many years, you may find that the tuning pin turns but the pitch doesn't rise – even when you've confirmed that you're working on the correct string. If so, *stop turning the pin immediately*, as any more tension on the string will snap it. The string is probably stuck to the top bridge, thanks to a tiny patch of corrosion caused by electrochemical reaction between the drawn steel string and cast iron bridge. Even if the string isn't fully stuck, it may be reluctant to slide over the bridge and under the

▥ How to stabilise a piano – if you dare!

A piano string has three parts:

- ■ The *speaking length* between the top and bottom bridges.
- ■ The *live end* between the top bridge and tuning pin.
- ■ The *dead end* between the bottom bridge and hitch pin.

The photo on page 103 shows the dead end of some upright bass strings, while the live end – upper bridge to tuning pin – is shown here.

A piano won't be stable until the string tension is equal in all three sections. But much friction is generated in pulling the wire over the top bridge and under the pressure bar, and over the bottom bridge and around the bridge pins. The tuner must do his or her best to even out all these sources of resistance as the string tension is raised. It's usually a losing battle, as there will always tend to be high tension in the live end, less in the speaking length and even less in the dead end. This is why multiple tunings are often necessary to stabilise a piano.

But maybe there's a much quicker, 'lateral thinking' solution. I once ran a business hiring out battered but fundamentally sound pianos to entertainment venues. I transported them on a trailer with an agricultural suspension. Now, conventional wisdom says that moving a piano is likely to put it out of tune by releasing some of the string tensions. At first I assumed I'd need to turn up early

enough at each venue to do a full tuning job. To my amazement, all the pianos soon stabilised until I needed only enough time to unload and slightly adjust perhaps half a dozen strings. My explanation is that the jolting of the trailer helped equalise the tension in each section of the strings. The lesson may be that if you want a really stable piano quickly, you should tune it, then trundle it around on a crude trailer over about 40 miles of bad road, then tune it again.

pressure bar. There will sometimes be visual evidence to support intuition, like rust on the pins or strings.

In either case, turn the pin anticlockwise a little until the reduction in tension frees the string, often with a 'ping'. However, you're not out of trouble yet. While you've spared yourself a broken string, you now have a string so far below pitch that it may be difficult to raise the pitch *and make it stay there*.

Let's now try to do something with the piano.

Option A says tune it below pitch – but how far below?

1 Using your electronic tuner, decide how flat the piano is on average across the compass. (Treble strings are commonly flatter than bass strings, as any degree of 'give' will be a larger proportion of their length.)

2 When you've decided on a pitch, set your electronic tuner so that middle C is indicated as C. (Keep pressing the 'flatten' button until you get there. If your tuner doesn't have enough range, tune C on the piano to B on the electronic tuner. You may have to *sharpen* the tuner to get B into range as a C – in which case, every note you tune will be a semitone below the note name on the keyboard. Exceptionally, you may have to set C even lower – my record to date is piano C = A♭.)

3 Then simply follow the procedures in sections 5 and 6 above, with the proviso that *all the beat rates will be correspondingly lower*.

Option B says go for broke and raise the pitch. My preferred method is:

1 Set the electronic tuner 5–10 cents (hundredths of a semitone) sharp.

2 Tune rapidly and crudely and none too accurately.

3 Give the whole keyboard a loud, vigorous workout.

4 Leave the piano overnight. In that time the strings will lose some tension – with luck, an amount equal or close to the sharpening of the strings.

5 The next day, tune as in sections 5 and 6. Or at least try. If you've correctly anticipated the overnight fall in pitch, you may succeed in stabilising the piano – or it may take a second tuning.

6 Either way, tune the piano again a few weeks later.

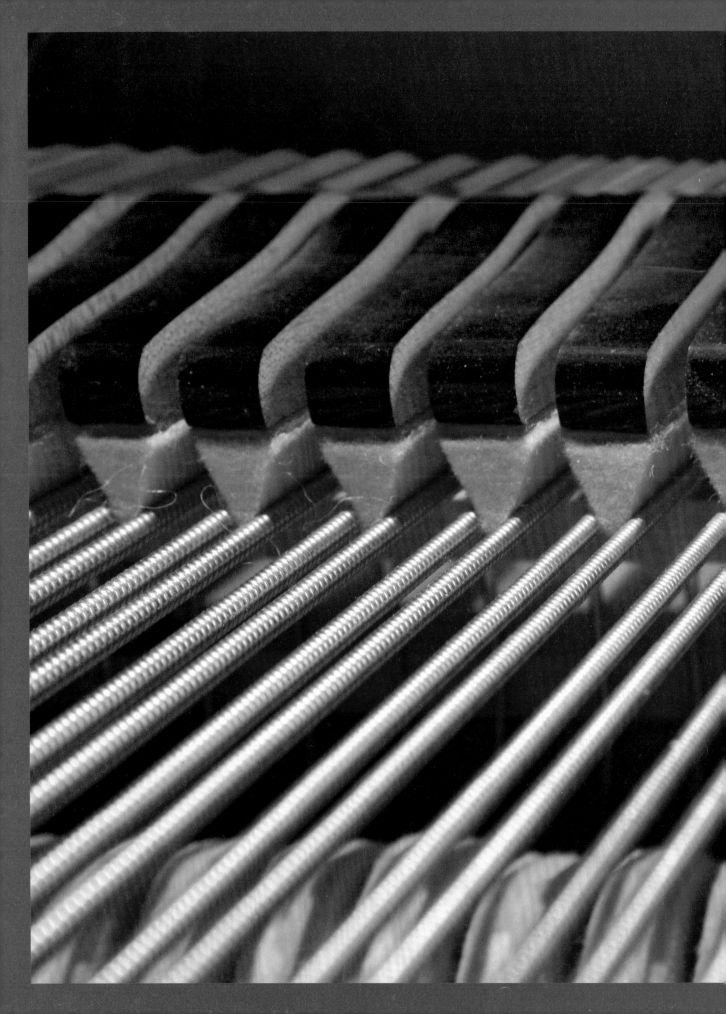

APPENDICES

Additional information

Appendices

■ **Appendix 1**

Frequency rates

Name	Note number	Frequency
A	1	27.5
A #	2	29.1
each successive rate is the previous one multiplied by the twelfth root of 2		
B	3	30.9
C	4	32.7
C #	5	34.6
D	6	36.7
D #	7	38.9
E	8	41.2
F	9	43.7
F #	10	46.2
G	11	49.0
G #	12	51.9
A	13	55.0
A #	14	58.3
B	15	61.7
C	16	65.4
C #	17	69.3
D	18	73.4
D #	19	77.8
E	20	82.4
F	21	87.3
F #	22	92.5
G	23	98.0
G #	24	103.8
A	25	110.0
A #	26	116.5
B	27	123.5
C	28	130.8
C #	29	138.6
D	30	146.8
D #	31	155.6
E	32	164.8
F	33	174.6
F #	34	185.0
G	35	196.0
G #	36	207.7
A	37	220.0
A #	38	233.1
B	39	246.9
MIDDLE C	40	261.6
C #	41	277.2
D	42	293.7
D #	43	311.1
E	44	329.6

Name	Note number	Frequency
F	45	349.2
F #	46	370.0
G	47	392.0
G #	48	415.3
A	49	440.0
A #	50	466.2
B	51	493.9
C	52	523.3
C #	53	554.4
D	54	587.3
D #	55	622.3
E	56	659.3
F	57	698.5
F #	58	740.0
G	59	784.0
G #	60	830.6
A	61	880.0
A #	62	932.3
B	63	987.8
C	64	1046.5
C #	65	1108.7
D	66	1174.7
D #	67	1244.5
E	68	1318.5
F	69	1396.9
F #	70	1480.0
G	71	1568.0
G #	72	1661.2
A	73	1760.0
A #	74	1864.7
B	75	1975.5
C	76	2093.0
C #	77	2217.5
D	78	2349.3
D #	79	2489.0
E	80	2637.0
F	81	2793.8
F #	82	2960.0
G	83	3136.0
G #	84	3322.4
A	85	3520.0
A #	86	3729.3
B	87	3951.1
C	88	4186.0

0 Correct to 1 decimal place

■ **Appendix 2**

Beat rates

Temperament: Middle two octaves of the piano around middle C.
Beat rates of the fifths.

Name	Note number	Fifth	Note number	Beat rate
C	28	G	35	0.44
C#	29	G#	36	0.47
D	30	A	37	0.5
D#	31	A#	38	0.53
E	32	B	39	0.56
F	33	C	40	0.59
F#	34	C#	41	0.63
G	35	D	42	0.66
G#	36	D#	43	0.7
A	37	E	44	0.75
A#	38	F	45	0.79
B	39	F#	46	0.84
Middle C	40	G	47	0.89
C#	41	G#	48	0.94
D	42	A	49	1
D#	43	A#	50	1.06
E	44	B	51	1.12
F	45	C	52	1.18
F#	46	C#	53	1.26
G	47	D	54	1.33
G#	48	D#	55	1.41
A	49	E	56	1.49
A#	50	F	57	1.58
B	51	F#	58	1.67
C	52	G	59	1.77

Name	Note number	Frequency	1	2	3	4	5	6	7	8
C	28	130.813	261.6	392.439	523.3	654.1	784.88	915.69	1046.5	1177.32
C #	29	138.6	277.2	415.775	554.4	692.96	831.55	970.14	1108.73	1247.32
D	30	146.8	293.7	440.498	587.3	734.16	881	1027.83	1174.66	1321.49
D #	31	155.6	311.1	466.691	622.3	777.82	933.38	1088.95	1244.51	1400.07
E	32	164.8	329.6	494.442	659.3	824.07	988.88	1153.7	1318.51	1483.33
F	33	174.6	349.2	523.843	698.5	873.07	1047.69	1222.3	1396.92	1571.53
F #	34	185.0	370.0	554.993	740.0	924.99	1109.99	1294.98	1479.98	1664.98
G	35	196.0	392.0	587.994	784.0	979.99	1175.99	1371.99	1567.98	1763.98
G #	36	207.7	415.3	622.958	830.6	1038.26	1245.92	1453.57	1661.22	1868.87
A	37	220.0	440.0	660.001	880.0	1100	1320	1540	1760	1980
A #	38	233.1	466.2	699.247	932.3	1165.41	1398.49	1631.58	1864.66	2097.74
B	39	246.9	493.9	740.826	987.8	1234.71	1481.65	1728.59	1975.54	2222.48
Middle C	40	261.6	523.3	784.878	1046.5	1308.13	1569.76	1831.38	2093.01	2354.63
C #	41	277.2	554.4	831.549	1108.7	1385.92	1663.1	1940.28	2217.46	2494.65
D	42	293.7	587.3	880.996	1174.7	1468.33	1761.99	2055.66	2349.32	2642.99
D #	43	311.1	622.3	933.382	1244.5	1555.64	1866.76	2177.89	2489.02	2800.15
E	44	329.6	659.3	988.884	1318.5	1648.14	1977.77	2307.4	2637.02	2966.65
F	45	349.2	698.5	1047.686	1396.9	1746.14	2095.37	2444.6	2793.83	3143.06
F #	46	370.0	740.0	1109.985	1480.0	1849.98	2219.97	2589.97	2959.96	3329.96
G	47	392.0	784.0	1175.988	1568.0	1959.98	2351.98	2743.97	3135.97	3527.96
G #	48	415.3	830.6	1245.916	1661.2	2076.53	2491.83	2907.14	3322.44	3737.75
A	49	440.0	880.0	1320.000	1760.0	2200	2640	3080	3520	3960
A #	50	466.2	932.3	1398.491	1864.7	2330.82	2796.98	3263.15	3729.31	4195.47
B	51	493.9	987.8	1481.650	1975.5	2469.42	2963.3	3457.18	3951.07	4444.95
C	52	523.3	1046.5	1569.753	2093.0	2616.26	3139.51	3662.76	4186.01	4709.26

Calculating beat rates

Beat rates are calculated by finding the closest coincidental harmonics in the two notes being tuned and subtracting one from the other.

In Appendix 2, sheet 2, I tabulate from Appendix 1 the fundamental frequencies of each note in the middle two octaves. The first harmonic in each row is this fundamental multiplied by two. The second harmonic is the fundamental multiplied by three, the third harmonic is the fundamental multiplied by four, and so on.

To give a specific example, based on values shown in red on the table:

C28 vibrates at 130.813cps
Its second harmonic vibrates at 130.813*3, which is 392.439

G35 vibrates at 196cps
Its first harmonic vibrates at 196*2, which is 392

When these notes are correctly tuned according to equal temperament, they will beat at a rate equal to the difference between them; that is, 0.439 of a beat per second, or one beat every 2.28 seconds. The note being heard in the beat is G above middle C, or G47 – which has the exact rate of 392. (For the sake of this example I'm assuming that the harmonics in this part of the piano won't be sharp, as explained in the 'Stretching the octaves' section in Chapter 10. In practice it can't be taken for granted that this will be true of all pianos.) Continuing the calculations from above:

The 5th harmonic of C28 will vibrate at 130.813*6 = 784.8766
The 3rd harmonic of G35 will vibrate at 196*4 = 784

This means that this almost common harmonic will beat at 0.87cps and will be heard as the note an octave and a half above middle C, or G59. It is an octave above the G47 beat identified above and will be at twice the rate of G47. It will be only a small fraction of the total volume of sound, but if your hearing is acute you may just be able to hear this beat within the original beat.

No further harmonics in this interval will produce much in the way of audible beats. The closest we get is the 9th harmonic of C28, which will vibrate at 1177.315 while the 6th harmonic of G35 vibrates at 1175.986. This common harmonic will vibrate at 1.33 times a second – quite close to, but sharp of, D66 at 1174.66. It would sound quite unpleasant but, mercifully, few of us would be able to hear it among all the other sounds going on.

By constructing such tables and performing such calculations, beat rates can be found for all intervals for tuning purposes. But before you rush off and do it, I must caution against too 'scientific' an approach to piano tuning. Every piano has its own idiosyncrasies and harmonic irregularities that confound 'one size fits all' solutions. If you want to coax the best out of a piano by tuning it, you have to go primarily with what your ears tell you, not what the calculations tell you.

■ Appendix 3
Music wire gauges

mwg	Thousandsths of an inch	mm
12	29	0.074
12.5	30	0.076
13	31	0.079
13.5	32	0.081
14	33	0.084
14.5	34	0.086
15	35	0.089
15.5	36	0.091
16	37	0.094
16.5	38	0.097
17	39	0.099
17.5	40	0.102
18	41	0.104
18.5	42	0.107
19	43	0.109
19.5	44	0.112
20	45	0.114
21	47	0.119
22	49	0.124
23	51	0.130
24	53	0.135
25	55	0.140
26	57	0.145

Piano wire and centre pins are measured in this gauge

■ **Appendix 4**
The piano technician's basic toolbox

Specialist tools can be bought new from piano supply houses (see *Useful contacts*), and used examples can sometimes be found on the internet. However, many of the tools and materials that you'll need will be either already in your DIY toolbox or can easily be bought in hardware stores.

General tools and materials for all work

- **Adhesives** – Various, but mainly for fabric.
- **Adjustable spanner or pipe wrench** – For removing grand piano legs, stubborn action screws and bolts, and other brute force tasks.
- **Blades** – Standard disposable blades for craft knives.
- **Blowlamp** – Rarely needed; a last resort for loosening some stubborn joints.
- **Car jack** – plus blocks of wood, for bracing grand pianos while new tuning pins are hammered in. See Photo 9.53. For the record, you can buy a specialist jack just for this job, but I've never felt the need to use one.
- **Chisel** – A wide one. Quality isn't too important, as you'll use it mostly for scraping off glue.
- **Clamps** – Various sizes for various tasks, but mainly small, self-gripping clamps to hold newly glued joints until the adhesive sets. See, for example, Photo 8a.3.
- **Craft knife or scalpel**.
- **Electric driver/drill** – Small size, with a good selection of drill bits.
- **Engineer's vice** – with some means of padding the jaws.
- **Micrometer** – Useful for accurate measurement of felt thickness.
- **Newspaper or old blankets** – For various padding and protective duties.
- **Parcel tape**.
- **Pencils** – You'll lose at least one.
- **Pliers** – At least two pairs, one standard and one round-nosed.
- **Sandpaper** – Of varying grades including the very finest.
- **Sandpaper-covered sticks** – See Photo 8b.70.
- **Scissors** – A very sharp pair.
- **Screwdrivers** – Several types and sizes. At least two should be very long and thin – one standard, one Phillips – and with fairly small working ends (Photo 8b.51 shows why they need to be long). At the other end of the scale, you'll need a 'stubby' for tightening keyblocks.
- **Tweezers** – Ideally, big dental tweezers with ends bent at 45°. My pair is probably my most used tool (see Photo 8b.11). Also the longest tweezers you can find, for reaching in to recover stray objects.

Specialist tools for regulation and repairs

With the possible exception of the multi-tool kit, buy these only as you need them.

- **Action centre bearings reamer** – See Photo 8b.35.
- **Broach** – See Photo 8b.36.
- **Capstan tool** – See Photo 7.4.
- **Centre pin cutter** – See Photos 8b.35 and 8b.61.
- **Coil lifter** – See Photo 8c.12.
- **Decentring tool** – A bench model allows more rapid and accurate work than the hand model shown in Photo 8b.42.
- **Grand hammer remover** – See Photo 8b.83.
- **Hammer needling tool** – For voicing pianos. See Photo 8b.75.
- **Hammer shank cutting tool** – See Photo 8b.91.
- **Hammer shank remover (uprights)** – See Photo 8b.9.
- **Key easing pliers** – For use when key bushings are too tight. The smaller jaw squeezes the bushing, the larger one spreads the load on the side of the key to avoid crushing it. See Photo 7.39.
- **Let-off rack** – See Photo 9.42.
- **Multi-tool kit with detachable handle** – See Photos 7.26 and 8b.21. Clockwise: Handle, general bender (in use in Photo 8b.26), key spacer, check bender, grand backcheck bender (in use in Photo 9.48).
- **Piano wire gauge** – See Photo 8b.32.
- **Set-off regulating tool** – Photo 8b.22 shows one type in use.
- **T-shaped tuning key** – For winding on new strings.
- **Wrest pin metal bushings or sleeve** – See Photo 8c.23.
- **Wrest pin punch** – See Photo 8c.21.

Specialist tools for tuning

- **Digital piano tuner** – Optional if your piano is already in a reasonable state of tune but essential if it's well below pitch. See *Digital piano tuner: yes or no?* in Chapter 10. Seek advice before buying, as tuners aimed at professionals may have features you'll pay for but never need.
- **Mutes** – Rubber or felt wedges (Photo 10.5) are used in grand pianos, but in an upright the cast iron frame prevents wedges from being pushed far enough through the strings and you'll need Papp's mutes (see Chapter 10). You'll need two mutes because the strings in modern uprights are too close together for them to be used singly. Try to buy nylon mutes. Most Papp's mutes are now made of plastic, which is far less durable than nylon.
- **Tuning lever** – Don't be tempted to buy the cheapest because you're 'only a beginner'. Many cheap levers are too short for accurate tuning and the heads break off easily. Look for something more like the lever in Photo 10.1. It has an extending handle for greater leverage, and interchangeable heads for different-sized pins and different access problems. If you have a modern, compressed piano look for a lever with a square rather than star-shaped drive, as its (usually) smaller tool end diameter will give you better access to some of the tuning pins. Many tuners also prefer a square drive for its more positive grip on the pins.
- **Tuning fork** – Tuning forks can be bought cheaply at most musical instrument stores. Even if you use a digital tuner, it's a good idea to have a tuning fork to check it occasionally.

Glossary

Action – The mechanical assembly that converts the small downward motion of the keys into the larger motion of the hammers – forward in an upright, upward in a grand. The feat of 18th-century engineering genius that makes the piano what it is.

Action bracket – See 'action posts'.

Action posts (US 'action brackets') – The end supports that hold the action components in place. Usually cast metal in modern pianos, wooden in older ones.

Agraffes – On pianos fitted with them, each note has its own individual mini-bridge called an agraffe, a brass stud with holes through which the strings pass to keep them in perfect alignment. Inserted into the frame, agraffes are used instead of, and are usually considered superior to, a bridge cast into the frame.

Aliquot stringing – Any method that allows sympathetic vibration to occur in the part(s) of the string not struck by the hammer (the live ends and dead ends). In older Blüthner grands this is positively encouraged by the addition of extra strings mounted over the top of the normal strings.

Backcheck (US 'catcher') – The component that is part of the action in an upright, but on the back end of each key in a grand, which catches the hammer as it rebounds off the strings. Often shortened to 'check'.

Backtouch – The felt-covered crosspiece in the keybed on which the keys rest when not being played.

Balance hammer – The part of the hammer mechanism in an upright that is caught on the backcheck after the hammer rebounds off the strings.

Balance pin – Small, vertical, nickel-plated pin on which the key pivots when played.

Balance rail – The wooden crosspiece in the keybed into which the balance pins are inserted.

Beats – The regular modulation, or variation in volume, audible when there is interaction between two strings in close proximity that are not quite in tune.

Bichord stringing – The section of the piano in which there are two strings for each note. The hammer strikes both simultaneously.

Blubbering – The sound made when the piano action is so out of regulation that the hammer strikes the string more than once.

Bottom board – On an upright, the removable external section of the piano case under the keybed.

Bridge – Hardwood strips attached to the soundboard over which the strings are stretched. The bridges transfer the vibrations from the strings to the soundboard.

Bridge pins – Small, headless nails driven into the bridge to secure the strings. In an ageing bridge, splits tend to start around these pins.

Bushed frame – Exact meaning depends on the age of the piano. In older pianos, a bushed frame is one that includes a thin layer of cast iron over the wrest plank portion. Holes are drilled through the metal for the tuning pins, which are thus held more firmly than in wood alone. In modern pianos the tuning pin holes are lined, or bushed, with a hardwood plug.

Bushing – General engineering term for the lining in a hole through which another component passes or moves. Its function is usually to ease motion and reduce friction and wear. In pianos, the most common bushings are of cloth to allow the smooth movement of a metal part inside a wooden part, specifically in the moving parts of the action and in the keys themselves. See also 'tuning pin bushings'.

Butt plate – In some better quality upright actions the hammer centre pin is not simply forced through the hammer butt, but is held by a small metal plate screwed on to the butt.

Cap or capping piece – A dubious past practice of some manufacturers of three-quarter frame (US 'half plate') pianos. They would 'cap' it with a piece of purely cosmetic cast iron to make the piano look as though it had a full frame. Naughty.

Capo d'astra – A bar, usually cast into the frame of a grand piano, that the strings pass under. In some grands all the strings pass under a *capo* but in most it's just the top three or so octaves. This allegedly overcomes the tone problems created by the hammers trying to force the strings away from the frame.

Capstan – A small, usually wooden component mounted on a vertical metal screw. Resembles a ship's capstan in shape, though a minute fraction of the size. It may be adjusted by screwing it up or down to close a gap between two components. It usually has two holes through it and can be adjusted with a pointed tool.

Case or casework (US 'cabinet') – The 'furniture' part of the piano – all the external woodwork, the main job of which is to make the piano look good and shield its workings from view.

Catcher – US term for backcheck.

Celeste – A crude soft pedal mechanism in older, cheaper uprights. It brings a felt pad up in front of the hammers. Similar in some respects to a practice pedal.

Centre pins – Tiny nickel-plated pins around which all the articulated parts of the action turn.

Check – See 'backcheck'.

Compass – The full playing range of the piano, usually designated from A1 (the lowest bass note) to C88 (the highest treble note).

Damper – The mechanism that mutes the sound when the key is released.

Damper pedal – The pedal on the right. It lifts all the dampers at once, so that struck strings continue to sound until they fade or the pedal is released, and strings not struck are free to vibrate sympathetically. Also called 'sustain', but never 'loud pedal' – or at least, not in knowledgeable company.

Damper spoon – The mechanism on the back of the upright action that raises the damper off the string when a note is played.

Dead end – The non-playing section of the string between the bridge and the hitch pin. Usually deadened by a strip of felt woven through all the dead ends.

Double duplex scaling – An arrangement patented by Steinway. The two ends of the string not struck by the hammer (the live end and the dead end) are allowed to vibrate sympathetically, rather than being deliberately deadened with felt as in most pianos.

Double escapement action – The type of action used in all modern grands. It allows notes to be repeated at full force without complete release of the key. Also called colloquially, but widely and acceptably, 'roller action'.

Downbearing – The angle formed by the strings as they pass over the bridges.

Drop screw – A screw through the grand piano hammer flange that limits the upward movement of the repetition lever when a key is played.

Dropper action (US 'spinet' or 'indirect blow action') – An arrangement, doomed by design to be awful to play, in which the action is situated under the back end of the keys.

Duplex scaling – An arrangement by which the parts of the string not struck by the hammer are allowed to vibrate sympathetically. It's called 'single duplex' when just the dead ends of the strings are allowed to vibrate; 'double duplex' when both dead and live ends are allowed to vibrate.

Escapement – The action mechanism that propels the hammer towards the strings but releases it just before it actually strikes. The hammer is thus free to fly through the air, hit the string and rebound.

Fall or fallboard – Technical term for what most people call the lid over the keyboard. Strictly speaking, the lid of a piano – a distinction not worth trying to remember, unless you're paid to know these things.

Fall plate – The plates that allow the fallboard of a grand piano to swivel and also attach it to the piano at each end.

False beat – The sound made when a single string produces beats. If there are just one or two false beats in a piano, the probable cause is an irregularity in string manufacture. If there are many, the bridge may have been poorly manufactured.

Flange – A small hardwood hinge to which piano action components are attached and which allows them to move around the centre pins.

Fly – See 'jack'.

Fly damper – In some better quality uprights, an additional damper attached to the shorter dampers near the overstringing break. This compensates for the small damper size necessary in this area.

Frame (US 'plate') – The principal structural component of any piano. The strings are stretched across it and it has to be strong enough to bear the entire string load. In all modern pianos it's made of cast iron.

Front board – The removable front section of the piano case just above the keyboard.

Front rail – The front strip of the keyframe. It grips the pins which project into the bottom of the keys at the front to prevent sideways movement.

Full frame – A cast iron frame that occupies the full height of an upright or the full length of a grand, and which encloses the wrest plank or pin block. See also 'three-quarter frame' or 'half plate frame'.

Glides – The domed metal projections in the bottom of a grand piano keyframe assembly which enable it to slide laterally when the *una corda* pedal is depressed.

Half-blow – The soft pedal mechanism in all modern uprights that slows hammer acceleration and thus reduces the volume of the note produced. Found on some older grands as a cheap substitute for *una corda*.

Half plate frame – US preferred term for three-quarter frame, though pedants might argue that the latter is mathematically more accurate.

Hammer rail – US term for rest rail.

Hammer shank – Hardwood (usually maple) dowel connecting the hammer butt to the hammer itself. The usual breaking point during excessive rock'n'roll.

Hitch pin – Steel pin or projection inserted near the bottom of the cast iron frame, around which the string turns or is fastened. (In most pianos each treble wire goes around the hitch pin and back again, to serve as a second string.)

In check – The position of the hammer when a note is played and the key held down. From this position the key has to be released, at least partially, to repeat the note.

Jack or fly – The action component mounted on the whippen that pushes the hammer forward as the key is depressed but disengages before the hammer strikes.

Key dip – The distance the keys travel from their rest position when fully depressed. Usually $^3/_8$in to $^7/_{16}$in (9.5mm to 11.1mm).

Key easing pliers – Pliers with jaws that move in parallel, for use when key bushings are too tight. One jaw squeezes the bushing; the other is larger, to spread the load on the side of the key to avoid crushing it.

Keybed – The flat part of the interior of the piano on which the keyframe and keyboard rest.

Keyblocks – The wooden blocks at each end of the keyboard that fill the gap between the ends of the piano and the ends of the keyboard. In a grand piano, they also secure the steel projections on the keyframe assembly so it can move laterally for the *una corda*, but in no other direction.

Keyframe – The wooden frame that supports the keys. It consists of three cross rails: the front rail, the balance rail and the backtouch.

Keyslip – The decorative wooden strip just below the keyboard. Usually permanently fixed in uprights, but in grand pianos it has to be removed to take out the keyframe assembly.

Keystrip (US 'keystop rail') – In grand pianos only, and it can't be seen with the fallboard in place. A narrow strip of wood with felt on the bottom, running right across the keys and suspended just above them. It acts as a buffer during vigorous playing, to prevent the keys bouncing up too far. It also stops the keys falling out when the piano is placed on its side during transportation.

Knuckle or roller – Small cylinder of leather with a wooden core, attached to the bottom of the grand hammer shank. The jack pushes against it when the key is depressed, thus raising the hammer.

Live end – The non-played length of string between the tuning pin and the upper bridge.

Lost motion – Any circumstance in which the correct movement of component parts is impaired, usually as a result or wear or shrinkage. Most commonly refers to the gap between the keys and the action, but can apply to any moving part(s).

Lyre – Formal term for the pedal mechanism of a grand piano, so called because on early grands it was shaped to resemble a lyre (ancient Greek harp).

Lyre rod – Metal or wooden supports on the back of the grand piano pedal mechanism (or lyre) to offer a counterforce to the player's pedal pressure. If the lyre rod goes missing, a regularly used pedal mechanism will soon break away from the piano.

Monochord stringing – One string per note, rather than two (bichord) or three (trichord). Monochords are found only in the bass section.

Music desk – The fold-out part of the piano on which the player rests his or her sheet music. The ones on modern uprights are sometimes disparagingly called trays.

Nameboard tape – The felt strip that separates the keyboard from the casework immediately above it. Now almost universally red, but green and blue were once permitted. In uprights it is both functional and decorative: it prevents any noise from the keys as they bounce up during vigorous playing.

Needling – Literally, sticking a needle into the ends of hammers to loosen the felt as part of voicing a piano. Must be done with great skill or the hammer felt can be ruined.

Oblique strung frame – Essentially a straight-strung frame but with the strings at a slight angle to the vertical to make them longer. Few pianos were made like this and they were considered no real improvement on straight-strung frames.

Overdamper action (US 'squirrel cage') – A deservedly obsolete arrangement of the dampers of an upright above, rather than under, the hammers. Unsatisfactory because it produced harsh harmonics and took too long for the sound to die.

Overstringing break – The gap in the stringing of a piano between the bass strings and the treble strings.

Overstrung frame – A frame designed so that the bass strings cross diagonally over the treble strings, at about an octave below middle C. This lengthens the bass strings relative to the height of the piano, and enables the bass bridge to be located away from the bottom edge of the soundboard. Now used in all pianos and significantly better in most respects than the straight-strung frame.

Pilot cloth – Usually the cloth covering the regulating screws in the keys of nasty, cheap pianos. However, the term may be used wherever there is a cloth interface between working surfaces in order to reduce noise and abrasion.

Pin block – US term for wrest plank.

Plain strings – Strings without copper windings.

Plate – US term for the cast iron frame.

Practice pedal – A mechanism found on modern uprights, similar to the celeste. Operating the lockable middle pedal introduces a thin felt pad between hammers and strings, reducing the sound to a volume tolerable to family and neighbours. Or so it is claimed.

Regulation – The state of adjustment of the many variables in a piano that affect the way it performs. Most commonly refers to the correct adjustment between keyboard and action, but may refer to other aspects of the action or pedals.

Repetition lever – Part of the action of the grand piano. When a key is played and released *slightly*, this sprung component raises the hammer *slightly*. This allows the jack to return under the roller, thus enabling rapid repetition.

Repetition spring – Spring below each repetition lever that gives it upward force when the key is released a little.

Rest rail (US 'hammer rail') – The felt-covered rail behind the hammer shanks. In an upright, the hammer shanks at rest should just touch the rest rail. In a grand, the hammer shanks at rest should be $1/8$in (3.1mm) above the rest rail and should make contact only on the rebound from the strings during vigorous playing.

Roller – See 'knuckle'.

Roller action – See 'double escapement action'.

Set-off or let-off – The point in the action cycle at which the hammer flies off the jack and is free to strike the strings and rebound. The usual setting is $^1/_8$in (3.1mm) from the string in uprights, $^1/_{16}$in (1.5mm) in grands.

Shank – See 'hammer shank'.

Shelf bridge – The bass bridge is mounted on a shelf fastened to the soundboard, rather than directly onto the soundboard. The advantage is better sound quality, as the point of bridge contact is now closer to the middle of the soundboard. Common in uprights and smaller grands.

Simplex action – See 'spring and loop action'.

Single duplex – See 'duplex scaling'.

Slap rail – A felt-covered wooden strip behind the dampers in an upright action. It prevents excessive movement of the dampers.

Soft pedal – See 'half-blow' and 'celeste'.

Sostenuto – Found mainly in three-pedal grands, and is the middle pedal. It acts like the sustain pedal but sustains only those notes whose keys are already depressed when the pedal is operated.

Soundboard – The large expanse of (usually) spruce under the strings to which the bridges are attached. It amplifies the sound produced by the strings.

Speaking length – The portion of string between the bridges that is struck by the hammer. See also 'dead end', 'live end' and 'aliquot stringing'.

Spring and loop action – This term has two meanings: a type of upright action, obsolete from around 1870 but still encountered occasionally; and the action of grand pianos by Herrburger Brooks and others, made from 1885 (when they were already obsolete) to around the 1950s. Also known as 'simplex actions', these were essentially an upright action and not the double escapement action that characterises a grand. Wretched to play but cheaper to make.

Squirrel cage – Descriptive US term for overdamper action.

Stickers – In uprights that are too tall for the action to be located right next to the keyboard, stickers (connecting rods, more or less) provide the extra reach needed to link each key to its corresponding part of the action.

Straight-strung frame – An upright piano frame in which all the strings are parallel and vertical to the ground. Long obsolete; replaced by overstrung frames.

Sustain – The length of time the sound produced by a string lasts if the key is struck and held down. See also 'damper pedal'.

Sustain pedal – See 'damper pedal'.

Swaging – A truly vile process that attempts to tighten up worn-out key bushings by damaging the wood surrounding them.

Sympathetic vibration – Sound waves from one source may cause a string or some other object to vibrate, creating one or more other sound sources. This is sometimes created deliberately in duplex scaling but often occurs when an object on or in the piano, or elsewhere in the room, produces sound when certain notes are played. Can be irritating, and the source difficult to find.

Three-quarter frame (US 'half plate frame') – A piano in which, for reasons of manufacturing economy, the cast iron frame does not extend to the top of the piano but stops just below the wrest plank. Much of the load on the wrest plank is thus thrown on to the wooden frame of the piano. Long obsolete but there are still plenty around.

Top board – See 'front board'.

Trichord stringing – The treble section of the piano, where each note is produced by the hammer striking three strings all tuned to the same note.

Tuning pin or wrest pin – The means by which a piano is tuned. Each piano wire has its end wound on to a tuning pin, which during manufacture or rebuild has been hammered into a very tight hole in the wrest plank.

Tuning pin bushings – Doughnut-shaped hardwood plugs in the holes for the tuning pins in the cast iron frame. The bushings are drilled and the pins inserted through them. This arrangement produces more grip on the pins while making it easier to turn them, and thus tune the piano.

Una corda – The soft (left) pedal mechanism in most grand pianos. When depressed, the whole keybed assembly shifts slightly to the right (except for Rud Ibach grands, where it shifts to the left). In consequence the hammer strikes one string less in the trichord and bichord sections, reducing the volume of the note. The monochords are still struck, but with a different part of the hammer that is likely to be softer in tone.

Underdamper action – All modern uprights have their damper mechanism under the hammer and thus nearer the middle of the string than is the case with the obsolete overdamper action. This ensures a more effective muting of the sound when the key is released.

Vertically-strung frame – See 'straight-strung frame'. In UK terminology 'vertical' means specifically straight-strung. A possible source of misunderstanding is the US practice of calling all uprights 'verticals', whether straight-strung or overstrung.

Voicing – The technique of needling the hammer felt to soften the tone of a piano, or to make the tone more uniform if some notes sound harsher than others.

Whippen – The moving part of the action that converts the upward motion of the back end of the key into hammer motion.

Wound strings – Bass strings that have copper wire wound round a drawn steel core. This makes the strings thicker, which slows the vibration rate. If the drawn steel cores were made that thick to begin with, they'd be too inflexible to vibrate at all.

Wrest plank (US 'pin block') – The laminated wooden board into which the tuning pins or wrest pins are hammered when a piano is manufactured or rebuilt.

Further reading

Books on piano tuning and technology tend to drift in and out of print, sometimes in revised editions and sometimes from different publishers. This can make it difficult to keep track of what is or is not currently available, so the years of publication given here are those of the first edition.

Crombie, David. *Piano: Evolution, Design and Performance*, 1999.
A superb book with an erudite text and full of wonderful photos of great pianos: presidential Steinways and the like. But not of much practical use to owners of less exalted pianos.

Duffin, Ross W. *How Equal Temperament Ruined Harmony (And Why You Should Care)*, 2006.
Worth reading by those with an academic interest in equal temperament tuning. The author's argument is interesting but, I think, misguided. His main hypothesis is that those who can, such as string players, should play out of tune sometimes.

Fine, Larry. *The Piano Book: Buying and Owning a New or Used Piano*, 1987.
An excellent book, the main feature of which is a model by model evaluation of new and recently-made pianos available in the USA (though most are also available globally), based on feedback from working piano technicians. Good section on Steinway grands.

Fischer, J. Cree. *Piano tuning: a simple and accurate method for amateurs*, 1907.
A classic; so good that I base my own chapter on tuning on his system, though with some modifications. But ignore his advice on repairs unless you want to wreck your modern piano.

Pierce, Bob. *Pierce Piano Atlas*, 1947.
A truly great undertaking. Long before computer databases, Pierce scoured the world amassing information about piano manufacturers, models, serial numbers and dates. Regularly revised.

An essential tool for anyone who is serious about pianos.

Reblitz, Arthur A. *Piano Servicing, Tuning, and Rebuilding*, 1976.
Indispensable reference for the piano technician, and the logical next step from this book if you want to rebuild a piano. However, although it claims to be suitable for the hobbyist, it makes no concessions to anyone not already up to professional standard.

Wolfenden, Samuel. *A Treatise on the Art of Pianoforte Construction*, 1916.
In my opinion the best book ever produced about piano construction – and wonderfully well written. No detail too small to dwell on; for example, three pages of correct technique for putting in a wood screw. For modern tastes this may be slightly overdoing it, but Wolfenden really knew how to make a piano.

Useful contacts

Suppliers of piano parts, tools etc.

Fletcher and Newman
www.fletcher-newman.co.uk
Long-established company that supplies all piano tools and parts. Exemplary and friendly service but mainly trade oriented.

In Tune
www.getintune.co.uk
John Bishop's own business. In Tune will supply any piano owner with tools and parts in small quantities sufficient to do all the jobs described in this book.

Association of Blind Piano Tuners
www.uk-piano.org
Wealth of piano-related information. Includes comprehensive directory of UK specialist companies, including those that will make actions and other parts to pattern.

Steve's Piano Service
www.stevespianoservice.com/piano.htm
US online repair and restoration parts service. Great catalogue and refreshingly irreverent website. Highly recommended for its entertainment value alone. Associated – somehow – with www.balaams-ass. com.

AcryliKey Ivory Repair System
www.acrylikey.co.uk
Ivory piano key repair system using synthetics.

Websites

Any search engine will, of course, quickly identify piano related websites of varying degrees of specialisation, depending on the search terms you use. The following is a sample, in no particular order, of sites I have found interesting or useful during the preparation of this book. There are many, many more.

Murray's Piano Tuning
http://members.cruzio.com/~fmurray/id19.htm
Click on 'Shop tour' to see detailed workshop photos of the various stages of piano rebuilding.

Ray's Piano Service
www.rayspiano.com/B-NiendorfGrand1925.htm
Includes over 60 photos of a grand rebuild in progress.

Courteney Pianos
www.courtneypianos.co.uk/more-restoration.html
More wonderful photos of piano restoration in progress.

The Blue Book of Pianos
www.bluebookofpianos.com
Treasure trove of historical, technical and buying information.

Kawai
www.kawai.net.au/makingof.html
Watch a short movie of a Kawai grand being made.

Brian Capleton
www.amarilli.co.uk
Site of music teacher and writer Brian Capleton. Includes much well-presented information on harmonic theory and tuning.

Period Piano Company
www.periodpiano.com/restoration.htm
Many wonderful photos of restored period pianos, including Beethoven's 1817 Broadwood.

The Piano-Forte
www.geocities.com/threesixesinarow
Links to an extraordinary collection of articles about various aspects of the piano, published between 1819 and 1880.

Piano Gen
www.uk-piano.org/piano-gen/piano-serial-numbers.html
Includes much useful information about dating and identifying pianos.

Piano String Scale Optimization
www.cs.ioc.ee/~stulov/lisboa.pdf
A 2005 technical paper on piano scale modelling by Anatoli Stulov.

The Piano Hammer as a Nonlinear Spring
www.kettering.edu/~drussell/Piano/NonlinearHammer.html
A 1997 technical paper on the behaviour of hammer felt by Daniel A. Russell.

Index